NOTHING OF IMPORTANCE

J B P Adams

NOTHING OF IMPORTANCE

A RECORD OF EIGHT MONTHS AT THE FRONT WITH A WELSH BATTALION
OCTOBER, 1915, TO JUNE, 1916

BY

BERNARD ADAMS

WITH A PORTRAIT AND THREE MAPS

METHUEN & CO. LTD.
36 ESSEX STREET W.C.
LONDON

First Published in 1917

Printed and bound by Antony Rowe Ltd, Eastbourne

TO

T. R. G.

WHO TAUGHT ME HOW TO THINK

In Memoriam

BERNARD ADAMS

JOHN BERNARD PYE ADAMS was born on November 15th, 1890, at Beckenham, Kent. From his first school at Clare House, Beckenham, he obtained an entrance scholarship to Malvern, where he gained many Classical and English prizes and became House Prefect. In December, 1908, he won an open Classical scholarship at St John's College, Cambridge, where he went into residence in October, 1909. He was awarded in 1911 Sir William Browne's gold medals (open to the University) for a Greek epigram and a Latin ode, and in 1912 he won the medal for the Greek epigram again, and graduated with a First Class in the Classical Tripos. In his fourth year he read Economics.

On leaving Cambridge he was appointed by the India Office to be Warden and Assistant Educational Adviser at the Hostel for Indian Students at Cromwell Road, South Kensington. "He threw himself," writes Dr. T. W. Arnold, C.I.E., Secretary of Indian Students, "with the enthusiasm of his ardent nature into the various activities connected with 21 Cromwell Road, and endeared himself both to the Indian students and to his colleagues." Adams was always a quiet man, but his high abilities, despite his unobtrusiveness, could not be altogether hidden ; and in London, as in Cambridge, his intellect and his gift for friendship had their natural outcome. Mr. E. W. Mallet, of the India Office, bears testimony to "the very high value which we all set on his work. He had great gifts of sympathy and character, strength as well as kindliness, influence as well as understanding; and these qualities won him—in the rather difficult work in which he helped so loyally and well—a rare and noticeable measure of esteem." On his side, he felt that the choice had been a right one; he liked his work, and he learned a great deal from it.

His ultimate purpose was missionary work in India, and the London experience brought him into close touch with Indians from every part of India and of every religion.

In November, 1914, he joined up as lieutenant in the Welsh regiment with which these pages deal, and he obtained a temporary captaincy in the following spring. When he went out to the front in October, 1915, he resumed his lieutenancy, but was very shortly given charge of a company, a position which he retained until he was wounded in June, 1916, when he returned to England. He only went out to the front again on January 31st of this year. In the afternoon of February 26th he was wounded while leading his men in an attack and died the following day in the field hospital.

These few sentences record the bare landmarks of a career which, in the judgment of his friends, would have been noteworthy had it not been so prematurely cut short. For instance, here is what his friend, T. R. Glover, of St John's, wrote in *The Eagle* (the St John's College magazine) and elsewhere :

" Bernard Adams was my pupil during his Classical days at St John's, and we were brought into very close relations. He remains in my mind as one of the very best men I have ever had to teach —best every way, in mind and soul and all his nature. He had a natural gift for writing—a natural habit of style ; he wrote without artifice, and achieved the expression of what he thought and what he felt in language that was simple and direct and pleasing. (A College Prize Essay of his of those days was printed in *The Eagle* (vol. xxvii, 47–60)—on Wordsworth's *Prelude.*) He was a man of the quiet and reserved kind, who did not talk much, for whom, perhaps, writing was a more obvious form of utterance than speech.

It was clear to those who knew him that he put conscience into his thinking—he was serious, above all about religion, and he was honest with himself. Other people will take religion at second-hand; he was of another type. He thought things out quietly and clearly, and then decided. His choice of Economics as a second subject at Cambridge was dictated by the feeling that it would prepare him for his life's work in the Christian ministry. There was little hope in it of much academic distinction—but that was not his object. A man who had thought more of himself would have gone on with Classics, in the hope (a very reasonable one) of a Fellowship. Adams was not working for his own advancement. The quiet simple way in which, without referring to it, he dismissed academic distinction, gives the measure of the man—clear, definite, unselfish, and devoted. His ideal was service, and he prepared for it—at Cambridge, and with his Indian students in London.

When the war came he had difficulties of decision as to the course he should pursue. Like others who had no gust for war, and no animosity against the enemy, he took a commission, not so much to fight *against* as to fight *for*; the principles at stake appealed to him, and with an inner reluctance against the whole business he went into it—once again the quiet, thought-out sacrifice."

In this phase of his career his characteristic conscientiousness was shown by the thoroughness and success with which he performed his military duties "He is a real loss to the regiment," wrote a senior officer; "everybody who knew him had a very high opinion of his military efficiency."

As is so often the case, a quiet and reserved manner hid a brave heart. When it came to personal danger he impressed men as being unconscious of it. "I never met a man who displayed coolly more utter disregard for danger." And in this spirit he led his men against the enemy—and fell. From the last message that he gave the nurse for his people, "Tell them I'm all right," it is clear that he died with as quiet a mind and as surrendered a will as he lived.

"What we have lost who knew him," writes Mr. Glover, "these lines may hint—I do not think we really know the extent of our loss. But we keep a great deal, a very great deal—*quidquid ex illo amavimus, quidquid mirati sumus, manet mansurumque est.* Yes, that is true; and from the first my sorrow (it may seem an odd confession) was for those who were not to know him, whose chance was lost, for the work he was not to do. For himself, if ever a man lived his life, it was he; twenty-five or twenty-six years is not much, perhaps, as a rule, but here it was life and it was lived to some purpose; it told and it is not lost."

CONTENTS

MAPS

ILLUSTRATION

PREFACE

"THEN," said my friend, "what *is* this war like? I ask you if it is this, or that; and you shake your head. But you will not satisfy me with negatives. I want to know the truth; what *is* it like?"

There was a long silence.

"Express that silence; that is what we want to hear."

"The mask of glory," I said, "has been stripped from the face of war."

"And we are fighting the better for that," continued my friend.

"You see that?" I exclaimed. "But of course you do. We know it, and you at home know it. And you want to know the truth?"

"Of course," was the reply.

"I do not say that what you have read is not true," said I; "but I do say that I have read nothing that gives a complete or proportioned picture. I have not yet found a perfect simile for this war, but the nearest I can think of is that of a pack of cards. Life in this war is a series of events so utterly different and disconnected, that the effect upon the actor in the midst of them is like receiving a hand of cards from an invisible dealer. There are four suits in the pack. Spades represent the dullness, mud, weariness, and sordidness. Clubs stand for another side, the humour, the cheerfulness, the jollity, and good-fellowship. In diamonds I see the glitter of excitement and adventure. Hearts are a tragic suit of agony, horror, and death. And to each man the invisible dealer gives a succession of cards ; sometimes they seem all black ; sometimes they are red and black alternately ; and at times they come red, red, red ; and at the end is the ace of hearts."

" I understand," said my friend. " And now tell me your hand."

" It was a long hand," I replied ; " I think I had better try and write it down in a book. I have never written a book. I wonder how it would pan out ? At first my hand was chiefly black with a sprinkling of diamonds ; later I received more diamonds, but the hearts began to come as well ; at last the hearts seemed to be squeezing out the clubs and diamonds. There were always plenty of spades."

There was another silence.

" There was one phrase," I resumed, " in the daily communiqués that used to strike us rather out there ; it was, " Nothing of importance to record on the rest of the front." I believe that a hundred years hence this phrase will be repeated in the history books. There will be a passage like this: "Save for the gigantic effort of Germany to break through the French lines at Verdun, nothing of importance occurred on the western front between September, 1915, and the opening of the Somme offensive on the 1st of July, 1916." And this will be believed, unless men have learnt to read history aright by then. For the river of history is full of waterfalls that attract the day excursionist—such as battles, and laws, and the deaths of kings; whereas the spirit of the river is not in the waterfalls. There are men who were wounded in the Somme battle, who had only seen a few weeks of war. I have yet to see a waterfall; but I have learned something of the spirit of the deep river in eight months of "nothing of importance."

This, then, is the book that I have written. It is the spirit of the war as it came to me, first in big incoherent impressions, later as a more intelligible whole. Perhaps it will seem that the first chapters are somewhat light in tone and inclined to gloss over the terrible side of War. But that is just what happens; at first, the interest and adventure are paramount, and it is only after a time, only after all the novelty has worn away, that one gets the real proportion. If the first chapters do not bite deep, remember that this was my experience. This book does not claim to be always sensational or thrilling. One claim only I make for it: from end to end it is the truth.

The events recorded are real and true in every detail. I have nowhere exaggerated; for in this war there is nothing more terrible than the truth.

All the persons mentioned are also real, though I have thought it better to give them pseudonyms.

January, 1917.

NOTHING OF IMPORTANCE

NOTHING OF IMPORTANCE

CHAPTER I

FIRST IMPRESSIONS

"GOOD-BYE!"

"Good-bye. Don't forget to send me that Hun helmet!"

"All right! Good-bye!"

. . . . . .

The train had long ago recovered from the shock of its initial jerk; a long steady grinding noise came up from the carriage wheels, as though they had recovered breath and were getting into their stride for Folkestone, regardless of the growing clatter of the South-Eastern rhythm;—if, indeed, so noble a word may be used for the noise made by the wheels as they passed over the rail-joints of this distinguished line.

"Don't believe it's a good thing having one's people to see you off," said Terry, whose people had accompanied him in large numbers to Charing Cross.

"They *will* come, though," remarked Crowley very wisely.

"I tried to persuade my people not to come," said I; "but they think you like it, I suppose. I would certainly rather say good-bye at home, and have no one come to the station."

And so I started off my experience of "the great adventure" with a "lie direct": but it does not weigh very heavily upon my conscience.

Six of us sat in a first-class carriage on the morning of the 5th of October, 1915: for months we had been together in a reserve battalion waiting to go out to the front, and now at last we had received marching orders, and were bound for Folkestone, and thence for France. For which battalion of our regiment any or all of us twelve officers were destined, we had no knowledge whatever; but even the most uncongenial pair of us would, I am sure, have preferred each other's company to that of complete strangers. I, at any rate, have never in my life felt more shy and self-conscious and full of stupid qualms: unless, indeed, it was on the occasion, ten months before, when I had stood shaking in front of a platoon of twenty men!

The last few days I had gone about feeling as though the news that I was going to the front were printed in large letters round my cap. I felt that people in the railway carriages, and in the streets, were looking at me with an electric interest; and the necessary (and unnecessary!) purchases, as well as the good-byes, were of the kind to make one feel placed upon a pedestal of importance! Now, in company with five other officers in like predicament, I felt already that I had climbed down a step from that pedestal; in fact, the whole experience of the first few days was one of a steady reduction from all-importance to complete insignificance!

As soon as we had recovered from the silence that followed my remarks upon the disadvantages of prolonged valedictions, we commenced a critical survey of our various properties and accoutrements. Revolvers leapt from brand new holsters; feet were held up to show the ideal trench-nails; flash lamps and torches, compasses, map-cases, pocket medicine-cases, all were shown with an easy confidence of manner that screened a sinking dread of disapprobation. The prismatic compass was regarded rather as a joke by some of us; its use in trench warfare was a doubtful quantity; yet there were some of us who in the depths of our martial wisdom were half expecting that the Battle of Loos was the prelude of an autumn campaign of open-country warfare. There was only one man whose word we took for law in anything, and that was Barrett. He had spent five days in the trenches last December; he had then received his commission in our battalion. He was the "man from the front." And I noticed with secret misgivings that he had not removed the badges of rank from his arm, or sewed his two stars upon his shoulder-straps; he had not removed his bright buttons, and substituted for them leather ones such as are worn on golfing-jackets; and in his valise, he told us, he had his Sam Browne belt.

"But you never wear Sam Brownes out there," I said: "all officers now dress as much as possible like the men."

That was so, we were informed; but officers used to wear them in billets, when they were out of the firing-line.

"Well," said Crowley, "we could get them sent out, I expect."

"Yes," said I; "I expect they would arrive safely."

But this infantile conversation is not worthy of record! Suffice to say we knew nothing about war, and were just beginning to learn that fact!

The first check to our enthusiasm was at Folkestone. We reported to the railway transport officer, whom we then regarded as a little demi-god; he told us to report in time for the boat at a certain hour. This we did, signed our names with a feeling of doing some awful and irrevocable deed, and then were told to wait another three hours: there was no room for us on this boat! We retired to an hotel with a feeling that perhaps after all there was no such imperious shouting for our help over in France, such as we had all, I think (save only Barrett, who was cynical and pessimistic!) secretly imagined.

Darkness came ere we started. The crossing did not seem long, and I stood up on deck with Barrett most of the time. Two destroyers followed a little astern, one on either side ; and there were lights right across the Channel. We were picked out by searchlights more than once, although all lights were forbidden on board. I felt that I was now fair game for the Germans ; and it was exciting to think that they would give anything to sink me ! At last I was in for " the great adventure."

At Boulogne we had to wait a long time on a dismal quay and in a drizzling rain to interview an irritated and sleepy railway transport officer. After a long, long queue had been safely negociated we were given tickets to —— ; and then again we had to wait quite an hour on the platform. Some of our party were excited at their first visit to a foreign soil ; but their enthusiasm abated when at the buffet they were charged exorbitant prices and their English money was rejected as " dam fool money."

Then there came a long jerky journey through the night in a crowded carriage. (As I am out for confessions, I will here state that I did not think this could be an ordinary passenger train, and I wondered vaguely who these men and women were who got in and out of other carriages !) At Étaples there was a still longer wait, and a still longer queue ; but, fortunately, my signature had not lengthened. I remember sitting tired and dazed on the top of a valise, and asking Barrett what the time was.

" Three forty-five ! "

" What a time to arrive ! " I replied. But in war

three forty-five is as good a time as any other, I was soon to discover.

We walked to a camp a mile distant from the station ; our arrival seemed quite unlooked for, and a quartermaster-sergeant had to be procured, by the officer who was our guide, in order to gain access to the tent that contained the blanket stores. Wearily, at close on five o'clock, we fell asleep on the boarded bottom of a bell-tent.

It must have been about 10 a.m. on the 6th when we turned out and found ourselves in a sandy country ; behind us was a small ridge, crowned by a belt of fir trees ; the sun was well up and shone warm on the face as we washed and shaved in the open. The feeling of camp was exhilarating, and I was in good spirits.

But two blows immediately damped my ardour most effectively. When I learned that I was posted to our first battalion, and I alone of all of us twelve, the thought of my arrival among the regulars, with no experience, and not even an acquaintance, far less a friend, was distinctly chilling ! To add to my discomfiture there befell a second misfortune : my valise was nowhere to be seen !

Indeed, the rest of the day was chiefly occupied in searching for my valise, but to no purpose whatever. I did not see it until ten days later, when by some miracle it appeared again ! I can hardly convey the sense of depression these two facts cast over me the next few days ; the interest and novelty of my experiences made me forget for short periods, but always there would return the thought of my arrival alone into a line regiment, and with the humiliating necessity of borrowing at once. Unknown and inexperienced I could not help being; but as a fool who lost all his property the first day, I should not cut a brilliant figure!

We obtained breakfast at an *estaminet* by the station; omelettes, rolls and butter, and *café noir*. I bought a French newspaper, and thought how finely my French would improve under this daily necessity; but I soon found that one could get the Paris edition of the *Daily Mail*, and my French is still as sketchy as ever! I remember watching the French children and the French women at the doors of the houses, and wondering what they thought of this war on their own soil; I knew that the wild enthusiasms of a year ago had died down; I did not expect the shouting and singing, the souvenir-hunting, and the generous impulses that greeted our troops a year ago; but I felt so vividly myself the fact that between me and the Germans lay only a living wall of my own countrymen, that I could not help thinking these urchins and women must feel it too! The very way in which they swept the door-steps seemed to me worth noting at the moment.

In the course of my wild peregrinations over the camp in search of my valise, I came upon a group of Tommies undergoing instruction in the machine-gun. Arrested by a familiar voice, I recognised as instructor a man I had known very well at Cambridge! He recognised me at the same moment, and in a few seconds we parted, after an invitation from him to dinner that evening; he was on "lines of communication" work, he told me.

Sitting in his tent after Mess, I was amazed at the apparent permanence of his abode; shelves, made out of boxes; novels, an army list, magazines, maps; bed, washstand, candlesticks, a chair; baccy, and whisky and soda! It was all so snug and comfortable. I was soon to find myself accumulating a very similar collection in billets six miles behind the firing-line, and taking most of it into the trenches! I remember being impressed by the statement that the cannonade had been heard day after day since the 25th, and still more impressed by references to "the plans of the Staff!"

I left Étaples early on the morning of the 7th, after receiving instructions, and a railway warrant for "Chocques," from a one-armed major of the Gordons. Of our original twelve only Terry and Crowley remained with me; with a young Scot, we had a grey-upholstered first-class carriage to ourselves.

In the train I commenced my first letter home; and I should here like to state that the reason for the inclusion in these first chapters of a good many extracts from letters is that they do really represent my first vague, rather disconnected, impressions, and are therefore truer than any more coherent

To face page 9

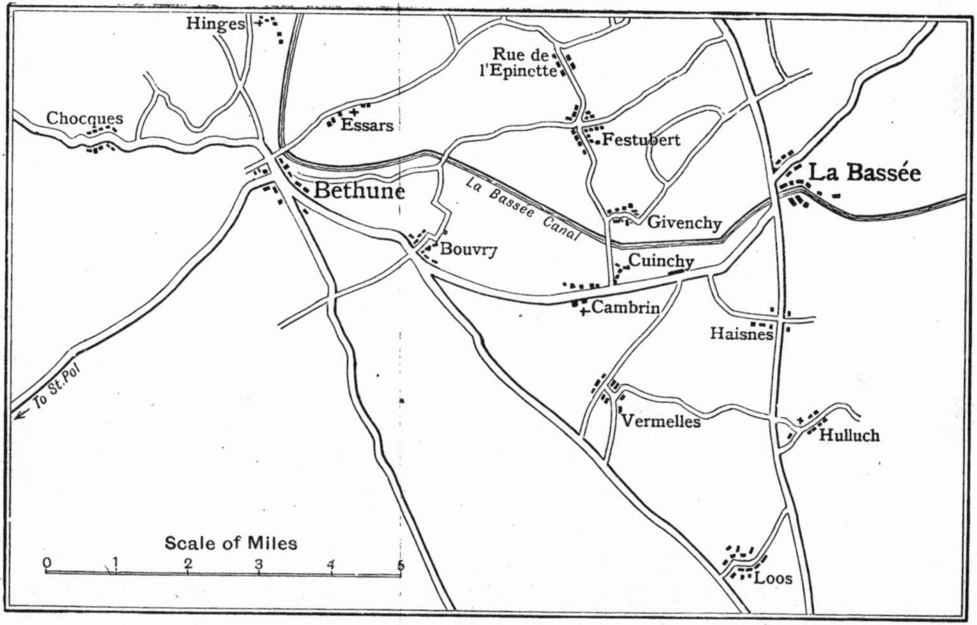

MAP. I.

account I might now give. First impressions of people, houses, places, are always interesting; I hope that the reader will not find these without interest, even though he may find them at times lacking in style.

"I am now in the train. We are passing level-crossings guarded by horn-blowing women; the train is strolling leisurely along over grass-grown tracks, and stopping at platformless stations. It is very hot. At midday I shall be about ten miles from the firing-line, and I expect the cannonade will be pretty audible. I feel strangely indifferent to things now, though I have the feeling that all this will be stamped indelibly on my memory." How well I remember the thrill of excitement when I found the name Chocques on my map, quite close to the firing-line! And as we got nearer, and saw R.A.M.C. and cavalry camps, and talked to Tommies guarding the line, saw aeroplanes, and yes! a captive balloon, excitement grew still greater! At last we reached Chocques, and the railway transport officer calmly informed us that we had another four miles to go. He brilliantly suggested walking. But an A.S.C. lorry was there, and in we climbed, only to be ejected by the corporal! Eventually we tramped to Béthune with *very* full packs in a hot sun.

Walking gave us opportunity for observation; and that road was worth seeing to those who had not seen it before. There were convoys of A.S.C. lorries, drawn up (or "parked") in twenties or thirties alongside the road, each with its mystical marking, a scarlet shell, a green shamrock, etc., painted on its side; Red Cross ambulances passed, impelling one to turn back and look in them, sometimes containing stretcher-cases (feet only visible), or sitting cases with bandaged head or arm in sling. Then there were motor-cars with Staff officers; motor-cars with youthful officers in immaculate Sam Brownes and "slacks"; and as we drew nearer Béthune, we saw canteens with Tommies standing and lounging outside, small squads of men, English notices, and boards with painted inscriptions,

such as

BILLETS.
Officers—2
Men—30

or

H.Q.
117th Inf. Bde.

and in the distance loomed the square tower of the cathedral, which I thought then to be a decapitated spire.

And so we came into the bustle of a French city.

I had never heard of Béthune before. As the crow flies it is about five to six miles from the front trenches. The shops were doing a roaring trade, and I was amazed to see chemists flaunting autostrop razors, stationers offering "Tommy's writing-pad," and tailors showing English officers' uniforms in their windows, besides all the goods of a large and populous town. We were very hungry and tired, and fate directed us to the famous tea-shop, where, at dainty tables, amid crowds of officers, we obtained an English tea ! I was astounded ; so were we all. To think that I had treasured a toothbrush as a thing that I might not be able to replace for months ! Here was everything to hand. Were we really within six miles of the Germans ? Yet officers were discussing " the hot time we had yesterday " ; while " we only came out this morning," or " they whizz-banged us pretty badly last night," were remarks from officers redolent of bath and the hairdresser ! Buttons brilliantly polished, boots shining like advertisements, swagger-canes, and immaculate collars, gave the strangest first impression of " active service " to us, with our leather equipment, packs, leather buttons, and trench boots !

" Old Barrett was right about the Sam Brownes," I said to Terry, vainly trying to look at my ease.

" Let's look at your map," he answered. Then, after a moment :

" Oh, we're not far from the La Bassée Canal. I've heard of that often enough ! "

" So have I," I replied. " Is La Bassée ours or theirs ? "

" Ours, of course " ; but he borrowed the map again to make sure !

Refreshed, but feeling strangely " out " of everything, we eventually found our way to the town major. Here my letter continues :

" I was told an orderly was coming in the evening to conduct me to the trenches, to my battalion ! Suddenly, however, we were told to go off—seven of us in the same division—to our brigades in a motor-lorry. So we are packed off. I said good-bye to Crowley and Terry. This was about 7 p.m. We went rattling along till within a short distance of our front trenches. There was a lot of cannonading going on around and behind us, and star-shells bursting continuously, with Crystal-Palace-firework pops ; we could hear rifles cracking too. At length we got to where the lorry could go no further, and we halted for a long time at a place where the houses were all ruins and the roofs like spiders'-webs, with the white glare of the shells silhouetting them against the sky. The houses had been shelled yesterday, but last night no shells were coming our way at all. My feelings were exactly like they are in a storm—the nearer and bigger the flashes and bangs the more I hoped the next would be really big and really near." Of course, all this cannonade was *our* artillery ; at the time we were quite muddled up as to what it all was ! The snarling bangs were the 18-pounders quite close to us, about one thousand yards behind our front line ; the cracking bullets were spent bullets, though it sounded to us as if they were from a trench about twenty yards in front of us ! Nothing is more confusing at first than the different sounds of the different guns. I think several of us would have been ready to say we had been under shell-fire that night ! The " star-shells " should be more accurately described as " flares ' or " rockets." But to continue my letter :

"Well, the next few hours were a strange mixture of sensations. We could nowhere find our brigades, and after *ten hours* in the lorry we landed here at a place sixteen miles back from the firing line; here our division had been located by a signaller, whom we had consulted when we stopped by the cross-roads! We were left by the lorry at 5.0 a.m. at a field ambulance station 'close to H.Q.,' where we slept wearily till 8.0, to awake and find ourselves miles from our division, which is really, I believe, quite near where we had been in the firing-line! Now we are sitting in a big old château awaiting a telephone-message; we are in a dining-room, walls peeling, and arm-chairs reduced to legless deformities! It is a jolly day: sun, and the smell of autumn." I shall not forget that long ride. I was at the back, and could see out; innumerable villages we passed; innumerable mistakes we made; innumerable stops, innumerable enquiries! But always there was the throbbing engine while we halted, and the bump and rattle as we plunged through the night. Eight officers and seven valises, I think we were; one or two were reduced to grumbling; several were asleep; a few, like myself, were awake, but all absolutely tired out. It was too uncomfortable to rest, cramped up among bulky valises and all sorts of sprawling limbs! Once, at about four o'clock, we halted at a house with a light in the window, and found a miner just going off to work. An old woman brewed some very black coffee, and we hungrily devoured bits of bread and butter, coffee, and cognac ; while the old woman, fat and smiling, gabbled incessantly at us ! A strange weird picture we must have made, some of us in kilts and bonnets, standing half-awake in the flickering candle-light.

We were at the Château all the morning. " The R.A.M.C. fellows were very decent to us ; gave us breakfast (eggs, bread and butter, and tinned jam) and also lunch (bully-beef, cheese, bread and butter, and beer). These were eaten off the dining-room table in style. I explored the Château during the morning ; just a big ordinary empty house inside ; outside, it is white plaster, with steep slate roofs, and a few ornamental turrets. The garden is mostly taken up with lines of picketed horses ; outside the orchards and enclosures the country is bare and flat ; it is a mining district, and pyramids of slag stand up all over the plain."

I cannot do better than continue quoting from these first letters of mine ; of course, I did not mention places by name :

" Well, at 2.0 p.m. the same old lorry and corporal turned up and took us back to Béthune. I gather he got considerable ' strafing ' for last night's performance, although I think he was not given clear enough instructions. Then, with seven other officers, we were sent off again in daylight, and dropped by twos and threes at our various Brigade Headquarters. Our " Brigade H.Q." was in one of the few houses left standing. Here I reported, and was told that an orderly would take me to my battalion transport. In half an hour the orderly arrived on a bicycle, and by 6.0 p.m. I was only half a mile from our transport. We were walking along, when suddenly there was a scream like a rocket, followed by a big bang, and the sound of splinters falling all about. I expected to see people jump into ditches; but they stood calmly in the street, women and all, and watched, while several shells (whizz-bangs, I believe)"—No, dear innocence, HIGH-EXPLOSIVE SHRAPNEL—" burst just near the road about a hundred yards ahead. We were four miles back from the firing-line. It was just the 'evening hate,' I expect. It didn't last long. Just near us was one of our own batteries firing intermittently."

This was my first experience of being under fire. I hadn't the least idea what to do. The textbooks, I believe, said "Throw yourself on the ground." I therefore looked at my orderly; but he was ducking behind his bicycle, which I am sure is not recommended by any manual of military training! I ducked behind nothing, copying him. This all took place in the middle of the road. But when I saw women opening the doors of their houses and standing calmly looking at the shells, ducking seemed out of the question; so we both stood and watched the bursting shells. Then the salvo ceased, and I, thinking I must show some sort of a lead, suggested that we should proceed. But my orderly, wiser by experience, suggested waiting to see if another salvo were forthcoming. After ten minutes, however, it was clear that the Germans had finished, and we resumed our journey in peace.

My letter continues : " At the transport I had a very comfortable billet. The quartermaster and two other new officers and myself had supper in an upstairs room. The quartermaster seemed very pessimistic, and told us a lot about our losses. We turned in at ten o'clock, and I slept well. It was ' very quiet ' ; that is to say, only intermittent bangs such as have continued ever since the beginning of the war, and will continue to the end thereof !

" October 9th. This morning a cart took us at nine o'clock to within about a mile of the firing-line, putting us down at the corner of a street that has been renamed ' H—— Street.' The country was dead flat ; the houses everywhere in ruins, though some were untouched and still inhabited. Thence an orderly conducted us to H.Q., where we reported to the Adjutant and the C.O. (who is quite young by the way) ; they were in the ground-floor room of a house, to which we came all the way from H—— Street along a communication trench about seven feet deep. These trenches were originally dug by the French, I believe. I was told I was posted to ' D ' Company, so another orderly took me back practically to H—— Street, which must be six or seven hundred yards behind the firing-line. ' D ' is in reserve ; I am attached to it for the present.

There are two other officers in it, Davidson and Symons. Both have only just joined."

So at last I was fairly lodged in my battalion. I had been directed, dumped, shaken, and carried, in a kindly, yet to me most amazingly haphazard, way to my destination, and there I found myself quite unexpected, but immediately attached somewhere until I should sort myself out a little and find my feet. I had a servant called Smith. In the afternoon I went with Davidson to supervise a working party, which was engaged in paving a communication trench with tiles from the neighbouring houses. In the evening I set to and wrote letters. I will close this chapter with yet one more quotation :

" Now I am in the ground-room of one of the few standing houses in H—— Street. Next door is a big ' École des filles,' which I am quite surprised to find empty ! Really the way the people go about their work here is amazing. Still, I suppose to carry on a girls' school half a mile from the Boche is just beyond the capacity of even their indifference ! I've already got quite used to the *noise*. There are two guns just about forty yards away, that keep on firing with a terrific bang ! I can see the flashes just behind me. I think the noise would worry you, if you heard these blaring bangs at the end of the back garden, which is just about the distance this battery is from me ! We are messing here in this room ; half a table has been propped up, and three chairs discovered and patched up for us. All the windows facing the enemy have been blocked up with sand-bags. I sleep here to-night. If the house is shelled, I shall flee to the dug-out twenty yards away. Orders have not yet come, but I believe we go back to billets to-morrow.

A free issue of 'Glory Boys' cigarettes has just arrived: two packets for each officer and man. Please don't forget to send my Sam Browne belt."

CHAPTER II

CUINCHY AND GIVENCHY

THROUGHOUT October and November our battalion was in the firing-line. This meant that we spent life in an everlasting alternation between the trenches and our billets behind, just far enough behind, that is, to be out of the range of the light artillery; always, though, liable to be called suddenly into the firing-line, and never out of the atmosphere of the trenches. Always before us was dangled a promised "rest," and always it was being postponed. Rumours were spread, dissected, laughed at, and eventually treated with bored incredulity. The battalion had had no rest, I believe, since May. Men, and especially N.C.O.'s, who had been out since October, 1914, were tired out in body and spirit.

With the officers and certain new drafts of men, it was different. We came out enthusiastic and keen. On the whole, I thoroughly enjoyed those first two months. I am surprised now to see how much detail I wrote in my letters home. Everything was fresh, everything new and interesting. And things were on the whole very quiet. We had a few casualities, but underwent no serious bombardment. And, most important to us, of course, we had no casualties among the officers.

Givenchy and Cuinchy are two small villages, north and south, respectively, of the La Bassée Canal, which runs almost due east and west between La Bassée and Béthune. Givenchy stands on a slight rise in the flattest of flat countries. A church tower of red brick must have been the most noticeable feature as one walked in pre-war days from the suburbs of Béthune along the La Bassée road. Cuinchy is a village straggling along a road. Both are as completely reduced to ruins as villages can be, the firing-line running just east of them. Between them flows the great sluggish canal.

During an afternoon in Béthune one could do all the shopping one required, and get a hair-cut and shampoo as well. Expensive cocktails were obtainable at the local bar ; there was also a famous tea-shop. We were billeted in one of the small villages around. Sometimes we only stayed one night at a billet : there was always change, always movement. Sometimes I got a bed ; often I did not ; but a valise is comfortable enough, when once its tricks are mastered. Anyhow it is "billets" and not "trenches," that is the point ; a continuous night's rest in pyjamas, the facilities of a bath, very often a free afternoon and evening, and no equipment and revolver to carry night and day ! It was in billets the following letters were written, which are really the best description of my life at this period.

"19th October, 1915. Our battalion went into the trenches on the 14th and came out on the 17th. Our company, 'B,' was in support. The front line was about 300 yards ahead, and we held the second line, everything prepared to meet an attack in case the enemy broke through the first line. Half-way between our first and second lines was a kind of redoubt, to be held at all costs. Here you are :

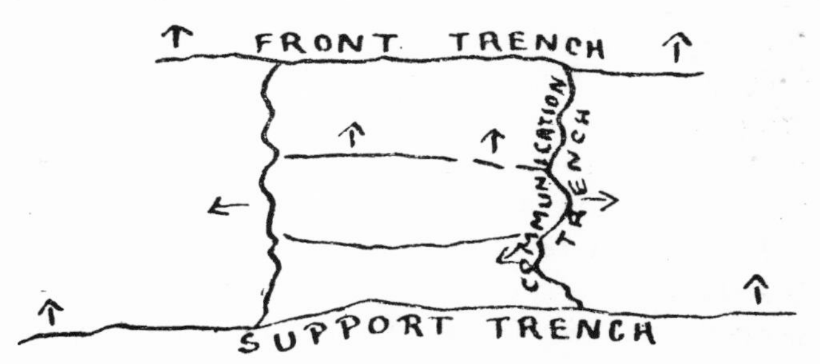

The arrows indicate the direction in which the fire-trenches point.

The line here forms a big salient, so that we often used to get spent bullets dropping into the redoubt, from right behind, it seemed. Here, another drawing will show what I mean :

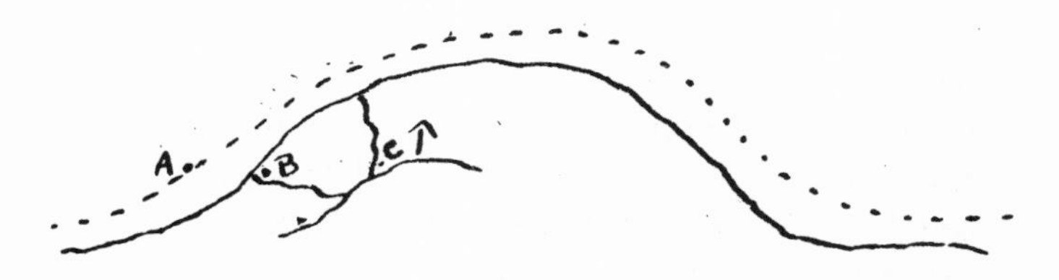

The dotted line is the German front trench. If the enemy A fires at the English B, the bullet will go on and fall at about C, who is facing in the direction of the arrow, in the support line. So C has to look out for *enfilading spent bullets*.

For three days and nights I was in command of this redoubt, isolated, and ready with stores, ammunition, water, barbed wire and pickets, bombs, and tools, to hold out a little siege for several days if necessary. I used to leave it to get meals at Company H.Q. in the support line; otherwise, I had always to be there, ready for instant action. No one used to get more than two or three hours' *consecutive* sleep, and I could never take off boots, equipment, or revolver.

Here is a typical scene in the redoubt.

Scene. A dug-out, 6′×4′×4′: smell, earthy.

Time. 2.30 a.m.

I awake and listen. Deathly stillness.

A voice. 'What's the time, kid?'

Another voice. 'Dunno. About 2 o'clock, I reckon.'

'Past that.'

Long silence.

'Rum job, this, ain't it, kid?'

'Why?'

'Well, I reckon if the —— Huns were coming over, we'd know it long afore they got 'ere. I reckon we'd 'ear the boys in front firing.'

Long pause.

'I dunno. 'Spose there's some sense in it, else we wouldn't be 'ere.'

Silence.

'—— cold on this —— fire step. Guess it's time they relieved us.'

Long silence.

'Don't them flares look funny in the mist?'

'Yus, I guess old Fritz uses some of them every night. Hullo, there they go again. 'Ear that machine-gun?'

Long pause, during which machine-guns pop, and snipers snipe merrily, and flares light up the sky. Trench-mortars begin behind us 'whizz-sh-sh-sh-h-h'—silence—'THUD.' Then the Germans reply, sending two or three over which thud harmlessly behind. The invisible sentries have now become clearly visible to me as I look out of my dug-out. Two of them are about ten yards apart standing on the fire-platform. Theirs is the above dialogue.

With a sudden *thud*, a trench-mortar shell drops fifteen yards behind us.

'Hullo, Fritz is getting the wind up.'

'Getting the wind up' is slang for getting nervous: this stolid comment from a sentry is typical of the attitude adopted towards 'Fritz' (the German) when he starts shelling or finding. He is supposed to be a bit jumpy! It seems hard to realise that Fritz is really trying to kill these sentrics: the whole thing seems a weird, strange play.

I make an effort, and crawl out of the dug-out. The 'strafing' has died down. Only occasional flares climb up from the German lines, and 'pop,' 'pop' in the morning mist. I go round the sentries, standing up by them and looking over the parapet. It is cold and raw, and the sentries are looking forward to the next relief. Ah! there is the corporal on trench duty coming. I can hear him routing out the snoring relief.

'Ping-g-g-g' goes a stray bullet singing by—a ricochet by its sound.

'A near one, sir.'

'Yes, Evans. Safer in the front line.'

'I guess it is, sir.'

Then, the sentries changed, I turn back again to my dug-out. Sleeping with revolvers and equipment requires some care of position.

'Half-past four, sir,' comes after a pause and some sleep.

Out I get, and everybody 'stands to' arms for an hour, each man taking up the position allotted to him along the fire-platform. Gradually it gets light. Some brick-stacks grow out of the mist in front, and ruined cottages loom up in the rear, and what was a church. The fire-platform being here pretty high, one can look back over the parados over bare flat country, cut up by trenches and run to waste terribly. 'Parados,' by the way, is the name given to the back of a trench; here is a drawing in section:

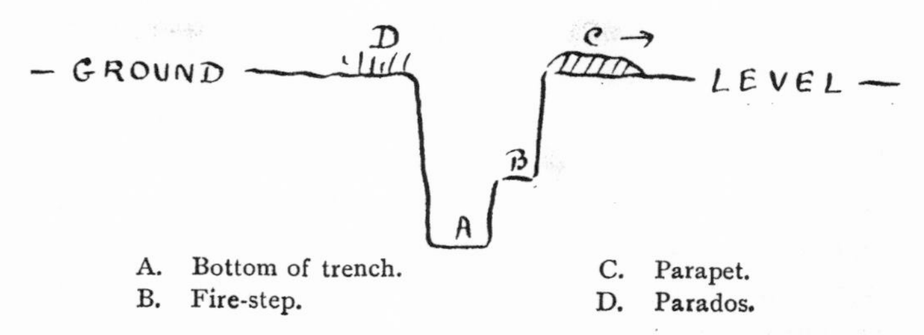

A. Bottom of trench.
B. Fire-step.
C. Parapet.
D. Parados.

At 5.30 ' Stand down and clean rifles ' is the order given, and the cleaning commences—a process as oft-repeated as ' washing up ' in civilised lands, and as monotonous and unsatisfactory, for a few hours later the rifles are a bit rusty and muddy again, and need another inspection.

7.30. ' Tell Sergeant Summers I'm going down to Company Headquarters.'

' Very good, sir.' Then I take a long mazy journey down the communication trench, which is six feet deep at least, and mostly paved with bricks from a neighbouring brick-field. There are an amazing lot of mice about the trenches, and they fall in and can't get out. Most of them get squashed. Frogs too, which make a green and worse mess than the mice. Our C.O. always stops and throws a frog out if he meets one. Tommy, needless to say, is not so sentimental. These trenches have been built a long time, and grass-stalks, dried scabious, and plantain-stalks grow over the edges, which must make them very invisible from above. ' H—— Street,' ' L—— Lane,' ' C—— Road,' ' P—— Lane ' are traversed, and so into S—— Street,' where, in the cellar of what was once a house, are two hungry officers already started on bacon and eggs, coffee (with condensed milk), and bread and tinned jam. We are lucky with three chairs and a table. A newspaper makes an admirable tablecloth, and a bottle a good candlestick, and there is room in a cellar to stand up. Breakfast done, a shave is manipulated, Meadows, my servant, getting ready my tackle and producing a mug of hot water.

9.30 finds me back in the redoubt and starting a 'working party' on repairing a communication trench and generally improving the trenches. Working parties are unpopular; Tommy does not believe in improving trenches he may never see again. And so the day goes on. Sentries change and take their place, sitting gazing into a scrap of mirror. Ration parties come up with dixies carried on wooden pickets, and the pioneer generally cleans up, sprinkling chloride of lime about in white showers, which seems as plentiful as the sand of the seashore, and the odour of which clings to the trenches, as the smell of seaweed does to the beach.

. . . . . .

The redoubt was in the Cuinchy trenches, and that old cellar was really a delightful headquarters. The first time we were in it we found a cat there; on the second occasion the same cat appeared with three lusty kittens! These used to keep the place clear of rats and get sat on every half-hour or so.

I soon learned to get used to smoke; on one occasion the smoke from our brazier became so thick that Gray, the cook, threatened to resign. For all the smoke gathers at the top of a dug-out and seems impossibly suffocating to anyone first entering; yet it is often practically clear two or three feet from the ground, so that when lying or sitting one does not notice the smoke at all; but a new-comer gets his eyes so stung that it seems impossible that anyone can live in the dug-out at all! (Gray, by the way, was not allowed to resign.)"

Here follows a letter describing the front trenches at Givenchy:

"7th November. On the 29th we marched off at 9.0 and halted at 11.0 for dinner. Luckily it was fine, and the piled arms, the steaming dixies, and the groups of men sitting about eating and smoking formed a pleasant sight. Our grub was put by mistake on the mess-cart which went straight on to the trenches! Edwards, however, our Company mess-president, came up to the scratch with bread, butter, and eggs. Tea was easily procured from the cookers. Then off we went to our H.Q. There we got down into the communication trench, and in single file were taken by guides into our part of the trenches: these guides were sent by the battalion we were relieving. I told you that all the trenches have names (which are painted on boards hung up at the trench corners). The first thing done was to post sentries along our company front: until this was done the outgoing battalion could not 'out-go.' Each man has his firing position allotted to him, and he always occupies it at 'stand to' and 'stand down.' We were three days and three nights in the trenches. Each officer was on duty for eight hours, during which he was responsible for a sector of firing-line and must be actually in the front trench. My watch was 12 to 4, a.m. and p.m. Work that out with 'stand to' in the morning and also in the evening and you will see that consecutive sleep is not easy! On paper 6–12 (midnight) looks good; but then, remember, dinner at 7.0 or 7.30 according to the fire, while you may have to turn out any time if you are being shelled at all. For instance, one night I was just turning in early at 7.0, when a mine went up on our right, and shelling and general 'strafing' kept me out till 9.30, after which I couldn't sleep! So at midnight I was tired when I started my four hours, turned in at 4.0, out again for 'stand to,' 8.0 breakfast, 9.0 rifle inspection, and so it goes on! That is why you can appreciate *billets*, and bed from 9.0 to 7.0 if you want it.

Imagine a cold November night—with a ground fog. What bliss to be roused from a snug dug-out at midnight, and patrol the Company's line for four interminable hours. It is deathly quiet. Has the war stopped? I stand up on the fire-step beside the sentry and try to see through the fog. 'Pip-

pip-pip-pip-pip ' goes a machine-gun. So the war's still on.

' Cold ? ' I ask a sentry. ' Only me feet, sir.' ' Why don't you stamp your feet, then ? ' This being equivalent to an order, Tommy stamps feebly a few times until made to do so energetically. Unless you *make* him stamp, he will not stamp ; would infinitely prefer to let his feet get cold as ice. Of course, when you have gone into the next bay, he immediately stops. Still, that is Tommy.

I gaze across into No Man's Land. I can just see our wire, and in front a collection of old tins—bully tins, jam tins, butter tins—paper, old bits of equipment. Other regiments always leave places so untidy. You clean up, but when you come into trenches you find the other fellows have left things about. You work hard repairing the trenches : the relieving regiment, you find on your return, has done ' damn all,' which is military slang for ' nothing.' And all other regiments, it seems, have the same complaint.

' Swish.' A German flare rocket lights up everything. You see our trenches all along. Everything is as clear as day. You feel as conspicuous as a cromlech on a hill. But the enemy can't see you, fog or no fog, if you only keep still. The light has fallen on the parapet this time, and lies sizzling on the sand-bags. A flicker, and it is gone ; and in the fog you see black blobs, the size and shape of the dazzling light you've just been staring at.

'Crack—plop.' 'Crack—plop.' A couple of bullets bury themselves in the sand-bags, or else with a long-drawn 'ping' go singing over the top. Why the sentries never get hit seems extraordinary. I suppose a mathematician would by combination and permutation tell you the chances against bullets aimed 'at a venture' hitting sentries exposing one-fourth of their persons at a given elevation at so many paces interval. Personally I won't try, as my whole object is to keep awake till four o'clock. And then I shall be too sleepy. Only remember, it is night and the sentries are invisible.

'Tap—tap—tap.' 'There's a wiring party out, sir. I've heard 'em these last five minutes.' Undoubtedly there are a few men out in No Man's Land, repairing their wire. I tell the sentries near to look out and be ready to fire, and then I send off a 'Very' flare, fired by a thick cartridge from a thick-barrelled brass pistol. It makes a good row, and has a fair kick, so it is best to rest the butt on the parapet and hold it at arm's length. Even so it leaves your ears singing for hours. The first shot was a failure—only a miserable rocket tail which failed to burst. The second was a magnificent shot. It burst beautifully, and fell right behind the party, two Germans, and silhouetted them, falling and burning still incandescent on the ground behind. A volley of fire followed from our waiting sentries. I could not see if the party were hit ; most of the shots were fired after the light had died out. Anyhow, the working party stopped. The two figures stood quite motionless while the flare burned.

The Germans opposite us were very lively. One could often hear them whistling, and one night they were shouting to one another like anything. They were Saxons, who are always at that game. No one knows exactly what it means. It was quite cold, almost frosty, and the sound came across the 100 yards or so of No Man's Land with a strange clearness in the night air. The voices seemed unnaturally near, like voices on the water heard from a cliff. 'Tommee—Tommee. Allemands bon—Engleesh bon.' 'We hate ze *Kron*prinz.' (I can hear now the nasal twang with which the 'Kron' was emphasised.) 'D—— the Kaiser.' 'Deutschland *unter* Alles.' I could hear these shouts most distinctly: the same sentences were repeated again and again. They shouted to one another from one part of the line to another, generally preceding each sentence by 'Kamerad.' Often you heard loud hearty laughter. As 'Comic Cuts' (the name given to the daily Intelligence Reports) sagely remarked, 'Either this means that there is a spirit of dissatisfaction among the Saxons, or it is a ruse to try and catch us unawares, or it is mere foolery.' Wisdom in high places!

Really it was intensely interesting. 'Come over,' shouted Tommy. 'We—are—not—coming—over,' came back. Loud clapping and laughter followed remarks like 'We hate ze *Kron*prinz.'

Then they would yodel and sing like anything. Tommy replied with 'Tipperary.' They sang, 'God save the King,' or rather their German equivalent of it, to the familiar tune. Then, 'Abide with us' rose into the night air and starlight. This went on for an hour and a half; though almost any night you can hear them shout something, and give a yodel—

It is the strangest thing I have ever experienced. The authorities now try and stop our fellows answering. The *entente* of last Christmas is not to be repeated! One of the officers in our battalion has shown me several German signatures on his pay-book (he was in the ranks then), given in friendly exchange in the middle of No Man's Land last Christmas Day.

I have had my baptism of mud now. It tires me to think of it, and I have not the effort to write fully about it! The second time we were in these trenches the mud was two feet deep. Even our Company Headquarters, a cellar, was covered with mud and slime. Paradoses and communication trenches had fallen in, and the going was terrible. The sticky mud yoicked one's boots off nearly, and it felt as if one's foot would be broken in extricating it. We all wore gum-boots, of blue-black rubber, that come right up to the waist like fishermen's waders. But the mud is everywhere, and we get our arms all plastered with it as we literally " reel to and fro " along the trench, every now and again steadying ourselves against slimy sand-bags. One or two men actually got stuck, and had to be helped out with spades ; one fellow lost heart and left one of his gum-boots stuck in the mud, and turned up in my platoon in a stockinged foot, of course plastered thick with clay ! We worked day and night. Gradually the problem is being tackled. Trench-boards, or ' mats,' are the best, like this :

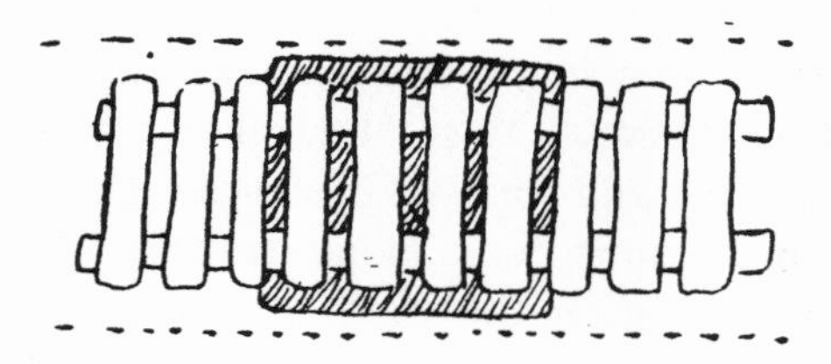

They are put along the bottom of the trench, the long ' runners ' resting on bricks taken from ruined houses, so as to raise the board and allow drainage underneath. If possible, a deep sump-pit is dug under the centre of the board. (The shaded part represents the sump-pit : the dotted lines are the sides of the trench ; the whole drawing in plan.)"

Weariness. Mud. The next experience (not mentioned in my letter) was Death. On our immediate right was " C " Company. Here our trench runs out like this __Λ_, more or less, and the opposite trenches are very close together. Consequently it is a great place for "mining activity." One evening we put up a mine; the next afternoon the Germans put up a counter-mine, and accompanied it with a hail of trench-mortars. I was on trench duty at the time, and had ample opportunity of observing the genus trench-mortar and its habits. One can see them approaching some time before they actually fall, as they come from a great height (in military terms, "with a steep trajectory"), and one can see them revolving as they topple down. Then they fall with a *thud*, and black smoke comes up and mud spatters all about. Most of them were falling in our second line and support trenches. I was patrolling up and down our front trench. We were "standing to" after the mine, and for half an hour it was rather a "hot shop." I was delighted to find that I rather enjoyed it: seeing one or two of the new draft with the "wind up" a bit steadied me at once. I have hardly ever since felt the slightest nervousness under fire. It is mainly temperament. Our company had four casualties: one in the front trench, the three others in the platoon in support. "C" Company suffered more heavily. At 6.0 Edwards came on duty, and I was able to go in quest of two bombers who were said to be wounded. Getting near the place I came on a man standing half-dazed in the trench. "Oh, sirrh," he cried, in the burring speech of a true Welshman. "A terench-mohrterh hass fall-en ericht in-ter me duck-out." For the moment I felt like laughing at the man's curious speech and look, but I saw that he was greatly scared: and no wonder. A trench mortar had dropped right into the mouth of his dug-out, and had half buried two of his comrades. We were soon engaged in extricating them. Both had bad head wounds, and how he escaped is a miracle. I helped carry the two men out and over the debris of flattened trenches to Company Headquarters. So, for the first time I looked upon two dying men, and some of their blood was on my clothes. One died in half an hour—the other early next morning. It was really not my job to assist: the stretcher-bearers were better at it than I, yet in this first little bit of "strafe" I was carried away by my instinct, whereas later I should have been attending to the living members of my platoon, and the defence of my sector. I left the company sergeant-major in difficulties as to whether Randall, the man who had so miraculously escaped, and who was temporarily dazed, should be returned as "sick" or "wounded."

Another death that came into my close experience was that of a lance-corporal in my platoon. I had only spoken to him a quarter of an hour before, and on returning found him lying dead on the fire-platform. He had been killed instantaneously by a rifle grenade. I lifted the waterproof sheet and looked at him. I remember that I was moved, but there was nothing repulsive about his recumbent figure. I think the novelty and interest of these first casualties made them quite easy to bear. I was so busy noticing details: the silence that reigned for a few hours in my platoon; the details of removing the bodies, the collecting of kit, etc. These things at first blunted my perception of the vileness of the tragedy; nor did I feel the cruelty of war as I did later.

Weariness. Mud. Death. So it was with great joy that we would return to billets, to get dry and clean, to eat, sleep, and write letters; to drill, and carry out inspections. Company drill, bayonet-fighting, gas-helmet drill, musketry, and lectures were usually confined to the morning and early afternoon. We thought that we had rather an overdose of lecturing from our medical officer (the M.O.) on sanitation and the care of the feet. "Trench feet," one lecture always began, "is that state produced by excessive cold or long standing in water or liquid mud." We soon got to know too much, we felt, about the use of whale-oil and anti-frostbite grease, the changing of socks and the rubbing and stamping of feet. We did get rather "fed up" with it; yet I believe we had only one case of trench feet in our battalion throughout the winter; so perhaps it was worth our discomfort of attending so many lectures! Our C.O.'s lectures on trench warfare were always worth hearing: he was so tremendously keen and such a perfect and whole-hearted soldier.

A chapter might be written on billet-life. Here are a few more extracts from letters :

"Oct. 13th. All day long this little inn has shaken from top to bottom : there is one battery about a hundred yards away that makes the whole house rattle like the inside of a motor-bus. The Germans might any time try and locate the battery, and a shell would reduce the house to ruins. Yet the old woman here declares she will not leave the house as long as she lives !

It is a strange place, this belt of land behind the firing-line. The men are out of the trenches for three days, and it is their duty, after perhaps a running parade before breakfast and two or three hours' drill and inspection in the morning, to rest for the remainder of the day. In the morning you will see all the evolutions of company drill carried out in a small meadow behind a strip of woodland ; in the next field an old man and woman are unconcernedly hoeing a cabbage-patch ; then behind here are a battalion's transport lines, with rows of horses picketed. Along the road an A.S.C. convoy is passing, each lorry at regulation distance from the next. In the afternoon you will see groups of Tommies doing nothing most religiously, smoking cigarettes, writing letters home. From six to eight the *estaminets* are open, and everyone flocks to them to get bad beer. They are also open an hour at midday, and then the orderly officer, accompanied by the provost-sergeant, produces an electric silence with 'Any complaints?' It does not pay an *estaminet*-keeper to dilute his beer too much, or else he will lose his licence.

I often wonder if these peasants think much. Think they must have done at the beginning, when their men were hastily called up. But now, after fifteen months of war? It is the children, chiefly, who are interested in the aeroplanes, shining like eagles silver-white against the blue sky; or in the boom from the battery across the street. But for their mothers and grandparents these things have settled into their lives; they are all one with the canal and the poplar trees. If a squad starts drilling on their lettuces, they are tremendously alert; but as for these other things, they are not interested, only unutterably tired of them. And after awhile you adopt the same attitude. The noise of the guns is boring and you hardly look up at an aeroplane, unless it is shrapnelled by the 'Archies' (anti-aircraft guns); then it is worth watching the pin-prick flashes dotting the sky all round it, leaving little white curls of smoke floating in the blue."

That billet was close to the firing-line. Here is a letter from a village, eight miles back:

"20th Oct., 1915. We came out here on Monday. The whole division marched out together. It was really an impressive sight, over a mile of troops on the march. Perfect order, perfect arrangement. Where the road bent you could often see the column for a mile in front, a great snake curling along the right side of the road. Occasionally an adjutant would break out of the line to trot back and correct some straggling; or a C.O. would emerge for a gallop over the adjacent ploughland.

Our company is billeted in a big prosperous farm. The men are in a roomy barn and look very comfortable. We are in a big room, on the right as you enter the front door of the farm: on a tiled floor stands a round table with an oilcloth cover, originally of a bright red pattern, but now subdued by constant scrubbings to the palest pink with occasional scarlet dottings. There are big tall windows, a wardrobe and sideboard, a big chimney-place fitted with a coke stove, and on the walls hang three very dirty old prints. The only war touch (beside our scattered possessions) is a picture from a French Illustrated of *L'Assaut de Vermelles*. Outside is a yard animated by cows, turkeys, geese, chicken, and ducks: also a donkey and a peacock, not to mention the usual dogs and cats. At 5 a.m. I am awakened by an amazing chorus.

The 'patron' is a strong, competent man, with many fine buxom daughters, who do the farm work with great capacity and energy. Henriette with a pitchfork is strength and grace in action. Tommy is much in awe of her. She hustles the pigs relentlessly. The sons are at the war. Etienne and Marcelle, aged ten and eight respectively, complete the family; with Madame, of course, who makes inimitable coffee; and various grandparents who appear in white caps and cook and bake all day.

I have just 'paid out'—all in five and twenty-franc notes. 'In the field' every man has his own pay book which the officer must sign, while the company quartermaster-sergeant sees that his acquittance roll is also signed by Tommy. We had a small table and chair out in the yard, and in an atmosphere of pigs and poultry I dealt out the blue-and-white oblongs which have already in many cases been converted into bread. For that is where most of the pay money goes, there and in the *estaminets.* The bread ration is always small, the biscuit ration overflowing. Bully beef, by the way, is simply ordinary corned beef. I watched cooking operations yesterday, and saw some fifty tins cut in half with an axe, clean hewn asunder, and the meat deftly hoicked with a fork into the field-kitchen, or 'cooker,' which is a range and boiler on wheels. This was converted into a big stew, and served out into dixies (camp kettles) and so to the men's canteens.

This afternoon our company practised an attack over open country. I was surprised to find the men so well trained. I had imagined that prolonged trench-warfare would have made them stale. The country is *very* flat. There are no hedges. The only un-English characteristics are the poplar rows, the dried beans tied round poles like mother-gamp umbrellas, and the wayside chapels and crucifixes.

Yesterday afternoon Edwards and I got in a little revolver practice just near; and afterwards we had an energetic game of hockey, with sticks and an empty cartridge-case."

Altogether, billet life was very enjoyable. On November 1st Captain Dixon joined our battalion and took over "B" Company. For over four months I worked under the most good-natured and popular officer in the battalion. We were always in good spirits while he was with us. "I can't think why it is," he used to say, "I'm not at all a jolly person, yet you fellows are always laughing; and in my old regiment it was always the same!" He was a fearful pessimist, but a fine soldier. His delight used to be to get a good fire blazing in billets, sit in front of it with a novel, and then deliver a tirade against the discomfort of war! The great occasion used to be when the arch-pessimist, our quartermaster, was invited to dinner. Then Edwards, the Mess president, would produce endless courses, and the two pessimists would warm to a delightful duologue on the fatuity of the Staff, the Army, and the Government.

"By Jove, we are the biggest fools on this earth!" Dixon would say at last.

"We're fools enough to be led by fools," Jim Potter would reply.

And somehow we were all more cheerful than ever!

CHAPTER III

WORKING-PARTIES

"FALL in the brick-party."

The six privates awoke from a state of inert dreaming, or lolling against the barn that flanked the gateway of battalion headquarters, to stand in two rows of three and await orders. At last the A.S.C. lorry had turned up, an hour late, and while it turned round I despatched one of the privates to our transport to get six sand-bags. By the time he returned the lorry had performed its about-wheel, and, all aboard, myself in front and the six behind, we are off for C——.

We pass through Béthune. As we approach through the suburbs, we rattle past motor despatch riders, A.S.C. lorries, Red Cross carts, columns of transport horses being exercised, officers on horse-back, officers in motor-cars, small unarmed fatigue parties, battalions on the march ; then there are carts carrying bricks, French postmen on bicycles, French navvies in blue uniforms repairing the road, innumerable peasant traps, coal waggons, women with baskets, and children of course everywhere. " Business as usual "—yet, but for a line of men not so many miles away the place would be a desolate ruin like the towns and villages that chance has doomed to be in the firing-line.

So I moralise. Not so the Tommies, sprawling behind, inside the lorry, and caring not a jot for anything save that they are on a " cushy " or soft job, as the rest of the battalion are doing four hours' digging under R.E. supervision. A good thing to be a Tommy, to be told to fall in here or there, and not to know whether it is for a bayonet-charge, or a job of carting earth !

" Bang—Bang-bang." We are nearing the firing-line, having left Béthune, where military police stand at every corner directing the traffic with flags, one road " up," another " down " : we are once more within the noisy but invisible chain of batteries. " Lorries 6 miles per hour." The shell-holes in the road, roughly filled with stones, would make quicker going impossible anyhow. We are entering C——, and I keep an eagle eye open for ruined houses, and soon stop by a house with two walls and half a roof. Out come the six Tommies and proceed to fill a sand-bag each with bricks and empty it into the lorry. The supply is inexhaustible, and in half an hour the A.S.C. corporal refuses to take more, declaring we have the regulation three-ton load, so I stop work and prepare to depart.

The corporal, however, has heard of a sister-lorry near by, which has unfortunately slipped into a ditch and, so to speak, sprained its ankle. Though extraordinarily unromantic in appearance, the corporal shows himself imbued with a spirit of knight errantry, and, having obtained my permission to rescue the fair damsel, sets off for what he declares cannot take more than ten minutes. As I thought the process would take probably more like twenty minutes, I let the men repair to a house on the opposite side of the road, where was a rather more undamaged piece of roof than usual (it was now raining), and myself explored the place I happened to be in.

Occasionally, at home one comes across a deserted cottage in the country ; a most desolate spirit pervades the place. Imagine, then, what it is like in these villages half a mile or a mile behind what has been the firing-line for now twelve months. A few steps off the main road brought me into what had formerly been a small garden belonging to a farm. There had been a red-brick wall all along the north side with fruit trees trained along it. Now, the wall was mostly a rubble-heap, and the fruit trees dead. One sickly pear tree struggled to exist in a crumpled sort of heap, but its wilted leaves only added to the desolation of the scene. An iron gate, between red brick pillars, was still standing, strangely enough ; but the little lawn was run to waste, and had a crater in the middle of it about five feet across, inside of which was some disintegrating animal, also empty tins, and other refuse. Trees were broken, weeds were everywhere. I tried to reconstruct the place in my imagination, but it was a chaotic tangle. I came across a few belated raspberries, and picked one or two ; they were tasteless and watery. Rubbish and broken glass were strewn everywhere. It was a dreary sight in the grey rain ; the only sign of life a few chattering blue-tits.

The house was an utter ruin, only a ground-room wall left standing ; some of the outhouses had not suffered so much, but all the roofs were gone. I saw a rusty mangle staring forlornly out of a heap of débris ; and a manger and hayrack showed what had been a stable. The pond was just near, too, and gradually I could piece together the various elements of the farm. Who the owners were I vaguely wondered ; perhaps they will return after the war ; but I doubt if they could make much of the old ruins. These villages will most likely remain a blighted area for years, like the villages reclaimed by the jungle. Already the virginia creeper and woodbine are trying to cover the ugliness. . . .

The Tommies meanwhile had been smoking Gold Flakes, and one or two had also been exploring ; one had discovered a child's elementary botany book, and was studying the illustrations when I came up. Our combined view now was " Where is the lorry ? " and this view held the field, with increasing curiosity, annoyance, and vituperation, for one solid hour and a half. It was dinner-time, and a common bond of hunger held us, until at last in exasperation I marched half the party in quest of our errant conveyance. I was thoroughly annoyed with the gallant corporal. Three-quarters of a mile away I found the two lorries. My little corporal had rescued his lorn princess, but she, being a buxom wench, had brought her rescuer into like predicament! And so we came up just in time to see the rescue of *our* lorry from the treacherous ditch! I felt I could not curse, especially as the little corporal had winded himself somehow in the stomach during the last bout. It had been a feeble show; yet there was the lorry, and in it the bricks, on to which the fellows climbed deliberately as men who recover a lost prize. And so we arrived at our transport (the bricks were for a horse-stand in a muddy yard) at half-past two; after which I dismissed the party to its belated dinner.

The above incident hardly deserves a place in a chapter headed "working-parties," being in almost every respect different from any other I have ever conducted. I think the "working-party" is realised less than anything else in this war by those who have not been at the front. It does not appeal to the imagination. Yet it is essential to realise, if one wants to know what this war is like, the amount of sheer dogged labour performed by the infantry in digging, draining, and improving trenches.

The "working-party" usually consists of seventy to a hundred men from a company, with either one or two officers. The Brigadier going round the trenches finds a communication trench falling in, and about a foot of mud at the bottom. "Get a working-party on to this at once," he says to his Staff Captain. The Staff Captain consults one of the R.E. officers, and a note is sent to the Adjutant of one of the two battalions in billets: "Your battalion will provide a working party of . . . officers . . . full ranks (sergeants and corporals) and . . . other ranks to-morrow. Report to Lt. . . ., R.E., at . . . at 5.0 p.m. to-morrow for work on . . . Trench. Tools will be provided." The Staff Captain then dismisses the matter from his head. The Adjutant then sends the same note to one or more of the four company commanders, detailing the number of men to be sent by the companies specified by him. (He is scrupulously careful to divide work equally between the companies, by the way.) The company commander on receiving the note curses volubly, declares it a "d—d shame the hardest worked battalion in the brigade can't be allowed a moment's rest, feels sure the men will mutiny one of these days," etc., summons the orderly, who is frowsting in the next room with the officers' servants, and says, "Take this to the sergeant-major," after scribbling on the note "Parade outside Company H.Q. 3.30 p.m.," and adding, as the orderly departs, "Might tell the quartermaster-sergeant I want to see him." Meanwhile the three subalterns are extraordinarily engrossed in their various occupations, until the company commander boldly states that it is

" rotten luck, but he supposes as So-and-so took the last, it is So-and-so's turn, isn't it ? " and details the officers ; if they are new officers he tells them the sergeants will know exactly what to do, and if they are old hands he tells them nothing whatever. The " quarter " (company quartermaster-sergeant) then arrives, and is told the party will not be back, probably, till 10.0 p.m., and will he make sure, please, that hot soup is ready for the men on return, and also dry socks if it turns out wet ; he is then given a drink, and the company commander's work is finished.

Meanwhile the company sergeant-major has received the orders from the orderly, and summons unto him the orderly-sergeant, and from his " roster," or roll, ticks off the men and N.C.O.'s to be warned for the working party. This the orderly-sergeant does by going round to the various barns and personally reading out each man's name, and on getting the answer, saying, " You're for working party, 3.15 to-day." The exact nature of the remarks when he is gone are beyond my province. Only, as an officer taking the party, one knows that at 3.25 p.m. the senior sergeant calls the two lines of waiting " other ranks " to attention, and with a slap on his rifle, announces " Working-party present, Sir," as you stroll up. Working-parties are dressed in " musketry order " usually—that is to say, with equipment, but no packs ; rifles and ammunition, of course, and waterproof sheets rolled and fastened to the webbing belt. The officer then tells the sergeant to " stand them easy," while he asks one or two questions, and looks once more at " orders " which the senior sergeant has probably brought on parade, and at 3.30, with a " Company-Shern! Slo-o-ope hip! Right-in-fours: form-fórs! Right! By the right, Quick *march!* " leads off his party, giving " March at *ease*, march-easy! " almost in one breath as soon as he rounds the corner. Then there is a hitching of rifles to the favourite position, and a buzz of remarks and whistles and song behind, while the sergeant edges up to the officer or the officer edges back to the sergeant, according to their degree of intimacy, and the working-party is on its way.

One working-party I remember very well. We were in billets at ——, and really tired out. It was Nov. 6th, and on looking up my letters I find our movements for the last week had been as follows:

Oct. 29th.	9.0 a.m. Moved off from billets.
	12.0 midday. Lunch.
	3.0 p.m. Arrived in front trenches.
Oct. 30th.	Front trenches.
Oct. 31st.	Front trenches.
Nov. 1st.	Relieved at 3.0 p.m. (The Devons were very late relieving us, owing to bad rain and mud.)
	5.30 p.m. Reached billets.

Nov. 2nd. Rain all day. Morning spent by men in trying to clean up. Afternoon, baths.

Nov. 3rd. 9.0 a.m. Started off for trenches again. It had rained incessantly. Mud terrible.

1.0 p.m. Arrived in front trenches.

Nov. 4th. Front trenches. Rained all day.

Nov. 5th. 2.30 p.m. Relieved late again. Mud colossal. Billets 5.0 p.m.

Nov. 6th. Morning. Cleaning up. Inspection by C.O.

Afternoon. SUDDEN AND UNEXPECTED WORKING-PARTY. 3.0 p.m.—11.0 p.m.!!

Yet I thoroughly enjoyed those eight hours, I remember. There were, I suppose, about eighty N.C.O.'s and men from "B" Company. I was in charge, with one other officer. We halted at a place whither the "cooker" had been previously despatched, and where the men had their tea. Luckily it was fine. The men sat about on lumps of trench-boards and coils of barbed wire, for the place was an "R.E. Dump," where a large accumulation of R.E. stores of all description was to be found. I apologised to the R.E. officer for keeping him a few minutes while the men finished their tea; he, however, a second-lieutenant, was in no hurry whatever, it seemed, and waited about a quarter of an hour for us. Then I fell the men in, and they " drew tools," so many men a pick, so many a shovel (the usual proportion is one pick, two shovels), and we splodged along through whitish clay of the stickiest calibre in the gathering twilight. An R.E. corporal and two R.E. privates had joined us mysteriously by now, as well as the second-lieutenant, and crossing H—— Street we plunged down into a communication trench, and started the long mazy grope. The R.E. corporal was guide. The trench was all paved with trench-mats, but these were not " laid," only " shoved down " anyhow ; consequently they wobbled, and one's boot slipped off the side into squelch, rubbing the ankle. Continually came up the message from behind, " Lost touch, Sir ! " This involved a wait—one, two minutes—until the " All-up " or " All-in " came up. (One hears it coming in a hoarse whisper, and starts before it actually arrives. Infinite patience is necessary. R.E. officers are sometimes eager to go ahead ; but once lose the last ten men at night in an unknown trench, and it may take three hours to find them.) The other officer was bringing up the rear.

At last we reached our destination, and the R.E. officer and myself told off the men to work along the trench. This particular work was clearing what is known as a " berm," that is, the flat strip of ground between the edge of the trench and the thrown-up earth, each side of a C.T. (communication trench).

When a trench is first dug, the earth is thrown up each side ; the recent rains were, however, causing the trenches to crumble in everywhere, and the weight of the thrown-up earth was especially the cause of this. Consequently, if the earth were cleared away a yard on each side of the trench, and

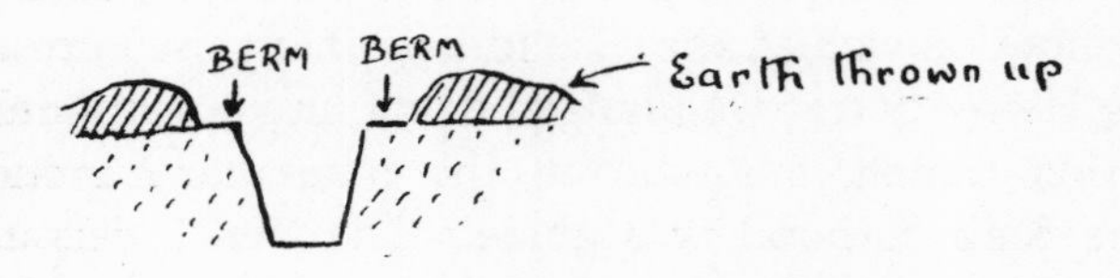

thrown further back, the trench would probably be saved from falling in to any serious extent, and the light labour of shovelling dry earth a yard or so back would be substituted for the heart-breaking toil of throwing sloppy mud or sticky clay out of a trench higher than yourself.

The work to be done had been explained to the sergeants before we left our starting-point. As we went along, the R.E. officer told off men at ten or five yards' interval, according to the amount of earth to be moved. Each man stopped when told off, and the rest of the company passed him. Sergeants and corporals stopped with their section or platoon, and got the men started as soon as the last man of the company had passed. At last up came the last man, sergeant, and the other officer, and together we went back all along. The men were on top (that is why the working-party was a night one) ; sometimes they had not understood their orders and were doing something wrong (a slack sergeant would then probably have to be routed out and told off). The men worked like fun, of course, it being known, to every one's joy, that this was a piece-job, and that we went home as soon as it was finished. There was absolute silence, except the sound of falling earth, and an occasional chink of iron against stone ; or a swish, and muttered cursings, as a bit of trench fell in with a slide, dragging a man with it ; for it is not always easy to clear a yard-wide " berm " without crumbling the trench-edge in. One would not think these men were " worn out," to see them working as no other men in the world can work ; for nearly every man was a miner. The novice will do only half the work a trained miner will do, with the same effort.

Sometimes I was appealed to as to the " yard." Was this wide enough ? One man had had an unlucky bit given him with a lot of extra earth from a dug-out thrown on to the original lot. So I re-divided the task. It is amazing the way the time passes while going along a line of workers, noticing, talking, correcting, praising. By the time I got to the first men of the company, they were half-way through the task.

At last the job was finished. As many men as space allowed were put on to help one section that somehow was behind ; whether it was bad luck in distribution or slack work no one knew or cared.

The work must be finished. The men wanted to smoke, but I would not let them ; it was too near the front trenches. And then I did a foolish thing, which might have been disastrous ! The R.E. corporal had remained, though the officer had left long ago. The corporal was to act as guide back, and this he was quite ready to do if I was not quite sure of the way. I, however, felt sure of it, and as the corporal would be saved a long tramp if he could go off to his dug-out direct without coming with us, I foolishly said I had no need of him, and let him go. I then lost my way completely. We had never been in that section before, and none of the sergeants knew it. We had come from the " R.E. Dump," and thither we must return, leaving our tools on the way. But I had been told to take the men to the Divisional Soup Kitchen first, which was about four hundred yards north of X, the spot where we entered the C.T. and which I was trying to find. For all I knew I was going miles in the wrong direction. My only guide was the flares behind, which assured me I was not walking to the Germans but away from them. The unknown trenches began to excite among the sergeants the suspicion that all was not well. But I took the most colossal risk of stating that I knew perfectly well what I was doing, and strode on ahead.

There was silence behind after that, save for splashings and splodgings. My heart misgave me that I was coming to undrained trenches of the worst description, or to water-logged impasses! Still I strode on, or waited interminable waits for the "All up" signal. At last we reached houses, grim and black, new and awfully unknown. I nearly tumbled down a cellar as a sentry challenged. I was preparing for humble questions as to where we were, the nearest way to X, and a possible joke to the sergeant (this joke had not materialised, and seemed unlikely to be of the easiest), when I recovered myself from the cellar, mounted some steps, and found myself on a road beside a group of Tommies emerging from the Soup Kitchen! My star (the only one visible, I believe, that inky night) had led me there direct! I said nothing, as every one warmed up in spirits as well as bodies with that excellent soup; and no one ever knew of the quailings of my heart along those unknown trenches! To lead men wrong is always bad; but when they are tired out it is unpardonable, and not quickly forgotten. As it was, canteens were soon brimming with thick vegetable soup, filled from a bubbling cauldron with a mighty ladle. In the hot room men glistened and perspired, while a regular steam arose from muddied boots and puttees; every one, from officer to latest joined private, was sipping with dangerous avidity the boiling fluid. Many charges have been laid against divisional staffs, but never a complaint have I heard against a soup kitchen! So in good spirits we tramped along, and dumped our tools in the place where we had found them. "Clank-clank, clank," as spade fell on spade. Then, " You may smoke " was passed down. The sergeant reported " All correct, Sir ! " and we tramped along in file. Soon the bursts of song were swallowed up in a great whistling concert, and we were all merry. The fit passed, and there was silence ; then came the singing again, which developed into hymns, and that took us into our billets. Here we were greeted with the most abominable news of réveillé at 5.0 a.m., but I think most of the men were too sleepy to hear it ; we two officers deplored our fate while eating a supper set out for us in a greenhouse, our temporary mess-room !

That is a working-party : interesting as a first experience to an officer ; but when multiplied exceedingly, by day, by night, in rain, mud, sleet, and snow, carrying trench boards, filling sand-bags, digging clay, bailing out liquid mud, and returning cold and drenched, without soup—then, working-parties became a monotonous succession of discomforts that wore out the spirit as well as the body.

The last six nights before the promised rest were spent in working-parties at Festubert. There the ground was low and wet, and it was decided to build a line of breastwork trenches a few hundred yards behind the existing line, so that we could retire on to dry ground in case of getting swamped out. For six nights in succession we left billets at 10.0 p.m. and returned by 4.0 a.m. The weather was the coldest, it turned out eventually, that winter. It started with snow; then followed hard frost for four nights; and, last but not least, a thaw and incessant sleet and rain. I have never before experienced such cold; but, on the other hand, I have never before had to stand about all night in a severe frost (it was actually, I believe, from 10° to 15° below freezing point). At 2.0 a.m. the stars would glitter with relentless mirth, as the cold pierced through two cardigans and a sheepskin waistcoat. I have skated at night, but always to return by midnight to fire and bed. Bed! At home people were sleeping as comfortably as usual; a few extra blankets, perhaps, or more coals in the grate!

I was out five nights of the six. Captain Dixon was on leave, so we only had three officers in "B," and two had to go every night. Every night at 9.30 the company would be fallen in and marched off to the rendezvous, there, at 10.0, to join the rest of the battalion. There was no singing; very little talking. In parts the road was very bad, and we marched in file. The road was full of shell-holes, and bad generally; the ice crackled and tinkled in the ruts and puddles; the frozen mud inclined you to stumble over its ridges and bumps. It took us the best part of an hour to reach our destination. The first night we must have gone earlier than the other nights, as I distinctly remember viewing by daylight those most amazing ruins. There was a barrier across the road just before you entered the village ; (a barrier is usually made like this—

you can defend the road without blocking it to traffic ; at the same time it cannot be rushed by motor-cycles or armoured cars) ; then just opposite were the few standing fragments of the church ; bits of wall and mullion here and there ; and all around tombstones leaning in every direction, rooted up, shattered, split. There was one of the crucifixes standing untouched in the middle of it all, about which so much has been written ; whether it had fallen and been erected again I cannot say. The houses were more smashed, crumpled, and chaotic than even Cuinchy or Givenchy

I remember that corner very vividly, because at that spot came one of the few occasions on which I had the " wind up " a little. Why, I know not. We were halted a few moments, when two whizz-bangs shot suddenly into a garden about twenty yards to our right, with a vicious " Vee-bm . . . Vee-bm." We moved on, and just as we got round the corner I saw two flashes on my left, and two more shells hissed right over us and fell with the same stinging snarl into the same spot, just twenty yards *over* us this time. I was, luckily, marching at the rear of the company at the time, as I ducked and almost sprawled in alarm. For the next minute or two I was all quivery. I am glad to know what it feels like, as I have never experienced since such an abject windiness! I believe it was mainly due to being so exposed on the hard hedgeless road; or, perhaps that last pair did actually go particularly near me. At any rate, such was my experience, and so I record it.

At the entrance to the communication trench R.E. officers told us off: "A" Company, "carrying party"; "B" Company to draw shovels and picks and "follow me." Then we started off along about a mile and a half of communication trenches. I have already said that Festubert is a very wet district, and it can easily be imagined that the drainage problem is none of the easiest. This long communication trench had been mastered by trench-mats fastened down on long pickets which were driven deep down into the mud. The result was that the trench floor was raised about two feet from the original bottom, and one walked along a hollow-sounding platform over stagnant water. The sound reminded me of walking along a wooden landing-stage off the end of a pier. Every few hundred yards were "passing points," pre-

sumably to facilitate passing other troops coming in the other direction; but as I never had the good fortune to meet the other troops at these particular spots, though I did in many others, I cannot say they were particularly useful. Another disadvantage about these water-logged trenches was that the bad rains had made the water rise in several places even over the raised trench-board platform ; others were fastened on top ; but even these were often not enough. And when the frost came and froze the water on top of the boards, the procession became a veritable cake-walk, humorous no doubt to the stars and sky, but to the performers, feeling their way in the thick darkness and ever slipping and plunging a boot and puttee into the icy water at the side, a nightmare of painful and jarring experiences.

There was one junction of trenches where one had to cross a dyke full of half-frozen water ; there was always a congestion of troops here, ration-parties, relieving-parties, and ourselves. All relieving had to be done at night, as the trenches with their artificially raised floors were no longer deep enough to give cover from view. This crossing had to be negociated in a most gingerly fashion, and several men got wet to their waists when compelled to cross while carrying an awkward-shaped hurdle. After this, the trench was worse than ever ; in parts it was built with fire-steps on one side, and one could scramble on to this and proceed on the dry for awhile ; but even here the slippery sand-bags would often treacherously slide you back into the worst part of the iced platform, and so gave but a doubtful advantage At last the open was gained ; then came the crossing of the old German trench, full of all kinds of grim relics from the spring fighting. And so to our destination.

On the open ground lay a tracing of white tape like this—

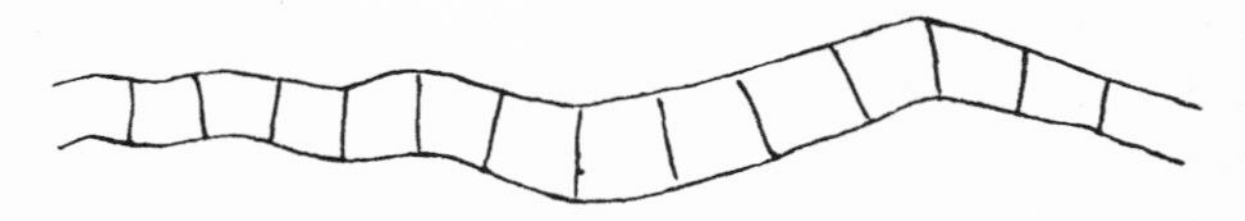

forming a serpentine series of contacting squares; in the blackness only two white-bordered squares were visible from one position. Each man was given a square to dig. I forget the measurements; about two yards square, I think, and two feet deep. The earth had to be thrown about eight yards back against a breastwork of hurdles. These hurdles were being brought up by the "carrying-parties" and fastened by wires by the R.E.'s; the R.E. officers had, of course, laid our white tapes for us previously. Eventually the sentries will stand behind the hurdle breastwork with a water-ditch ten yards in front of them, which obstacle will be suitably enhanced by strong wire entanglements.

But all this vision of completion is hid from the eyes of Private Jones, who only knows he has his white-taped square to dig. Arms and equipment are laid carefully on the side of the trench furthest from the breastwork; and nothing can be heard but the hard breathing and the shovelling and scraping of the "other ranks." For two hours those men worked their hardest ; indeed, it was much the best job to have on those cold nights. I did more digging then than I have ever done before or since. " Come on, Davies, you're all behind," and for ten minutes I would do an abnormal amount of shovelling, until, out of breath, I would hand the boy back his shovel, and tell him to carry on, while all aglow I went along the line examining the progress of the work. We had quite a number of bullets singing and cracking across, and there were one or two casualties every night. Sometimes flares would pop over, and every one would freeze into static posture ; but on the whole things were very quiet, the enemy doubtless as full of water as ourselves.

That intense cold ! Yet I did not know then that it is far worse being on sentry in the frost than marching and digging. And I am not sure that the last night, when it rained incessantly, was not worse than all the rest. We had a particularly bad piece of ground that night, pitted with shell-holes, full of frozen water : you were bound to fall in one at last, and get wet to the waist ; but even if you did escape that sticky humiliation, the driving sleet and rain were bad enough in themselves. That was a night when I found certain sergeants sheltered together in a corner ; and certain other sergeants in the middle of their men and the howling gale. I soon routed the former out, but did not forget ; and have since discovered how valuable a test of the good and the useless N.C.O. is a working.party in the rain.

Never have I longed for 2.0 a.m. as I did that night! My feet were wet, my body tired, my whole frame shivering with an approaching cold. The men could do nothing any longer in that stinking slush (for these old shell-holes of stagnant water were, to say the least of it, unsavoury!). I was so heavy with sleep I could scarce keep my eyes open. But when at last the order came from our second-in-command "Cease work," I was filled with a dogged energy that carried me back to billets in the best of spirits, though I actually fell asleep as I marched behind the company, and bumped into the last four, when they halted suddenly half-way home! And so at four o'clock the men tumbled upstairs to breakfast and braziers (thanks to a good quarter-master-sergeant). I drank Bovril down below, and then, in pyjamas, sweaters, and innumerable blankets, turned in till 11.0 a.m. Next afternoon we left Rue de l'Epinette and halted at a village on the road to Lillers, whence we were to train to "a more northern part of the line," and enjoy at last our long-earned rest.

CHAPTER IV

REST

RUMOURS were rife again, and mostly right this time. " The C.O. knew the part we were going to: a chalk country . . . rolling downs . . . four or five weeks' rest . . . field training thirty miles from the firing-line." Chalk downs! To a Kentish man the words were magic, after the dull sodden flats of Flanders. I longed for a map of France, but could not get hold of one. As we marched to Lillers I looked at the flat straight roads and the ditches, at the weary monotony, uninspired by hill or view, at the floods on the roads, and the uninteresting straightness of the villages; and I felt that I was at the end of a chapter. Any change must be better than this. And chalk! chalk! short dry turf, and slopes with purple woods! I had forgotten these things existed.

I forget the name of the village where we halted for two nights. I had a little room to myself, reached by a rickety staircase from the yard. One shut the staircase door to keep out the yard. Here several new officers joined us, Clark being posted to our company, and soon I began to see my last two months as history. For we began to tell our adventures to Clark, who had never been in the firing-line! Think of it! He was envious of our experiences! So I listened in awe and heard a tale develop, a true tale, the tale of the night the mine went up. It was no longer a case of disputing how many trench-mortars came over, but telling an interested audience that trench-mortars *did* come over! Clark had never seen one. And I listened agape to hear myself the hero of a humorous story. When the mine went up, I had come out of my dug-out rather late and asked if anything had happened. This tale became elaborated: I was putting my gloves on calmly, it seems, as I strolled out casually and asked if anyone had heard a rather loud noise! And so stories crystallised, a word altered here and there for effect, but true, and as past history quite interesting.

The move was made the occasion, by our C.O., of very elaborate and careful operation orders. No details were left to chance, and a conference of officers was called to explain the procedure of getting a battalion on a train and getting it off again. As usual, the officers' valises had to be ready at a very early hour, and the company mess-boxes packed correspondingly early. Edwards, I think, was detailed as O.C. loading-party. Everything like this was down in the operation orders. The adjutant had had a time of it.

Certainly the entraining went like clockwork, and

once more I was seated in a grey-upholstered corridor carriage; the men were in those useful adaptable carriages inscribed "Chevaux 10. Hommes 30." Our Tommies were evidently a kind of centaur class, for they went in by twenties. As far as I can remember, we entrained at 10.0 a.m.; we arrived at a station a few miles from Amiens at 9.0 p.m. A slow journey, but I felt excited like a child. I must keep going to the corridor to put my head out of the window. It was a sparkling, nippy air; the smell of the steam, the grit of the engine—these were things I had forgotten; and soon there were rolling plains, hills, clustering villages. The route, through St. Pol, Doullens, and Canaples, is ordinary enough, no doubt; and so, too, the gleam of white chalk that came at last. But if you think that ordinary things cannot be wonderful beyond measure, then go and live above ground and underground in Flanders for two months on end in winter; then, perhaps, you will understand a little of my good spirits.

It was quite dark when we arrived. Then for three and a half hours we waited in a meadow outside the station, arms piled, the men sitting about on their waterproof sheets. Meanwhile the transport detrained, a lengthy business. Tea was produced from those marvellous field-kitchens. The night was cold, though, and it was too damp to sit down. For hours we stood about, tired. Then came the news that our six-mile march would be more like double six; that the billets had been altered! . . . At half-past twelve we marched off. It was starlight, but pretty dark. Eighteen miles we marched, reaching Montagne at half-past seven; every man was in full marching kit, and most of them carried sandbagfuls of extras. It was a big effort, especially as the men had done nothing in the nature of a long march for months. Well I remember it—the tired silence, the steady tramp, along the interminable road. Sometimes the band would strike up for a little, but even bands tire, and cannot play continuously. Mile after mile of hard road, and then the hedges would spring up into houses, and from the opened windows would gaze down awakened women. Hardly ever was a light shown in any house. Then the village would be left behind, and men shifted their packs and exchanged a sand-bag, unslung a rifle from one shoulder to the other, and settled down to another stretch, wondering if the next village would be the last.

So it went on interminably all through the winter night. Once we halted in a village, and I sat on a doorstep with O'Brien discussing methods of keeping our eyes open. Edwards had been riding the horse, and had nearly tumbled off asleep. At another halt, half-way up a hill, I discovered a box of beef lozenges and distributed it among No. 6 platoon. All the last ten miles I was carrying a rifle and a sand-bag. Sergeant Callaghan had the same, besides all his own kit. Sergeant Andrews kept on as steady as a rock. There were falterers, but we kept them in ; only in the last two miles did one or two drop out. And all the while I was elated beyond measure ; partly at seeing men like Ginger Joe, with his dry wit flashing, and Tudor, with his stolid power ; but partly, too, at the climb uphill, the swing down, mysterious woods, and the unmistakable trunks of pines. And all the time we were steadily climbing ; we must be upon a regular tableland.

Dawn broke, and it got lighter and lighter—and so we entered Montagne. The quartermaster had had a nice job billeting at 2.0 a.m., but he had done it, and the men dropped on to their straw, into outhouses, anywhere. The accommodation seemed small and bad, but that could be arranged later. To get the men in, that was the main thing. One old woman fussed terribly, and the men looked like bayoneting her ! We soon got the men in somehow. Then for our own billets. We agreed to have a scratch breakfast as soon as it could be procured. Meanwhile I went to the end of the village and found myself on the edge of the tableland ; before me was spread out a great valley, with a poplar-lined road flung right across it ; villages were dotted about ; there were woods, and white ribbon by-roads. And over it all glowed the slant morning sun. I was on the edge of a chalky plateau ; it was all just as I had imagined. I slept from 11.0

a.m. to 7.0 p.m., when I got up for a meal at which we were all short-tempered! And at 9.0 p.m. I retired again to sleep till 7.0 next morning.

Montagne—How shall I be able to create a picture of Montagne? As I look back at all those eight months, the whole adventure seems unreal, a dream; yet somehow those first few days in the little village had for me a dream-like quality, unlike any other time. I think that then I felt that I was living in an unreality; whereas at other times life was real enough; and it is only now, afterwards, that these days are gradually melting through distance into dreams. At any rate, if the next few pages are dull to the reader, let him try and weave into them a sort of fairy glamour, and imagine a kind of spell cast over everything in which people moved as in a dream.

First, there was the country itself. The next day (after a day's sleep and a night's on top of it) was, if I remember right, rather wet, and we had kit inspection in billets, and tried to eke out the hours by gas-helmet drill, and arm-drill in squads distributed about the various farmyards and barns. Then Captain Dixon decided to take the company out on a short route march, and as it was raining very steadily we took half the company with *two* waterproof sheets per man. One sheet was thrown round the shoulders in the usual way; the other was tied kilt-wise round the waist. The result was an effective rainproof, if unmilitary-looking dress!

We set off and soon came to a large wood with a broad ride through it.

Along this ride we marched, two-deep now, and I at the rear as second-in-command. Here I felt most strongly that strange glamour of unreality. It was but three months ago, and I was in the heart of Wales, yet such was the effect of a few months that I looked on everything with the most exuberant sense of novelty. The rain-beads on the red-brown birch trees ; the ivy ; the oaks ; the strange stillness in the thick wood after the gusts of wind and slashes of rain ; especially the sounds—chattering jays, invisible peeping birds, the squelching of boots on a wet grass track—everything reminded me of a past world that seemed immeasurably distant, of past winters that had been completely forgotten. Then we emerged into a wide clearing along the edge of the wood, full of stunted gorse and junipers. Long coarse grass grew in tussocks that matted under foot ; and now I could see the whole company straggling along in front of me, slipping and sliding about on the wet grass in their curious kilt-like costumes, some of which were now showing signs of uneasiness and tending to slip in rings to the ground. Everyone was very pleased with life. A halt was called at length, and while officers discussed buying shot-guns at Amiens, or stalking the wily hare with a revolver, Tommy, I have reason to believe, was planning more effective means of snaring Brer rabbit. Next day in orders appeared an extract from corps orders *re* prohibition of poaching and destruction of game. It was all part of the dream that we were surprised, almost shocked, at this unwarranted exhibition of property rights! Not that there was much game about, anyhow.

The next day we did an advance guard scheme, down in the plain. It was a crisp winter day, and I remember the great view from the top of the hill, on the edge of the plateau as you leave Montagne. It was all mapped out, with its hedgeless fields, its curling white roads, and its few dark triangles and polygons of fir woods. But we had not long to see it, for we came into observation then (so this dream game pretended!) and were soon in extended order working our way along over the plain. It all came back to one, this "open warfare" business, the advancing in short rushes, the flurried messages from excited officers to stolid platoon-sergeants, the taking cover, the fire-orders, the rattling of the bolts, the lying on the belly in a ploughed field; and yes! the spectator, old man or woman, gazing in stupid amazement at the khaki figures rushing over his fields. Then came the assault, bayonets fixed, and the C.O.'s whistle, ending the game for that day. "Game," that was it: it is all a game, and when you get tired you go home to a good meal, and discuss the humour of it, and probably have a pow-wow in the evening in which the O.C. "A" is asked why he went off to the left, the real answer being that he lost direction badly, but the actual answer given explaining the subtlety of a detour round a piece of dead ground! Which is the dream? this, or the mud-slogging in the trenches and the interminable nights?

For, every night we went to bed! Think of it! Every night! Always that bed, that silence, that priceless privacy of sleep! I had a rather cold ground-floor billet with a door that would not shut; yet it was worth any of your beds at home! And I should be here for a month, perhaps six weeks! I wrote for my basin and stand, for books, for all sorts of things. I felt I could accumulate, and spread myself. It was like home after hotels! For always we had been moving, moving; even our six days out were often in two or even three different billets.

So, too, with our mess. The dream here consisted of a jolly little parlour that was the envy of all the other company messes. As usual, the rooms led into one another, the kitchen into the parlour, the parlour into a bedroom; I might almost continue, and say the bedroom into a bed! For the four-poster, when curtained off, is a little room in itself. It was a good billet, but best of all was Madame herself. Suffice it to say she would not take a penny for use of crockery; and she would insist on us making full use of everything; she allowed all our cooking to be done in her kitchen; and on cold nights she would insist on our servants sitting in the kitchen, though that was her only sitting-room. Often have I come in about seven o'clock to find our dinner frizzling merrily on the fire under the supervision of Gray, the cook, while Madame sat humbly in the corner eating a frugal supper of bread and milk, before retiring to her little room upstairs. Ah, Madame ! there are many who have done what you have done, but few, I think, more graciously. If we tried to thank her for some extra kindness, she had always the same reply " You are welcome, M. l'Officier. I have heard the guns, and the Germans passed through Amiens ; if it were not for the English, where should we be to-day ? "

So we settled down for our " rest," for long field days, lectures after tea, football matches, and week-ends ; I wrote for my Field Service Regulations, and rubbed up my knowledge of outposts and visual training. But scarcely had I been a week at Montagne when off I went suddenly, on a Sunday morning, to the Third Army School. I had been told my name was down for it, a few days before, but I had forgotten all about it, when I received instructions to bicycle off with Sergeant Roberts ; my kit and servant to follow in a limber. I had no idea what the " Third Army School " was, but with " note-book, pencil, and protractor " I cycled off at 11.0 a.m. " to fields and pastures new."

Most people, I imagine, have had the following

experience. They have a great interest in some particular subject, yet they have somehow not got the key to it. They regret that they were never taught the elements of it at school; or it is some new science or interest that has arisen since their schooldays, such as flying or motoring. They are really ashamed of asking questions; and all books on the subject are technical and presuppose just that elementary knowledge that the interested amateur does not possess. Then suddenly he comes on a book with those delicious phrases in the preface promising "to avoid all technical details," apologising for "what may seem almost childishly elementary," and containing at the end an expert bibliography. These are the books written by very wise and very kind men, and because they are worth so much they usually cost least of all!

Such was my delightful experience at the Army School. I will confess to a terrible ignorance of my profession—I did not know how many brigades made up a division; "the artillery" were to me vague people whom the company commander rang up on the telephone, and who appeared in gaiters in Béthune; a bomb was a thing I avoided with a peculiar aversion; and as to the general conduct of the war I was the most ignorant of pawns. The wildest things were said about Loos; the *Daily Mail* had just heard of the Fokker, and I had not the remotest idea whether we were hopelessly outclassed in the air, or whether perhaps after all there were people "up top" who were not so surprised or disconcerted at the appearance of the Fokker as the Northcliffe Press. Moreover, I had been impressed with the reiteration of my C.O., that my battalion was the finest in the Army, and that my division was likewise the best. Yet I had always felt that there were other good battalions, and that "K.'s Army" was, to say the least of it, in a considerable majority when compared with the contemptible little original which I had had the luck to join!

Imagine my delight, then, at finding myself one of over a hundred captains and senior subalterns representing their various battalions. Regulars, Territorials, and Kitcheners, we were all there together; one's vision widened like that of a boy first going to school. Here at least was a great opportunity, if only the staff was good. And any doubt on that question was instantly set at rest by the Commandant's opening address, explaining that the instructors were all picked men with a large experience in this war, that in the previous month's course mostly subalterns had been sent and this time it had been the aim to secure captains only (oh! balm in Gilead this!) and that apologies were due if some of the lectures and instructions were elementary; that bombing experts, for instance, must not mind if the bombing course started right at the very beginning, as it had been found in the previous course that it was wrong to presume *any* military knowledge to be the common possession of all officers in the school. Those who understood my simile of the expert's kind book to the amateur will understand that there were few of us who did not welcome such a promising bill of fare.

I do not intend to say much about the instruction at the Army School—a good deal of what I learnt there is unconsciously embodied in the rest of this book—but it is the spirit of the place that I want to record. I can best describe it as the opposite of what is generally known as academic. Theories and text-books about the war were at a discount : here were men who had been through the fire, every phase of it. It was not a question of opinions, but of facts. This came out most clearly in discussions after the lectures ; a point would be raised about advancing over the open : "We attacked at St. Julien over open ground under heavy fire, and such and such a thing was our experience" would at once come out from someone. And there was no scoring of debating points ! We were all out to pool our knowledge and experience all the time.

The Commandant inspired in everyone a most tremendous enthusiasm. His lectures on "Morale" were the finest I have ever heard anywhere. "Put yourself in your men's position on every occasion ; continually think for them, give them the best possible time, be in the best spirits always;" "long faces" were anathema! No one can forget his tale of the doctor who never laughed, and whom he put in a barn and taught him how to! "'Hail fellow well met' to all other officers and regiments" was another of his great points. "Give 'em a d—d good lunch—a *d—d* good lunch." "Get a good mess going." "Ask your Brigadier into lunch in the trenches: *make* him come in." "Concerts? —plenty of concerts in billets." "An extra tot of rum to men coming off patrol." All this was a "good show." But long faces, inhospitality, men not cheerful and singing, officers not seeing that their men get their dinners, after getting into billets, before getting their own; officers supervising working-parties by sitting under haystacks instead of going about cheering the men; brigadiers not knowing their officers; poor lunches—all these things were a "bad show, a d—d bad show!" These lectures were full of the most delicious anecdotes and thrilling stories, and backed up by a huge enthusiasm and a most emphatic practice of his preaching. We had a concert every Wednesday, and every Saturday the four motor-buses took the officers into Amiens, and the sergeants on Sundays—week-ends were in fact "good shows."

Then there were the lectures. The second week, for instance, was a succession of lectures on the Battle of Loos. These lectures used to take place after tea, and the discussion usually lasted till dinner. First was a lecture by an infantry major of the Seventh Division (who needless to say had been very much in it !). Then followed one by an artillery officer, giving his version of it ; then followed an R.E. officer. There was nothing hidden away in a corner. It was all facts, facts, facts. An enlarged map of our own and the German trenches was most fascinating to us who had for the most part never handled one before. I remember the Major's description of the fighting in the Quarries ; it was one of the most vivid bits of narrative I have ever heard. Then there were other fascinating lectures—Captain Jefferies, the big game hunter, on Sniping : the Commandant again on Patrol work and discipline, and Dealing with prisoners : two lectures from the Royal Flying Corps, perhaps most fascinating of all.

We drilled hard with rifles : we took a bombing course and threw live bombs : we went through the gas, and had a big demonstration with smoke bombs : we went to a squadron of the R.F.C., inspected the sheds, saw the aeroplanes, and had anything we liked explained : we went out in motor-buses and carried out schemes of attack and defence : we did outpost schemes : drew maps : dug trenches and revetted them. In short, there was very little we did not do at the School.

It was, in fact, a " good show." The School was in a big white château on the main road—a new house built by the owner of a factory. The village really lies like a sediment at the bottom of a basin, with houses clustering and scrambling up the sides along the high road running out of it east and west, getting thinner and fewer up the hill, to disappear altogether on the tableland. The jute factory was working hard night and day: we used to have hot baths in the long wooden troughs that are used for dyeing long rolls of matting, and I know no hot baths to equal those forty-footers!

Needless to say, we took advantage of our commandant's arrangement for free 'bus rides into Amiens every Saturday. Christmas Day falling on a Saturday, we all had a Christmas dinner at the Hôtel de l'Univers. This, needless to say, was a "good show." It was a pity, though, that turkey had been insisted on, as turkey with salad, minus sausages, bread-sauce, and brussels sprouts did not seem somehow the real thing; the chef had jibbed at sausages especially! Better at Rome to have done completely as Rome does. After all we cannot give the French much advice in cooking or in war. Otherwise the dinner was good, and unlike our folk at home we had a merry Christmas.

Of course I went to see the Cathedral that Ruskin has claimed to be the most perfect building in the world; indeed, each Saturday found me there; for like all true beauty the edifice does not attract merely by novelty but satisfies the far truer test of familiarity. Yet I confess to a thrill on first entering that dream in stone, which could not come a second time. For down in the mud I had forgotten, in the obsession of the present, man's dreams and aspirations for the future. Now, here again I was in touch with eternal things that wars do not affect. I remember once at Malvern we had been groping and choking in a thick fog all day; then someone suggested a walk, and three of us ventured out and climbed the Beacon. Half-way up the fog began to thin, and soon we emerged into a clear sunshine. Below lay all the plain wrapped in a great level blanket of white fog; here and there the top of a tall tree or a small hill protruded its head out of the mist and seemed to be laughing at its poor hidden companions; and in a cloudless blue the sun was smiling at mankind below who had forgotten his very existence. So in Amiens Cathedral I used to get my head out of the thick fog of war for a time, and in that stately silence recover my vision of the sun.

The cathedral is a building full of all the freshness of spring. I was at vespers there on Christmas afternoon, and was then impressed by the wonderful lightness of the building: so often there is gloom in a cathedral, that gives a heavy feeling. But Amiens Cathedral is perfectly lighted, and in the east window glows a blue that reminded me of viper's bugloss in a Swiss meadow. My imagination flew back to the building of the cathedral, and to the brain that conceived it, and beyond that again to the tradition that through long years moulded the conception; and behind all to the idea, the ultimate birth of this perfect creation. And one seemed to be straining almost beyond humanity, to see the first spring flowers looking up in wonder at the sky. The stately pillars were man's aspiration towards his Creator, the floating music his attempt at praise.

Yet it was only as I left the building that I found the key to the full understanding of this perfect expression of an idea. Round the chancel is a set of bas-reliefs depicting a saint labouring among his people. But what people! They live, they speak! The relief is so deep, that some of the figures are almost in the round, and several come outside the slabs altogether. They are the people of mediæval Amiens; they are the very people who were living in the town while their great cathedral rose stone by stone to be the wonder of their city, the pride of all Picardy. Almost grotesque in their vivid humanity, they are the same people who walk outside the cathedral to-day. The master-artist, greater in his dreams than his fellow men, was yet blessed with that divine sense of humour that made him love them for their quaint smallnesses! So in Amiens I felt a double inspiration: there was man's offering of his noblest and most beautiful to his Creator, and there was also the reminder, in the saint among the Amiens populace, that God's answer was not a proud bend of the head as He deigned to accept the offering of poor little man, but a coming down among them, a claiming of equality with them, even though they refuse still to realise their divinity, and choose to live in a self-made suffering and to degrade themselves in a fog of war.

All too quickly the month went by. The enthusiasm and interest of everybody grew in a steady crescendo, and no one, I am sure, will ever forget the impression left by the Major-General who was deputed to come and "tell us one or two things" from the General Staff. In a quiet voice, with a quiet smile, he compared our position with that of a year ago; told us facts about our numbers compared with the enemy's; our guns compared with his; the real position in the air, the temporary superiority of the Fokker that would vanish completely and finally in a month or so; in everything we were now superior except heavy trench-mortars, and in a month or so we should have a big supply of them too, and a d—d sight heavier! And we could afford to wait. One got the impression that all our grousings and doubtings were completely out of date, that up at the top now was a unity of command that had thought everything out and could afford to wait. Later on I forgot this impression, but I remember it so well now. Even through Verdun we could afford to wait. We had all the cards now. There was a sort of breathless silence throughout this quiet speech. And when it ended with a "Good luck to you, gentlemen," there was applause ; but one's chief desire was to go outside and shout. It was a bonfire mood : best of all would have been a bonfire of *Daily Mails !*

We returned to our units on Sunday, 9th January, 1916, by motor-bus, which conveyed us some sixty or seventy miles, when we were dropped, Sergeant Roberts, myself, and Lewis, my servant. Leaving Lewis with my valise, we walked in the moonlight up to Montagne, where I got the transport officer to send a limber for my valise. " O'Brien on leave " was the first thing I grasped, as I tried to acclimatise myself to my surroundings. Leave ! My three months was up, so I ought to get leave myself in a week or so ; in a few days in fact. My first leave ! The next week was rosy from the prospect. My second impression was like that of a poet full of a great sunset and trying to adjust himself to the dry unimaginative remarks of the rest of the community who have relegated sunsets to perdition during dinner. For every one was so dull ! They groused, they maligned the Staff, they were pessimistic, they were ignorant, oh ! profoundly ignorant ; they were in fact in a state of not having seen a vision ! I could not believe then that the time would come when I, too, should forget the vision, and fix my eyes on the mud ! Still, for the moment, I was immensely surprised, though I was not such a fool as to start at once on a general reform of everyone, starting with the Brigadier. For under the Commandant's influence one felt ready to tell off the Brigadier, if he didn't get motor-'buses to take your men to a divisional concert instead of saying the men must march three miles to it. But, as I say, I restrained myself.

A week of field days, of advance guards and attacks in open order, of battalion drill, company drill, arm-drill, gas-helmet drill ; lectures in the school in the evening, and running drill before breakfast. Yet all the time I felt chafing to get back into the firing-line. I felt so much better equipped to command my men. I wanted to practise all my new ideas. Then my leave came through.

Leave " comes through " in the following manner. The lucky man receives an envelope from the orderly room, in the corner of which is written " Leave." Inside is an " A " Form (Army Form C 2121) with this magic inscription : " Please note you will take charge of —— other ranks proceeding on leave to-morrow morning, 17th inst. They will parade outside orderly room at 7.0 a.m. sharp." Then follow instructions as to where to meet the 'bus. " Take charge ! " If you blind-folded those fellows they would find their way somehow by the quickest route to Blighty ! The officer is then an impossible person to live with. He is continually jumping about, upsetting everybody, getting sandwiches, and discussing England, looking at the paper to see " What's on " in town, talking, being unnecessarily bright and cheery. He is particularly offensive in the eyes of the man just come back from leave. Still, it is his day; abide with him until he clears off! So they abode with me until the evening, and next morning Oliver and I started off in the darkness with our four followers. As we left the village it was just beginning to lighten a little, and we met the drums just turning out, cold and sleepy. As we sprang down the hill, leaving Montagne behind us, faintly through the dawn we heard réveillé rousing our unfortunate comrades to another Monday morning!

Then came the long, long journey that nobody minds really, though every one grumbles at it. At B—— an hour's halt for omelettes and coffee and bread and jam, while the Y.M.C.A. stall supplied tea and buns innumerable. B—— will be a station known for all time to thousands. "Do you remember B——?" we shall ask each other. "Oh! yes. Good omelettes one got there." Then the port, and fussy R.T.O's again. Why make a fuss, when everyone is magnetised towards the boat? Under the light of a blazing gas-jet squirting from a pendant ball, we crossed the gangway.

. . . . . .

There were men of old time who fell on their native earth and kissed it, on returning after exile. We did not kiss the boards of Southampton pier-head, but we understood the spirit that inspired that action as we steamed quietly along the Solent over a grey and violet sea. There were mists that morning, and the Hampshire coast was grey and vague ; but steadily the engine throbbed, and we glided nearer and nearer, entered Southampton Water, and at last were near enough to see houses and fields and people. People. English women.

We disembarked. But what dull people to meet us ! Officials and watermen who have seen hundreds of leave-boats arrive—every day in fact ! The last people to be able to respond to your feelings. Still, what does it matter ? There is the train, and an English First ! Some one started to run for one, and in a moment we were all running ! . . .

But you have met us on leave.

CHAPTER V

ON THE MARCH

On this leave I most religiously visited relations and graciously received guests. For one thing, I felt it my duty to dispel all this ignorant pessimism that I found rolling about in large chunks, like the thunder in *Alice in Wonderland*. I exacted apologies, humble apologies from them. " How can we help it ? " they pleaded. " We have no means of knowing anything except through the papers."

" No, I suppose you can't help it," I would reply, and forgive them from my throne of optimism. Eight days passed easily enough.

After dinner sometimes comes indigestion : people enjoy the one and not the other. So after leave comes the return from leave, the one in Tommy-French *bon*, the other *no bon*. I hope I do not offend by calling the state of the latter a mental indigestion ! It was with a kind of fierce joy that we threw out our bully and biscuits to the crowds of French children who lined the railway banks crying out, " Bullee-beef," " Biskeet." The custom of supplying these rations on the leave train has long since been discontinued now, but in those days the little beggars used to know the time of the train to a nicety, and must have made a good trade of it.

As soon as I got back to Montagne I heard a "move" was in the air, and I was delighted. I was fearfully keen to get back into the firing-line again. I was full of life, and in the mood for adventure. I started a diary. Here are some extracts.

"29th January, 1916. Lewis (my servant) brought in a bucket of water this morning which contained 10% of mud. As the mud dribbled on to the green canvas of my bath during the end of the pouring, he saw it for the first time. Apparently the well is running dry. . . . He managed to get some clean water at length and I had a great bath. Madame asked me as I went in to breakfast why I whistled getting up that morning. I tried to explain that I was in good spirits. It was an exhilarating morning; outside was a great cawing of rooks, and the slant sunlight lit up everything with a rich colour; the mouldy green on the twigs of the apple trees was a joy to see. Later in the day I noticed how all this delicious morning light had gone.

"7 p.m. Orders have just come in for the move to-morrow. Loading party at 6.0 a.m. under Edwards, who is inwardly fed up but outwardly quite pleased. Valises to be ready by 6.45 a.m. Dixon grouses as usual at orders coming in late.

These moves always try the tempers of all concerned. O'Brien and Edwards are now on the rustle, collecting kit. We have accumulated rather a lot of papers, books, tins of ration, tobacco, etc."

Madame was genuinely sorry to see us go. We gave her a large but beautiful ornament for her mantelpiece, suitably inscribed. The dear soul was overwhelmed, and drew cider from a cellar hitherto unknown to us, which she pressed on our servants as well as on us. We made the fellows drink it, though they were not very keen on it !

"30 Jan., 1916. Montagne—Vaux-en-Amienois. I found myself suddenly detailed as O.C. rear party, in lieu of Edwards, who has to remain in Montagne and hand over to the incoming battalion. At 9.30 three A.S.C. lorries arrived, and we loaded up. I had about forty men for the job. It was good to see these boys heaving up rolls of many-coloured blankets, which filled nearly two lorries ; the third was packed with a mixture of boilers, dixies, brooms, spades, lamps, etc. The leather and skin waistcoats had to be left behind for a second journey : I left the shoemaker-sergeant and four men with these to await the return of one of the lorries. As we worked a fog rolled up, which was to stay all day. Edwards meanwhile saw to it that all the odd coal and wood left at the transport was taken to our good Madame ; this much annoyed the groups of women who peered like vultures from the doorways, ready to squabble over the pickings as soon as the last of us had departed.

Farewell to Montagne. All the fellows were dull. Even Sawyer the smiling, who had been prominent with his cheery face in the loading-up, was silent and dull. No life. No spirit. A mournful lot, save for the plum-pudding dog that galloped ahead and on either flank, smelling and pouncing and tossing his mongrel ears in delight. He belonged to one of the men, a gift from a warm-hearted daughter of France.

A dull lot, I say. I rallied them. I persuaded. I whistled, hoping to put a tune into their dull hearts ; and as we swung downhill into Riencourt they began to sing. It was but a sorry thin sort of singing though, like a winter sunshine ; there was no power behind it, no joy, no spontaneity. Suddenly, however, as we came into the village, there was a company of the Warwicks falling in, and everyone sang like fury. Baker, one of the last draft, was the moving spirit. But he is young to this life, and later on, when the fog had entered their souls again, he said he could not well sing with a pack on. Yet is not that the very time to sing, is not that the very virtue of singing, the conquest of the poor old body by the indomitable spirit ?

It was a fifteen-mile march. At the third halt I gave half an hour for the eating of bread and cheese. Then was the hour of the plum-pudding hound ; also appeared a sort of Newfoundland collie, very big in the hind-quarters, and very dirty as well as ill-bred. Between them they made rich harvest of crusts and cheese. We sat on a bank along the road, but after half an hour we were all getting cold in the raw air, and I fell them in again, and we got on our way. Soon they warmed up and whistled and sang for a quarter of an hour; then silence returned, and eyes turned to the ground again. This march began to tell on the older men. Halford fell out, and I sent Corporal Dewey to bring him along, hastily scribbling the name of our destination on a slip torn from my field-message book, and giving it to him. Then Riley fell out, and Flynn. I began to dread the appearance of Sergeant Hayman from the rear, to tell me of some one else. They were men, these, who had been employed on various jobs; the older and weaker men. There was no skrim-shanking, for there was no Red Cross cart behind us. But no one else fell out; the pace was steady and they were as fit as anything, these fellows. Then happened an incident. We had just turned off the main Amiens road, and come to a forked road. I halted a moment to make sure of the way by the map, and while I did so apparently some sergeant from a regiment billeted in the village there told Sergeant Hayman that the battalion had taken the left road. The way was to the right, and as I struck up a steep hill, Sergeant Hayman ran up and told me the battalion (which had started nearly two hours before us) had gone to the left. 'I'm going to the right, sergeant,' said I. And the sergeant returned to the rear. Up, up, up. Grind, grind, grind. I began to hear signs of doubt behind. 'Did you hear that? Said the battalion went t'other way,' and so on. 'Ain't 'e got a map all right?' from a believer. 'Three kilos more,' I said at the next stop. But some of the fellows had got it into their heads, I could see, that we were wrong. I studied the map; there was no doubt we were all right. Yet a mistake would be calamitous, as the men were very done. Ah! a kilo-stone! 'Two kilos to ——,' a place not named on the map at all. This gave me a qualm; and behind came the usual mispronunciations of this annoying village on the stone. But lo! on the left came a turning as per map. Round we swung, downhill, and suddenly we were in a village. Another qualm as I saw it full of Jocks. The doubters were just beginning to realise this fact, when we turned another corner, and almost fell on top of the C.O.! In five minutes we were in billets. . . ."

The next day we marched to the village of Querrieux. There I heard the guns again after two months.

"31st January. This evening was full of the walking tour spirit, the spirit of good company. We were billeted at a farmhouse, and the farmer showed Captain Dixon and me all round his farm. He was full of pride in everything ; of his horses first of all. There were three in the first stable, sleek and strong ; then we saw *la mère,* a beautiful mare in foal ; then lastly there was ' Piccaninny,' a yearling. All the stables were spotlessly clean, and the animals well kept. But to see him with his lambs was best of all. The ewes were feeding from racks that ran all along both sides of the sheds, and his lantern showed two long rows of level backs, solid and uniform and dull ; while in the middle of the shed was a jocund company of close-cropped lambs, frisking, pushing, jostling, or pulling at their dams ; as lively and naughty a crew as you could imagine. ' Ah ! *voleur,*' cried our friend, picking up a lamb that was stealing a drink from the wrong tap, and pointing to its dam at the other end of the shed ; he fondled and stroked it like a puppy, making us hold it, and assuring us it was not *méchant !*

At 7.0 we had our dinner in the kitchen. The farmer, his wife, and the *domestique* (a manservant, whose history I will tell in a few minutes) had just finished, and were going to clear off ; but we asked them to stay and let us drink their health in whiskey and soda. The farmer said this was wont to make the *domestique* go ' zigzag ' ; for himself, he would drink, not for the inherent pleasure of the whiskey, which was a strong drink to which he was unused, he being of the land of light wines, but to give us pleasure ! So the usual healths were given in

Old Orkney and Perrier. Then we were told the history of the *domestique,* which brought one very close to the spirit in which France is fighting. He had eight children in Peronne, barely ten miles the other side of the line. Called up in September, 1914, he was in the trenches until March, 1915, when he was released on account of his eight children. But by then the living line had set between them in steel and blood, and never a word yet has he heard of his wife and eight children, the youngest of whom he left nine days old ! There are times when our cause seems clouded with false motives ; but there seemed no doubt on this score to-night, as we watched this man in his own land, creeping up, as it were, as near as possible to his wife and children and home, and yet barred from his own village, and without the knowledge even that his own dear ones were alive. The farmer told us he had gone half crazed. Yet he had a fine face, though furrowed with deep lines down his forehead. 'Ten minutes in the yard with the Germans—ah ! what would he do ! ' And vividly he drew his hand across his throat. But the Germans would never go back : that was another of his opinions. No wonder he told us he doubted the *bon Dieu :* no wonder he sometimes went zigzag.

The farmer was well educated, and had very intelligent views on the war ; one son was a captain ; the other was also serving in some capacity. The wife made us good coffee, but got very sleepy. I learnt she rose every morning at 4.0 a.m. to milk the cows.

To-night we can hear the guns. There seems a considerable liveliness at several parts of the line, and strange rumours of the Germans breaking through, which I do not believe. To-morrow we shall be within the shell-zone again."

"Feb. 1st. To-day we marched to Morlancourt and are spending the night in huts. It is very cold, and we have a brazier made out of a biscuit tin, but it smokes abominably. We are busy getting trench-kit ready for the next day. From outside the hut I can see star-lights, and hear machine-guns tapping. It thrills like the turning up of the foot-lights."

And it was a long act. The curtain did not fall till June.

CHAPTER VI

THE BOIS FRANÇAIS TRENCHES

THIS is a chapter of maps, diagrams, and technicalities. There are people, I know, who do not want maps, to whom maps convey practically nothing. These people can skip this chapter, and (from their point of view) they will lose nothing. The main interest of life lies in what is done and thought, and it does not much matter exactly where these acts and thoughts take place. Maps are like anatomy: to some people it is of absorbing interest to know where our bones, muscles, arteries and all the rest of our interior lie; to others these things are of no account whatever. Yet all are alike interested in human people. And so, quite understanding (I think you are really very romantic in your dislike of maps: you associate them with the duller kind of history, and examination papers!), I bid you mapless ones farewell till page 117, promising you (again) that you shall lose nothing.

. . . . . .

Now to work. We understand each other, we map-lovers. The other folk have gone on to the next chapter, so we can take our time.

To face page 197

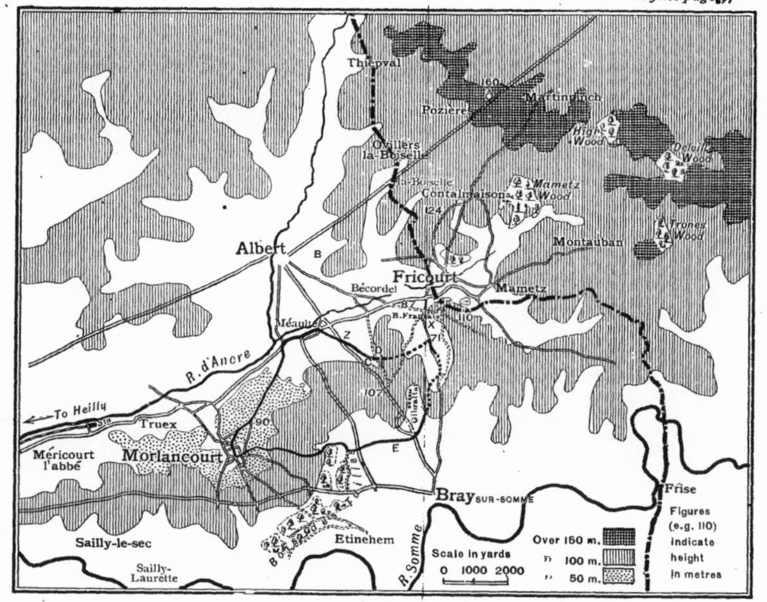

MAP II.

TRENCH LINE

Now look at Map II. The River Ancre runs down west of the Thiepval ridge, through Albert, and then in a south-westerly course through Méricourt-l'abbé down to Corbie, where it joins the Somme on its way to Amiens. On each side of the Ancre is high ground of about 100 metres. The high ground between the Ancre and the Somme forms a long tableland. There is no ridge, it is just high flat country, from three hundred and thirty to three hundred and forty feet, cultivated and hedgeless. Now look at Fricourt. It is a break in this high ground running on the left bank of the Ancre, and this break is caused by a nameless tributary of that river, that joins it just west of Méaulte. And now you will see that this little streamlet was for over a year and a half the cause of much thought and labour to very many men indeed: for this stream formed the valley in which Fricourt lies; and right across this valley, just south of that unimportant little village, ran for some twenty months or so the Franco-German and later the Anglo-German lines.

Now look at the dotted line (—·—·) which represents the trenches. From Thiepval down to Fricourt they run almost due north and south; then they run up out of the valley on to the high ground at Bois Français (a small copse, I suppose, once; I have never discovered any vestige of a tree-stump among the shell-holes), and then abruptly run due east. It is as though someone had appeared suddenly on the corner of the shoulder at Bois Français, and pushed them off, compelling them to make a détour. After five miles they manage to regain their direction and run south again.

It is these trenches at Bois Français that we held for over four months. I may fairly claim to know every inch of them, I think! It is obvious that if you are at Bois Français, and look north, you have an uninterrupted view not only of both front lines running down into Fricourt valley, but of both lines running up on to the high ground north of Fricourt, and a very fine view indeed of Fricourt itself, and Fricourt wood. It is also quite clear that from their front lines north of Fricourt the Germans had a good view of *our* front lines and communications in the valley; but of Bois Français and our trenches east of it they had no enfilade view, as all our communications were on the reverse slope of this shoulder of high ground. So as regards observation we were best off. Moreover, whereas they could not possibly see our support lines and communications at Bois Français, we could get a certain amount of enfilade observation of their trenches opposite from point 87, where was a work called Boute Redoubt and an artillery observation post.

The position of the artillery immediately becomes clear, when the lie of the ground is once grasped. For field artillery enfilade fire is far most effective, as the trajectory is lower than that of heavy artillery. That is to say, a whizz-bang (the name given to an

18-lb. shell) more or less skims along the ground and comes *at* you ; whereas howitzers fire up in the air, and the shell rushes down on top of you. To be explicit at the risk of boring :—

If a battery of eighteen-pounders can fire up a trench like this :—

it has far more effect against the nine men in that trench than if it fires like this :

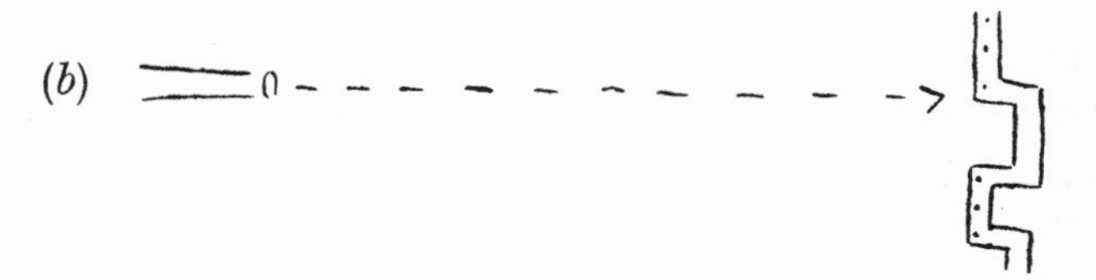

The same applies of course to howitzers, but as howitzers drop shells down almost perpendicularly, they can be used with great effect traversing along a trench, that is to say, getting the exact range of the trench in sketch (*b*), and dropping shells methodically from right to left, or left to right, so many to each fire-bay, and dodging about a bit, and going back on to a bit out of turn so that the enemy cannot tell where the next coal-box is coming. Oh ! it is a great game this for the actors, but not for the unwilling audience.

So you can see now why a battery of field artillery

was stationed in the gully called Gibraltar, and another just west of Albert (at B): each of these batteries could bring excellent enfilade fire on to the German trenches. There was another battery that fired from the place I have marked C, and another at D. The howitzers lived in all sorts of secret places, as far back as Morlancourt some of them. One never worried about them. They knew their own business. Once, in June, on our way into the trenches we halted close by a battery at E, and I looked into one of the gun-pits and saw the terrible monster sitting with its long nose in the air. And I saw the great shells (it was a 9·6) waiting in rows. But I felt like an interloper, and fled at the approach of a gunner. All these howitzers you see firing on the Somme films, we never saw or thought about; only we loved to hear their shells whistling and "griding" (if there is no such word, I cannot help it: there is an "r" and a "d" in the sound anyway!) over our head, and falling "crump," "crump," "crump" along the German support trenches. There were a lot of batteries in the Bois des Tailles; the woods were full of them, and grew fuller and fuller. I do not know what they all were.

As one brigade contains four battalions, we almost invariably had two battalions in the line, and two "in billets." So it was usually "six days in and six days out." During these six days out we also invariably supplied four working-parties per company, which lasted nine hours from the time of falling in outside company headquarters to dismissing after marching back. Still, it was " billets." One slept uninterruptedly, and with equipment and boots off. Now we were undeniably lucky in being invariably (from February to June, 1916) billeted in Morlancourt, which, as you can see from the map, is situated in a regular cup with high ground all round it. I have put in the 50-metre contour line to show exactly how the roads all run down into it from every quarter. It was a cosy spot, and a very jolly thing after that long, long weary grind up from Méaulte at the end of a weary six days in, to look down on the snug little village waiting for you below. For once over the hill and " swinging " down into Morlancourt, one became, as it were, cut off from the war suddenly and completely. It was somewhat like shutting the door on a stormy night: everything outside was going on just the same, but with it was shut out also a wearing, straining tension of body and mind.

Yes, we were very lucky in being billeted at Morlancourt. It was just too far off to be worth shelling, whereas Bray was shelled regularly almost every day. So was Méaulte. And there were brigades billeted in both Bray and Méaulte. There were troops in tents in the Bois des Tailles, and this too was sometimes shelled.

Now just look, please, at the two thick lines, which represent alternative routes to the trenches.

We were always able to relieve by day, thanks to the rolling nature of the country. (Where the line is dotted, this represents a trench.) We always used to go by the route through Méaulte at one time, until they took to shelling the road at the point I have marked Z; whether they could see us from an observation post up la-Boiselle way, or whether they spotted us by observation balloon or aeroplane, one cannot say. But latterly we always used the route by the Bois des Tailles and Gibraltar. In both cases we had to cross the high ground S.W. of point 71 by trench, but on arrival at that point we were again in a valley and out of observation. All along this road were a series of dug-outs, and here were companies in reserve, R.E. headquarters, R.A.M.C. dressing-station, field kitchens, stores, etc. And here the transport brought up rations every evening viâ Bray. One could walk about here, completely secure from view; but latterly they took to shelling it, and it was not a healthy spot then. It was also enfiladed occasionally by long-range machine-gun fire. But on the whole it was a good spot, and one had a curious sensation being able to walk about on an open road within a thousand yards of the Germans. The dug-outs called "71 North" were the best. The bank sloped up very steeply from the road, thus protecting the dug-outs along it from anything but shell-fire of very high trajectory. And this the Germans never used. However, one did not want to walk

To face page 103

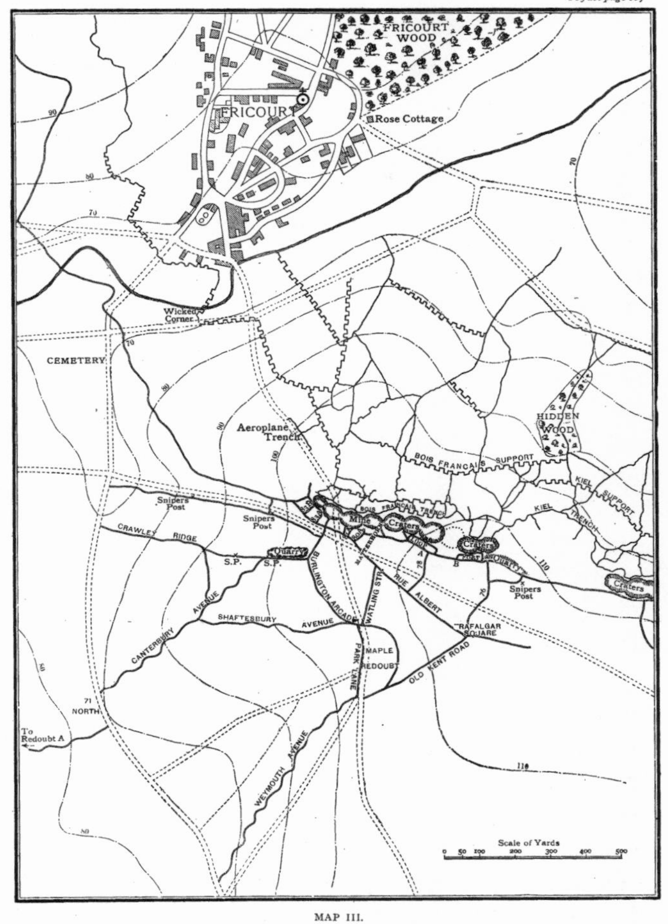

MAP III.

OUR TRENCHES

GERMAN TRENCHES

too far along the road, for it led round the corner into full view of Fricourt at X. There was a trench at the side of the road that ought to be hopped down into, but it could easily be missed, and there was no barrier across the road! I saw a motor-cyclist dash right along to the corner once, and return very speedily when he found himself gazing full view at Fricourt!

Map III is an enlargement of the area in Map II, and gives details of our trenches and the German trenches opposite. I wish I could convey the sense of intimacy with which I am filled when I look at this map. It is something like the feelings I should ascribe to a farmer looking at a map of his property, every inch of which he knows by heart; every field, every copse, every lane, every hollow and hill are intimate things to him. With every corner he has some association; every tree cut down, every fence repaired, every road made up, every few hundred yards of shaw grubbed up, every acre of orchard enclosed and planted—all these he can call back to memory at his will. So do I know every corner, every turning in these trenches; every traverse has its peculiar familiarity, very often its peculiar history. This traverse was built the night after P——'s death; this trench was dug because "75 Street" was so marked down by the enemy rifle-grenades; another was a terrible straight trench till we built those traverses in it; another was a morass until we boarded it. How well I remember being half buried by a canister at the corner of "78 Street"; and the night the mine blew in all the trench between the Fort and the Loop; what an awful dug-out that was at Trafalgar-Square; how we loathed the straightness of Watling Street. And so on, *ad infinitum.* We were in those trenches for over four months, and I know them as one knows the creakings of the doors at home, the subtle smell of the bath-room, the dusty atmosphere of the box-room, or the lowness of the cellar door. Particularly intimate are the recollections of dug-outs, with their good or bad conveniences in the way of beds and tables, their beams that smote you on the head as regularly as clockwork, or their peculiarly musty smell. One dug-out invariably smelt of high rodent; another of sand-bag, nothing but sand-bag.

From February, then, to June we kept on going into these trenches drawn on Map III, and then back to Morlancourt for rest and working-parties, all as regular as clockwork. Once or twice the actual front line held by our battalion was altered, so that I have been in the trenches all along from the Cemetery (down in the valley) to the end of the craters opposite Danube Trench. But every time except twice my company held part of the trench between 83 B (the end of the craters) and the Lewis gun position to the right of 76 Street. The usual distribution of the battalion was as follows :—

A Company.	From 80 A to L. G. (Lewis gun) on right of 76.
B	,,	Maple Redoubt.
C	,,	71 North.
D	,,	L. G. on right of 76 to 73 Street.

(After three days A and B, and C and D, relieved each other.)

Battalion Headquarters, Headquarter Bombers, M.O. and H.Q. Stretcher-bearers R.S.M.	Maple Redoubt.

Maple Redoubt was what is known as a "strong point." In case of an enemy attack piercing our front line, the company in Maple Redoubt held out at all costs to the last man, even if the enemy got right past and down the hill. There was a dug-out which was provisioned full up with bully-beef and water (in empty petrol cans) ready for this emergency. There was a certain amount of barbed-wire put out in front of the trenches to N., W., and E.; and there were two Lewis-gun positions at A and B. Really it was not a bad little place, although the "Defences of Maple Redoubt" were always looked on by us as rather more of a big joke than anything. No one ever really took seriously the thought of the enemy coming over and reaching Maple Redoubt. Raid the front line he was liable to do at any moment; but attack on such a big scale as to come right through, no, no one really ever (beneath the rank of battalion commander, anyway) worried about that. Still, if he did, there was the redoubt anyway; and there was another called "Redoubt A" on the hill facing us, as one looked from Maple Redoubt across the smoke rising from dug-outs which could just not be seen under the bank at 71 North. Here was rumoured to be bully-beef and water also, and the Machine-gun Corps had some positions in it which they visited occasionally; but even a notice "No one allowed this way," failed to tempt me to explore its interior. One saw it, traced out on the hill, from Maple Redoubt, and there I have no doubt it still is, with its bully-beef intact and its water a little stale!

So much for Maple Redoubt. In case of attack, as I have said, it was a strong point that must hold out at all costs, while the company at 71 North came up to Rue Albert, and would support either of the front companies as the C.O. directed. The front companies of course held the front line to the last man. Meanwhile, the two battalions in billets would be marching up from Morlancourt, to the high ground above Redoubt A (that is, just east of D on Map II). Up there were a series of entrenched "works," known as the "intermediate line." (The "second line" ran a little north of point 90, N.E. of Morlancourt. But no one took *that* seriously, anyway.) The battalions marching up from billets might have to hold these positions, or, what was more likely, be ordered to counter-attack immediately. Such was the defence scheme.

"Six days in billets: three days in support. Not particularly hard, that sounds," I can hear someone say. I tried to disillusion people in an earlier chapter about the easiness of the "rest" in billets, owing to the incessant working-parties. These were even more incessant during these four months. Let me say a few words then, also, about life in support trenches. I admit that for officers it was not always an over-strenuous time; but look at Tommy's ordinary programme:—

This would be a typical day, say, in April.

4 a.m. Stand to, until it got light enough to clean your rifle; then clean it.

About 5 a.m. Get your rifle inspected, and turn in again.

6.30 a.m. Turn out to carry breakfast up to company in front line. (Old Kent Road very muddy after rain. A heavy dixie to be carried from top of Weymouth Avenue, up viâ Trafalgar Square, and 76 Street to the platoon holding the trench at the Loop.)

7.45 a.m. Get your own breakfast.

9 a.m. Turn out for working-party; spend morning filling sandbags for building traverses in Maple Redoubt.

11.30 a.m. Carry dinner up to front company. Same as 6.30 a.m.

1 p.m. Get your own dinner.

1 to 4 p.m. (With luck) rest.
4 p.m. Carry tea up to front company.
5 p.m. Get your own tea.
5.15 to 7.15 p.m. (With luck) rest.
7.15 p.m. Clean rifle.
7.30 p.m. Stand to. Rifle inspected.
Jones puts his big ugly boot out suddenly, just after you have finished cleaning rifle, and upsets it. Result—mud all over barrel and nose-cap.
8.30 p.m. Stand down. Have to clean rifle again and show platoon sergeant.
9 p.m. Turn out for working-party till 12 midnight in front line.
12 midnight. Hot soup.
12.15 a.m. Dug-out at last till
4 a.m. Stand to.

And so on for three days and nights. This is really quite a moderate programme : it is one that you would aim at for your men. But there are disturbing elements that sometimes compel you to dock a man's afternoon rest, for instance. A couple of canisters block Watling Street ; you *must* send a party of ten men and an N.C.O. to clear it at once : or you suddenly have to supply a party to carry "footballs" up to Rue Albert for the trench-mortar man. The Adjutant is sorry; he could not let you know before; but they have just come up to the Citadel, and must be unloaded at once. So you have to find the men for this on the spur of the moment. And so it goes on night and day. Oh, it's not all rum and sleep, is life in Maple Redoubt.

Three days and nights in support, and then comes the three days in the front line.

Now we will take it that " B " Company is holding from 80 A to the Lewis-gun position to the right of 76 Street. You will notice at once that almost the whole of No Man's Land in front of this sector of trenches is a chain of mine craters. No one can have much idea of a crater until he actually sees one. I can best describe it as a hollow like a quarry or chalk hole about fifty yards in diameter and some forty or fifty feet deep. (They vary in size, of course, but that is about the average.) The sides, which are steepish, and vary in angle between thirty and sixty degrees, are composed of a very fine thin soil, which is, in point of fact, a thick sediment of powdered soil that has returned to earth after a tempestuous ascent into the sky. A large mine always causes a " lip " above the ground level, which appears in section somewhat like this :—

There is usually water in the bottom of the deeper craters. When a series of craters is formed, running into one another, you get a very uneven floor that appears in lengthwise section thus :—

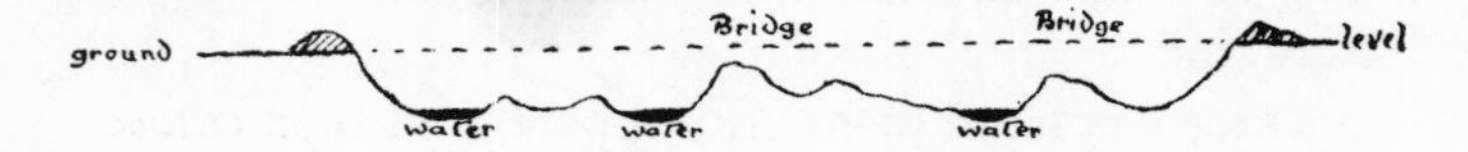

The dotted line is the ground level : the uneven line is the course that would be taken by a man walking along the bottom of the chain of craters, and keeping in the centre. Actually, of course, (on patrol) one would not keep in the centre where the crater contained water, but would skirt the water by going to one side of it. The " bridges " are important, as they are naturally the easiest way across the craters ; a bombing patrol, for instance, could crawl over a bridge, without having to go right down to the bottom level, and (which is more important) will not have a steep climb up over very soft and spongy soil. These bridges are

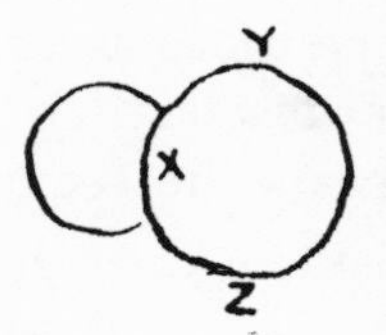

the " lips " of the larger craters where they join the smaller ; looking at a crater-chain *in plan* X is a " bridge," whereas Y and Z are " lips " rising above ground level.

This crater-chain being understood, the system of sentries is easily grasped. Originally, before mining commenced, our front line ran (roughly) from left to right along Rue Albert up 80 A Street and along to the top of 76 Street in a straight line. Then began the great game of mining under the enemy parapet and blowing him up; and its corollary countermining, or blowing up the enemy's mine galleries before he reached your parapet. Such is the game as played underground by the tunnelling companies, R.E. To the infantry belongs the work (if not blown up) of consolidating the crater, whether made by your or an enemy mine, that is to say, of seizing your side of the crater and guarding it by bombing-posts in such a way as to prevent the enemy from doing anything except hold his side of the crater.

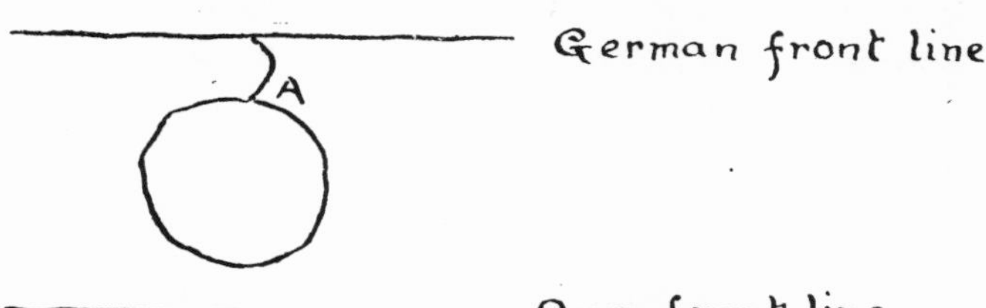

For instance, take a single crater, caused by us blowing up the German gallery before it reaches our parapet. If we do nothing, the enemy digs a trench into the crater at A, and can get into the crater any time he likes and bomb our front line, and return to his trench unseen. This, of course, never happens, as we dig a sap into the crater from our side, and the result is stale-mate; each side can see into the crater, so neither can go into it.

That is all. 83 B, 81 A, the Matterhorn sap, the Loop, the Fort—they are all saps up to crater-edges, in some cases joined up along the edge (as between 83 B and 83 A, or at the Loop and the Fort.) And these saps are held by bombing-posts. Where there are no craters in front (as, for instance, between the Fort and the Loop), there the trench is held by sentry groups in the ordinary way. The most important bombing-posts are at the "bridges," which are the points that most want guarding.

Each platoon has so many posts to "find" men for. No. 5 Platoon has three posts between the Lewis-gun position and the top of 76 Street; No. 6 finds two in the Fort and one between the Fort and the Loop; there is another post before you reach the Loop, found by No. 7, who also finds two in the Loop itself; while No. 8 finds the Matterhorn post and the top of 80 A. All these posts are composed of one bomber, who has a box of bombs with him and his rifle without bayonet fixed, and one bayonet man. There is no special structure about a "post": it is just the spot in the trench where the sentries are placed. Sometimes one or two posts could be dispensed with by day, if one post could with a periscope watch the ground in front of both. The sentry groups are relieved every two hours by the platoon N.C.O. on trench duty. There is always an N.C.O. on trench duty, going the rounds of his sentry groups, in every platoon; and one officer going round the groups in the company. Thus is secured the endless chain of unwinking eyes that stretches from Dunkirk to Switzerland.

There were two Lewis guns to every company. One had a position at the Fort, covering the ground between the Fort and the Loop; the other was just to the right of 80 A, where it had a good position sweeping the craters. The Lewis-gun teams found their sentries independently of the platoons, and had their dug-outs. A nice compact little affair was a Lewis-gun team; always very snug and self-contained.

Company Headquarters were at Trafalgar Square, though later we changed to a dug-out half-way up 76 Street. Each platoon had a dug-out about fifty yards behind the front line, and as far as possible one arranged to get the men a few hours' sleep in them every day; but only a certain percentage at a time. There were four stretcher-bearers and two signallers also at Trafalgar Square. Also a permanent wiring-party had its quarters here, a corporal and five men; they made up "concertina" or "gooseberry" wire by day, and were out three or four hours every night putting it out. They were, of course, exempt from other platoon duties. Each platoon had a pioneer to attend to sanitary arrangements, and other odd jobs such as fetching up soup; and each platoon had an orderly ready to take messages. At Company Headquarters, besides the officers' servants, were the company orderly, and company officers' cook. An officer on trench duty was accompanied by his servant as orderly.

This was the distribution of the company in the front line. Every morning from 9 to 12 all men not on sentry worked at repairing and improving the trenches; and the same for four hours during the night. Work done to strengthen the parapet can only be done by night. Every night wire was put out. Every night a patrol went out. Every day one "stood to" arms for an hour before dawn, and an hour after dusk. And day and night there was an intermittent stinging and buzzing of black-winged instruments between the opposing trenches. Of shells I have already spoken; next in deadliness were rifle-grenades, which are bombs with a rod attachment that is put down the barrel of an ordinary rifle. Four of these rifles are stood in a rack fixed to the ground, and fired by a string from a few yards away, at a very high trajectory. They are a very deadly weapon, as you cannot see them dropping on to you. Then there is a multiform genus called "trench-mortar," being projectiles of all kinds and shapes lobbed over from close range. The canister was the most loathed. It was simply a tin oil-can, the size of a lady's muff (large); one heard a thud, and watched the beast rising, rising, then stationary, it seemed, in mid-air, and then come toppling down, down, down on top of one with a crash—three seconds' silence—and then a most colossal explosion, blowing everything in its vicinity to atoms. These canisters were loathed by the men with a most personal and intense aversion. Yet they were really not nearly so dangerous as rifle-grenades, as one had time to dodge them very often, unless enfiladed in a communication trench. They were, moreover, very local in their effects. A shell has splinters that spread far and wide; a trench-mortar is a clumsy monster with a thin skin, no splinters, and an abominable, noisy, vulgar way of making the most of itself. "Sausages" were another but milder form of the vulgar trench-mortar; aerial torpedoes were daintier people with wings, who looked so cherubic as they came sailing over, that one almost forgot their deadly stinging powers; they, too, were a species of trench-mortar.

It is natural to write lightly of these things; yet they were no light matters. They were the instruments of death that took their daily toll of lives. In this chapter describing the system and routine of ordinary trench warfare, I have tried to prepare the canvas for several pictures I have drawn in bold bare lines; now I am putting in a wash of colour, the atmosphere of Death.

Sometimes we forgot it in the interest of the present activity; sometimes we saw it face to face, without a qualm; but always it was there with its relentless overhanging presence, dulling our spirits, wearing out our lives. The papers are always full of Tommy smiling: Bairnsfather has immortalised his indomitable humour. Yes, it is true. We laugh, we smile. But for an hour of laughter, there are how many hours of weariness, strain, and grim agony! It is great that Tommy's laughter has been immortalised; but do not forget that its greatness lies in this, that it was uttered beneath the canopy of ever-impending Death.

CHAPTER VII

MORE FIRST IMPRESSIONS

IT must not be imagined that I at once grasped all the essential details of our trench system, as I have tried to put them concisely in the preceding chapter. On the contrary, it was only very gradually that I accumulated my intimate knowledge of our maze of trenches, only by degrees that I learnt the lie of the land, and only by personal patrolling that I learnt the interior economy of the craters. At first the front line, with its loops and bombing-posts, and portions "patrolled only," its sand-bag dumps, its unexpected visions of R.E.'s scurrying like bolted rabbits from mine-shafts, its sudden jerk round a corner that brought you in full view of the German parapet across a crater that made you gaze fascinated several seconds before you realised that you should be stooping low, as here was a bad bit of trench that wanted deepening *at once* and had not been cleared properly after being blown in last night—all this, I say, was at first a most perplexing labyrinth. It was only gradually that I solved its mysteries, and discovered an order in its complexity.

I will give a few more extracts from my diary, some of which seem to me now delightfully naïve! Here they are, though.

"2nd Feb., 1916. In the trenches. Everything very quiet. We are in support, in a place called Maple Redoubt, on the reverse slope of a big ridge. Good dug-outs (*sic*), and a view behind, over a big expanse of chalk-downs, which is most exhilarating. A day with blue sky and a tingle of frost. Being on the reverse slope, you can walk about anywhere, and so can see everything. Have just been up in the front trenches, which are over the ridge, and a regular, or rather very irregular, rabbit-warren. The Boche generally only about thirty to forty yards away. The trenches are *dry*, that is the glorious thing. DRY. Just off to pow-wow to the new members of my platoon."

Here I will merely remark that the "good" dug-out in which we were living was blown in by a 4·2 shell exactly four days later, killing one officer and wounding the other two badly. With regard to the state of the trenches, it was dry weather, and "when they were dry they were dry, and when they were wet they were wet!"

"3rd Feb. Another beautiful February morning. Slept quite well, despite rats overhead. O'Brien and Dixon awfully dull and heavy; can't think why. Everything outside is full of life; there is a crispness in the air, and a delightful sharp shadow and light contrast as you look up Maple Redoubt.

Meditations on coldness, and how it unmans—on hunger, and how it weakens—on the art of feeding and warming, and how women realise this, while men do not usually know there is any art in keeping house at all!

Meditations, too, on the stupidity, slowness, and clumsiness of officers' servants.

Dixon's snores make me bucked with life; so, too, this same clumsiness of the servants. Lewis came in just now. 'Why are you waiting, Lewis?' I asked. 'I thought Watson was waiting to-day.' (This after a great strafing of servants for general stupidity and incompetence.) 'None of the others dared come in, sir,' he replied, in his high piping voice, and a broad grin on his face. Oh! they are good fellows! Why be fed up with life? Why long faces? Long faces, these are the bad things of life, the things to fight against. . . ."

So did my vision of the Third Army School bear fruit, I see now!

"Philosophy from the trenches. Does it cover everything? Does it explain the fellows I passed this morning being carried to the Aid Post, one with blood and orange iodine all over his face, and the other wounded in both legs? It always comes as a surprise when the bombs and shells produce wounds and death. . . .

Watched a mine go up this evening—great yellow-brown mass of smoke, followed by a beautiful under-cloud of orange-pink that steamed up in a soft creamy way. No firing and shelling followed as at Givenchy. . . .

Take over from 'A' to-morrow morning.

10 p.m. Great starlight. Jupiter and Venus both up, and the Great Bear and Orion glittering hard and clean in the steely sky. I wish I had a Homer. I am sure he has just one perfect epithet for Orion on a night like this. I shall read Homer in a new light after these times. I begin to understand the spirit of the Homeric heroes; it was all words, words, words before. Now I see. Billet life—where is that in the *Iliad?* In the tents, of course. And the eating and drinking, the 'word that puts heart into men,' the cool stolid facing of death, all those gruesome details of wounds and weapons, all is being enacted here every day exactly as in the Homeric age. Human nature has not altered.

And did not Homer tell, too, how utterly 'fed up' they were with it all? Can one not read between the lines and see, besides the glamour of physical courage, the strain, the weariness, the 'fed-upness' of them all! I think so. 'Νόστος' is a word I remember so well. They were all longing for the day of their return. As here, the big fights were few and far between ; and as here, there were the months and years of waiting.

And on them, too, the stars looked down, winking alike at Greeks and Trojans ; just as to-night thousands of German and British faces, dull-witted or sharp, sour-faced or smiling, sad or happy, are gazing up and wondering if there is any wisdom in the world yet.

Four thousand years ago ? And all the time the stars in the Great Bear have been hurtling apart at thousands of miles an hour, and the human eye sees no difference. No wonder they wink at us. . . .

And our mothers, and wives . . . the women-folk—Euripides understood their views on war. Ten years they waited. . . .

Must go to bed. D—— these scuffling rats."

Frequently I found my thoughts flying back through the years, and more especially on starlit nights, or on a breathless spring evening, to the Greeks and Romans. Life out here was so primitive ; so much a matter of eating and drinking, and digging, and sleeping, and so full of the elements, of cold, and frost, and wind, and rain ; there were so many definite and positive physical goods and bads, that the barrier of an unreal civilisation was completely swept away. Under the stars and in a trench you were as good as any Homeric warrior ; but you were little better. And so you felt you understood him. And here I will add that it was especially at sunset that the passionate desire to live would sometimes surge up, so intense, so clamorous, that it swept every other feeling clean aside for the time.

But to return to Maple Redoubt, or rather to Gibraltar, where the next entry in my diary was written.

"6th Feb. Rather an uncomfortable dug-out in Gibraltar. Yesterday was a divine day. I sat up in 'the Fort' most of the day, watching the bombardment. Blue sky, on the top of a high chalk down ; larks singing ; and a real sunny dance in the air. We watched four aeroplanes sail over, amid white puffs of shrapnel ; and a German 'plane came over. I could see the black crosses very plainly with my glasses. Most godlike it must have been up there on such a morning. I felt very pleased with life, and did two sketches, one of Sawyer, another of Richards. . . .

A dull thud, and then 'there goes another,' shouts someone. It reminds me of Bill the lizard coming out of the chimney-pot in *Alice in Wonderland*. Everyone gazes and waits for the crash ! Toppling through the sky comes a big tin oil-can, followed immediately by another ; both fall and explode with a tremendous din, sending up a fifty-foot spurt of black earth and flying débris, while down the wind comes the scud of sand-bag fluff and the smell of powder. This alternated with the 4·2's, which come over with a scream and wait politely a second or two before bursting so inelegantly." (I seem to have got mixed up a bit here: it was usually the canisters that "waited.")

"The mining is a great mystery to me at present. One part of the trench is only patrolled, as the Boche may 'blow' there at any moment. I must say it is an uncomfortable feeling, this liability to sudden projection skywards! The first night I had a sort of nightmare all the time, and kept waking up, and thinking about a mine going up under one. The second night I was too tired to have nightmares.

The rats *swarm*. I woke up last night, and saw one sitting on Edwards, licking its whiskers. Then it ran on to the box by the candle. It was a pretty brown fellow, rather attractive, I thought. I felt no repulsion whatever at sight of it. . . .

The front trenches are a *maze*. I cannot disentangle all the loops and saps; and now we are cut off from 'C,' as the front trench is all blown in; one has to have a connecting patrol that goes viâ Rue Albert. A very weird affair. The only consolation is that the Boche would be *more* lost if he got in!

I cannot help feeling that 'B' company has

been very lucky. We were in Maple Redoubt, Wednesday, Thursday, and Friday; everything was quite quiet with us, but 'D' had seven casualties in the front trench. On Friday we relieved 'A,' and all Saturday the enemy bombarded a spot just behind our company's left, putting over 4·2's and canisters all day long from 9.0 a.m. onwards, and absolutely smashing up our trenches there. Then Trafalgar Square has been rather a hot shop: two of our own whizz-bangs fell short there, and several rifle grenades fell *very* close—also, splinters of the 4·2's came humming round, ending with little plops quite close. O'Brien picked up a large splinter that fell in the trench right outside the dug-out. Again, at 'stand-down,' when Dixon, Clark, Edwards, and I were standing talking together at the top of 76 Street, two canisters fell most alarmingly near us, about ten yards behind, covering us with dirt. Yet we have not had a single casualty.

To-day we were to have been relieved by the Manchesters at midday, but this morning at 'stand to' we heard the time had been altered to 8.0 a.m. 'B' was duly relieved, and No. 5 Platoon had just changed gum-boots, while 6, 7, and 8 were sitting at the corner of Maple Redoubt enthralled in the same process, when over came two canisters, one smashing in Old Kent Road, down which we had just come, and the other falling right into an 'A' Company dug-out, twenty yards to my left, killing two men and wounding three others, one probably mortally. And now I have just had the news that the Manchesters have had twenty-three casualties to-day, including three officers, their R.S.M., and a company sergeant-major."

As I read some of these sentences, true in every detail as they are, I cannot help smiling. For it was no "bombardment" that took place on our left all day; it was merely the Germans potting one of our trench-mortar positions! And Trafalgar Square was really very quiet, that first time in. But what I notice most is the way in which I record the fall of *individual* canisters and rifle grenades, even if they were twenty yards away! Never a six days in, latterly, that we did not have to clear Old Kent Road and Watling Street two or three times; and we used to fire off a hundred rifle grenades a day very often, and received as many in return always. And the record of casualties one did not keep. We *were* lucky, it is true. Once, and once only, after, did "B" Company go in and come out without a casualty. Those first two days in Maple Redoubt, when "everything was quiet," were the most deceitful harbingers of the future that could have been imagined. "Why long faces?" I could write. The Manchesters had a ruder but a truer introduction to the Bois Français trenches, and especially to Maple Redoubt. For the dug-outs were abominable; not one was shell-proof; and there was no parados or traverse for a hundred and fifty yards. The truth of the matter was that these trenches had been some of the quietest in the line; for some reason or other, when our Division took them over, they immediately changed face about, and took upon themselves the task of growing in a steady relentless crescendo into one of the hottest sectors in the line.

On the 22nd of February the Germans raided our trenches on the left opposite Fricourt. They did not get much change out of it. I can remember at least four raids close on our left or right during those four months; they never actually came over on our front, but we usually came in for the bombardment. The plan is to isolate the sector to be raided by an intense bombardment on that sector, and on the sectors on each side; to "lift" the barrage, or curtain of fire, at a given moment off the front line of the sector raided "what time" (as the old phrase goes) they come over, enter the trench, if they can, make a few prisoners, and get back quickly. All the while the sectors to right and left are being bombarded heavily. It was this isolating bombardment that our front line was receiving, while we were left unmolested in 71 North. All this I did not know at the time. Here is my record of it.

"25 Feb., 1916. It is snowing hard. We are in a very comfortable tubular dug-out in 71 North. This dug-out is the latest pattern, being on the twopenny-tube model; very warm, and free from draughts. It is *not* shell-proof, but then shells never seem to come near here.

Let me try and record the raid on our left on the 22nd, before I forget it.

The Manchesters were in the front line and Maple Redoubt. During the afternoon the Boche started putting heavies on to Maple Redoubt, and the corner of Canterbury Avenue. 'Bad luck on the Manchesters again,' we all agreed—and turned in for tea. There was a wonderful good fire going.

'By Jove, they are going it,' I said, as we sat down and Gray brought in the teapot. Thud! Thud! Thud—thud! We simply had to go out and watch. Regular coal-boxes, sending up great columns of mud, and splinters humming and splashing right over us, a good hundred yards or more. 'Better keep inside,' from Dixon.

We had tea, and things seemed to quiet down.

Then about six o'clock the bombardment got louder, and our guns woke up like fun. 'Vee-bm . . . vee-bm' from our whizz-bangs going over, and then the machine-guns began on our left. Simultaneously, in came Richards (Dixon's servant) with an excited air. 'Gas,' he exclaimed. Instinctively, I felt for my gas helmet. Meanwhile Dixon had gone outside. 'Absurd,' he said in a quiet voice. 'The wind's wrong. Who brought that message?'

Then up came a telephone orderly. I heard

him running on the hard road. 'Stand to,' he said breathlessly, and Dixon went off to the 'phone with him. Nicolson appeared in a gas helmet. I was looking for my pipe, but could not find it. Then at last I went out without it.

Outside it was getting dark. It was a fairly nippy air. The bombardment was going strong. All the sky was flickering, and our guns were screaming over. 'Crump, crump,' the Boche shells were bursting up by Maple Redoubt. 'Scream, scream,' went our guns back; and right overhead our big guns went griding.

All this I noticed gradually. My first impression was the strong smell of gas helmets in the cold air. The gas alarm had spread, and some of the men had their helmets on. I felt undecided. I simply did not *know*, whether the men should wear them or not. What was happening? I wished Dixon would come back. Ah! there he was. What news?

'I can't get through,' he said, 'but we shall get a message all right if necessary.'

'What's happening?' I asked. 'Do you think they are coming over.'

'No. It won't last long, I expect. Still, just let's see if the men have got their emergency rations with them.'

A few had not, and were sent into the dug-outs for them. Gas helmets were ordered back into their satchels.

'No possibility of gas,' said Dixon; 'wind's dead south.'

I was immensely bucked now. There was a feeling of tenseness and bracing-up. I felt the importance of essentials—rifles and bayonets in good order—the men fit, and able to run. This was the real thing, somehow.

I made Lewis go in and get my pipe. I found I had no pouch, and stuffed loose baccy in my pocket.

I realised I had not thought out what I would do in case of attack. I did not know what was happening. I was glad Dixon was there. . . .

It was great, though, to hear the continuous roar of the cannonade, and the machine-guns rapping, not for five minutes, but all the time. That I think was the most novel sound of all. No news. That was a new feature. A Manchester officer came up and said all their communications were cut with the left.

I was immensely bucked, especially with my pipe. Our servants were good friends to have behind us, and Dixon was a man in his element. The men were all cool. 'Germans have broken through,' I heard one man say. 'Where?' said someone rather excitedly. 'In the North Sea,' was the stolid reply.

At last the cannonade developed into a roar on our left, and we realised that any show was there, and not on our sector. Then up came the quartermaster with some boots for Dixon and me, and we all went into the dug-out, where was a splendid fire. And we stayed there, and certain humorous remarks from the quartermaster suddenly turned my feelings, and I felt that the tension was gone, the thing was over; and that outside the bombardment was slackening. In half an hour it was 'stand down' at 7.40.

I was immensely bucked. I knew I should be all right now in an attack. And the cannonade at night was a magnificent sight. Of course we had not been shelled, though some whizz-bangs had been fired fifty yards behind us just above 'Redoubt A,' trying for the battery just over the hill.

My chief impression was, 'This is the real thing.' You must know your men. They await clear orders, that is all. It was dark. I remember thinking of Brigade and Division behind, invisible, seeing nothing, yet alone knowing what was happening. No news, that was interesting. An entirely false rumour came along, 'All dug-outs blown in in Maple Redoubt.'

I had sent Evans to Bray to try and buy coal: he returned in the middle of the bombardment with a long explanation of why he had been unable to get it.

'Afterwards,' I said. Somehow coal could wait.

All the while I have been writing this, there is a regular blizzard outside."

Such is my record of my first bombardment. The Manchesters, who were in the front line, suffered rather heavily, but not in Maple Redoubt. No dug-outs were smashed in at all there, though Canterbury Avenue was blocked in two places, and Old Kent Road in one. The Germans came over from just north of Fricourt, but only a very few reached our trenches, and of them about a dozen were made prisoners, and the rest killed. It was a "bad show" from the enemy point of view.

And now I will leave my diary. These first impressions are interesting enough, but later the entries became more and more spasmodic, and usually introspective. The remaining chapters are not exactly, though very nearly, chronological. From February 6th to March 8th I was Sniping and Intelligence officer to the battalion. Chapters VIII, IX, and XII describe incidents in that period. Then on March 8th Captain Dixon was transferred as Second-in-Command to our ——th Battalion, and on that date I took over the command of "B" Company, which I held until I was wounded on the 7th of June. These were the three months in which I learnt the strain of responsibility as well as the true tragedy of this war.

During all these four months I was fortunate in having as a commanding officer a really great soldier. The C.O. had inaugurated his arrival by a vigorous emphasis of the following principle:

"No Man's Land belongs to *US;* if the Boche dare show his face in it, he's going to be d—d sorry for it. We are top-dogs, and if there is any strafing, the last word must always be ours." Such was the policy of the man behind me during those four months. Meanwhile, from eight to midnight every night, trenches were being deepened, the parapet thickened, and fire-steps and traverses being put in the front line, which had hitherto been a maze of hasty improvisations; barbed wire was put out at an unprecedented pace, and patrols were going out every night. If things went wrong, there was the devil to pay; but if things went well, one was left entirely unmolested; and if there was a bombardment on, the orders came quick and clear. And any company commander will know that those three qualities in a commanding officer are worth almost anything.

CHAPTER VIII

SNIPING

I

THE snow was coming down in big white flakes, whirling and dancing against a grey sky. I shivered as I looked out from the top of the dug-out steps in Maple Redoubt. It was half-past seven, a good hour since the snipers had reported to me before going to their posts. It was quite dark then, for a sniper must always be up on his post a good hour before dawn to catch the enemy working a few minutes too late. It is so easy to miss those first faint glimmerings of twilight when you are just finishing off an interesting piece of wiring in "No Man's Land." I speak from experience. For so a sniper got me.

"U—u—u—gh," I shuddered, "it's no good keeping the men on in this"; so, putting my whiskey-bottle full of rum in my haversack, I set off up Old Kent Road to visit my posts and withdraw the men *pro tem.* I expected to find the fellows unutterably cold, shrivelled up, and bored. To my surprise, at No. 1 post Thomas and Everton were in a state of huge excitement, eyes glowing, and faces full of life. There seemed to be a great rivalry, too, for the possession of the rifle. For the snipers always worked in pairs : a man cannot gaze out at the opposing lines with acute interest for more than about half an hour on end ; so I used to work them by pairs, and give them shifts according to the weather. In summer you could put a pair on for four hours, and they would work well, taking half-hour shifts ; but in cold weather two hours was quite enough.

"We've got them, sir," from 75 Thomas ; "they was working in the trench over there—by all them blue sand-bags, sir—four of them, sir——"

"Yes, and I saw him throw up his arms, sir," put in Everton, excited for the first time I have ever seen him, and trying to push Thomas out of the box, and have another look. But Thomas would not be pushed.

"Splendid," I said : "by Jove, that's good work. Can I see ? " But it was snowing hard, and I could see very little. I tried the telescope. "Put it right up to your eye, sir," said Thomas, forgetting that I had myself taught him this in billets as he vainly tried to see through it holding it about four inches from his face, and declaring that he could see everything just as well with his own eyes !

"Yes, I think I see where you mean," said I ; "up by that sand-bag dump. There's a mine-shaft there, and they were probably some of their R.E.'s piling up sand-bags, or emptying them out. I believe that is what they usually do now, fill the sand-bags below in their galleries, bring them up, empty them, and use the same ones again."

Thomas and Everton gaped at this. It had not occurred to them to consider that the Boche had R.E.'s. They were of the unimaginative class of snipers, who "saw, did, and reported," and on the whole I preferred them to those who saw, and immediately "concluded." For their conclusions were usually wrong. To men like Thomas I was, I think, looked upon as one who had some slightly supernatural knowledge of the German lines; he did not realise that by careful compass-bearings I knew the exact ground visible from his post, and that my map of the German lines, showing every trench as revealed by aeroplane photographs, was accurate to a yard. He was like a retriever, who keeps to heel, noses out his bird with unerring skill, and brings it in with the softest of mouths; yet the cunning and strategy he leaves to his master, who is decidedly his inferior in nose and mouth. So 75 Thomas could see and shoot far better than I; but it was I who thought out the strategy of the shoot.

"Well," said I, as I doled out a rather more liberal rum ration than usual, "that's d—— good work, anyway. Two you got, you say? Not sure about the second? Anyway you had two good shots, and remember what I told you, a sniper only shoots to kill. So two it's going to be, anyhow." (They both grinned at this, which was the nearest they could get to a wink.) "I'm very pleased about it. Now it's not much good staying up here in this thick snow, so you can go off till I send word to your dug-out for you to go on again."

I turned to go away, thinking that the other posts, rumless, and in all probability quarryless, must be in a state of exasperating coldness by now. But Thomas and Everton did not move. There was something wanted.

"Well, what is it ? "

"Please sir, can we stay on here a bit ? P'raps one of those R.E. fellows may come back for something "

"Good heavens, yes," I said, "stay on as long as you like," and smiled as I made off to my other posts. (Later I used to get the snipers to report to me coming off their posts, and get their rum ration then ; as I found it gave a bad appearance and damaged the reputation of the snipers when people saw me going about with the nose of a bottle of "O.V.H." whiskey sticking out of my haversack !) There, as I expected, I found the men blue and bored.

"You can't see nothing to-day, sir, at all," was the sentence with which I was immediately greeted. Even the rum seemed to inspire very little outward enthusiasm.

"You can go off to your dug-outs till I send for you," I replied, carefully corking the bottle and not looking at them while I spoke : "if you like," I added after a pause, looking up. But the post was empty.

That afternoon I was up on No. 1 post, with a sniper who was new to the work. It was still freezing, but the snow-clouds had cleared right away, and the wind had dropped. There was a tingle in the air ; everything was as still as death ; the sun was shining from a very blue sky, and throwing longer and longer shadows in the snow as the afternoon wore on. It was a valuable afternoon, the enemy's wire showing up very clearly against the white ground, and I was showing the new sniper how to search the trench systematically from left to right, noting the exact position of anything that looked like a loophole, or steel-plate, and especially the thickness of the wire, what kind, whether it was grey and new, or rusty-red and old ; whether there were any gaps in it, and where. All these things a sniper should note every morning when he comes on to his post. Gaps are important, as patrols must come out through gaps, and the Lewis gunners should know these, and be ready to fire at them if a patrol is heard thereabouts in No Man's Land. Similarly, old gaps closed up must be reported.

It was very still. " Has the war stopped ? " one felt inclined to ask. No, there is the sound of shells exploding far away on the right somewhere ; in the French lines it must be, somewhere about Frise. Then a " phut " from just opposite, and a long whining " we'oo—we'oo—we'oo—we'-oo . . .

bzung," and a rifle-grenade burst with a snarl about a hundred yards behind. Then another, and another, and another. "They're trying for Trafalgar Square," said I. No. 1 post was a little to the right of the top of 76 Street. I waited. There were no more. It was just about touch and go whether we replied. If they went on up to about a dozen, the chances were that the bombing-corporal in charge of our rifle-grenade battery would rouse himself, and loose off twenty in retaliation. But, no. Perhaps the German had repented him of the evil of desecrating the peace of such an afternoon; or perhaps he was just ranging, and had an observer away on the flank somewhere to watch the effect of his shooting. Anyway he did not fire again, and the afternoon slumber was resumed, till the evening "strafe" came on in due course.

"I can see something over on the left, sir. It is a man's head, sir! Look!"

I looked. Yes!

"No," I almost shouted. "It's a dummy head. Just have a look. And don't, whatever you do, fire."

Sure enough, a cardboard head appeared over the front parapet opposite, with a grey cap on. Slowly it disappeared. Without the telescope it would have been next to impossible to see it was not a man. Again it appeared, then slowly sank out of view. It was well away on the left, just in front of where the "R.E.'s" had been hit at dawn. For this post was well-sited, having an oblique field of vision, as all good sniping-posts should. That is to say, they should be sited something like this :

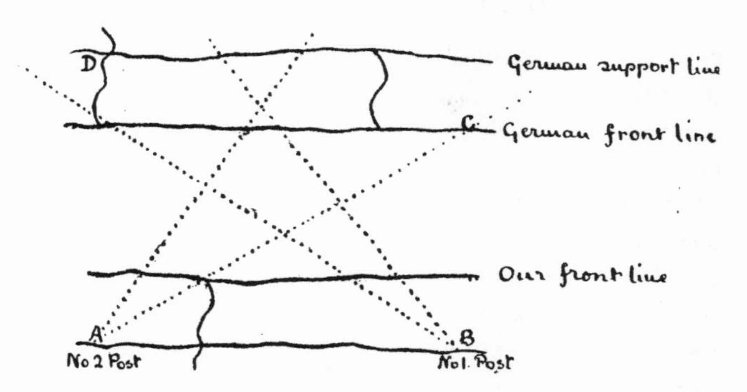

The ideal is to have all your posts in the supports, and *not* in the front line, and at about three hundred yards from the enemy front line. Of course if the ground slopes *away* behind you, you cannot get positions in the supports unless there are buildings to make posts in. By getting an *oblique* view, you gain two advantages :

(*a*) If A gets a shot at C, C's friends look out for "that d——d sniper opposite," and look in the direction of B, who is carefully concealed from direct view.

(*b*) A's loophole is invisible from direct observation by D, as it is pointing slantwise at C.

All this I now explained to my new sniper.

"But why not smash up his old dummy, sir ? Might put the wind up the fellow working it."

"No," I explained. "Look at the paper again. (I had drawn it out for him, as I have on the previous page.) Thomas shot at those R.E.'s this morning, don't you see? He was here (B), and they're at D. Now they're trying to find *you*, or the man who shot their pal; and you can bet anything you like they've got a man watching either at C or right away on the left to spot you if you fire at the dummy. No. Lie doggo, and see if you can spot that man on the flank. He's probably got a periscope."

"Can't see him, sir," at length.

"No. Never mind; he's probably far too well concealed. Always remember the Boche is as clever as you, and sometimes cleverer."

"Ah, but he wants me to shoot, sir, and I won't," came the cheery answer. "What about smashing up his old dummy?" I reminded him. His face fell. He had forgotten his old un-sniper-like self already. "Never mind," said I. "Now when Thomas and Everton come up here, mind you tell them all about the dummy; and tell Thomas from me that the Boche doesn't spend his time dummy-wagging for nothing. Probably it was an R.E. sergeant."

II

"Swis–s–sh—báng. Swis–s–sh—báng."

"That settles it," said I, as I scrambled hastily down into the trench, preceded by the sniper I had with me that day as orderly. I more or less pushed him along for ten yards—then halted; we faced each other both very much out of breath and "blowy." The whole place was reeking with the smell of powder, and the air full of sand-bag fluff.

"That settles it," I repeated: "I always thought that was a rotten post; and I object to being whizz-banged. 'A sniper's job is to see and not be seen.' Isn't that right, Morris?"

"Yes, sir," replied Morris, adding with a sad lack of humour "They must have seen us, sir!"

"Exactly: they did. And they weren't very far off hitting one of us into the bargain. As I say, that settles it. We'll leave that post for ever and ever; and to-night we'll build a new one that they *won't* see."

At ten o'clock that night we were well at work. Just on the one hundred metre contour line there was a small quarry, at the west end of which had been the too conspicuous post where the Boche had spotted us. Every loophole must by its very nature be "spottable"; but when the natural ground is so little disturbed that it looks exactly the same as it did before the post was made, then indeed this "spottability" is so much reduced that it verges on invisibility. So, leaving the old post exactly as before, we were building a new one about twenty yards to the west of it.

There was a disused support trench running west from the Quarry, and this suited my purpose admirably. It ran just along the crest of the hill, and commanded even a better view of Fricourt than the Quarry itself. Moreover, there was enough earth thrown up in front of the trench to enable us to fix in the steel-plate (at an angle of 45° : this increases its impenetrability) on ground level, without the top protruding above the top of the earth. The soil in front was not touched at all until the plate was fixed in, and then enough was carefully scooped away from the front of the actual loophole to secure a fair field of view. The earth in front of the loophole is then exactly like a castle wall, with a splay window. If you think of a Norman castle you will know exactly what I mean. The loophole represents the inch-wide aperture in the inner side of the splay. Similarly an embrasure is built behind the loophole, with room for one man to stand and fire, and the second man to sit by him. A rainproof shelter of corrugated iron is placed over this embrasure, and covered over with earth ; this prevents it being spotted by aeroplane ; also it makes the place habitable in the rain. Here is a section of a typical sniper's post :

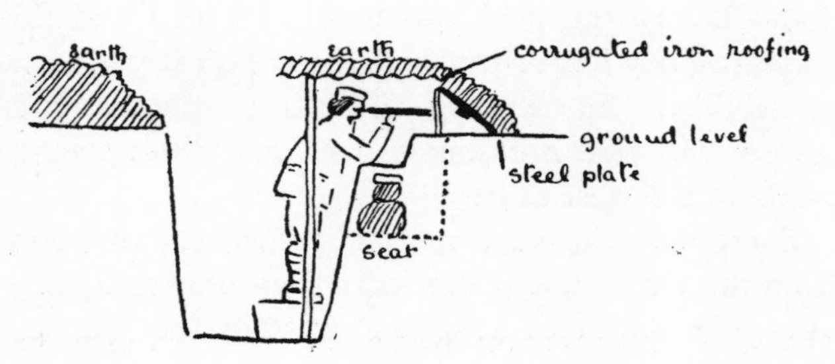

"Click, click click" went the pick into the chalk, cutting room for the embrasure ; there was a tinny sound as some of the loose surface soil came away with a spurt, spilling on to the two sheets of corrugated iron waiting to go on to the roof. Added to this were the few quiet whispers, such as "Where's that sand-bag ?" or "Is this low enough, sir ?", and the heavy breathing of Private Evans as he returned from the Quarry after emptying his sand-bag. For all the chalk cut away had to be carried to the Quarry and emptied there ; new earth on the top there would not give any clue to those gentlemen in Fricourt Wood who put the smell of powder in my nostrils a few hours back.

It was a darkish night, but not so dark but what you could see the top of the trench. There are very few nights when the sky does not show lighter than the trench-sides. There are a few, though, especially when it is raining ; and they are bad, very bad. But that night I could just distinguish the outline of the big crater-top, half-right, and follow the near skyline along the German parapet down into Fricourt valley. I was gazing down into that silent blackness, when a machine-gun started popping ; I could see the flashes very clearly from my position. Somewhere in Fricourt they must be.

Meanwhile the post was nearly finished ; the corrugated iron was being fixed to the wooden upright, and Jones was on the parapet sprinkling earth over it. The others were deepening the trench from the Quarry to the post.

"That's the machine-gun that goes every night, sir," said Jones. "Enfilading, that's what it is."

"Pop—pop—pop," answered the machine-gun.

"Look here, Jones," said I. "You know No. 5 post, opposite Aeroplane Trench ?"

"Yes, sir !"

"Well, go down there, and see if you can see the flashes from there ; and if you can, mark it down. See ?"

"Yes, sir !" and he had his equipment on in no time, and was starting off when I called him back.

"Be very careful to mark your own position," I warned him. "You know what I mean."

He knew, and I knew that he knew.

Meanwhile, I stuck an empty cartridge case in the parados behind my head and waited.

Five flashes spat out again, and "pop—pop—pop—pop—pop" came up out of the valley : and between me and them in the parapet I stuck a second cartridge case——

I looked at my watch. It was half-past twelve. The post was finished, and the trench deep enough to get along, crawling anyway.

"Cease work."

The next day was so misty that you could see practically nothing over five hundred yards, and the new post was useless. The following day it had frozen again, and an inch of snow lay on the ground. It was a sunny morning, and from the new post all Fricourt lay in full view before me. How well I remember every detail of that city of the dead ! In the centre stood the white ruin of the church, still higher than the houses around it, though a stubby stump compared to what it must have been before thousands of shells reduced it to its present state. All around were houses ; roofless, wall-less skeletons all of them, save in a few cases, where a red roof still remained, or a house seemed by some magic to be still untouched. On the extreme right was Rose Cottage, a well-known artillery mark ; just to its left were some large park-gates, with stone pillars, leading into Fricourt Wood ; and just inside the wood was a small cottage—a lodge, I suppose. The extreme northern part of the village was invisible, as the ground fell away north of the church. I could see where the road disappeared from view ; then beyond, clear of the houses, the road re-appeared and ran straight up to the skyline, a mile further on. A communication trench crossed this road : (I remember we saw some men digging there one morning). With my glasses I could see every detail ; beyond the communication trench were various small copses, and tracks running over the field ; and on the skyline, about three thousand yards away, was a long row of bushes.

And just to the left of it all ran the two white lace-borders of chalk trenches, winding and wobbling along, up, up, up until they disappeared over the hill to La Boiselle. Sometimes they diverged as much as three hundred yards, but only to come in together again, so close that it was hard to see which was ours and which the German. Due west of Fricourt church they touched in a small crater chain.

It was a fascinating view. I could not realise that there lay a *French* village ; I think we often forgot that we were on French soil, and not on a sort of unreal earth that would disappear when the war was over ; especially was No Man's Land a kind of neutral stage, whereon was played the great game. To a Frenchman, of course, Fricourt was as French as ever it had been. But I often forgot, when I watched the shells demolishing a few more houses, that these were not German houses deserving of their fate. Perhaps people will not understand this : it is true, anyway.

I was drawing a sketch of the village, when lo ! and behold ! coolly walking down the road into Fricourt came a solitary man. I had to think rapidly, and decide it must be a German, because the thing was so unexpected ; I could not for the moment get out of my head the unreasonable idea that it might be one of our own men ! However, I soon got over that.

" Sight your rifle at two thousand yards," said I to Morgan, who was with me. " Now, give it to me."

Carefully I took aim. I seemed to be holding the rifle up at an absurd angle. I squeezed, and squeezed——

The German jumped to one side, on to the grass at the side of the road, and doubled for all he was worth out of sight into Fricourt! Needless to say, I did not see him again to get another shot!

"They've been using that road last night, sir," said 58 Morgan, while I was taking a careful bearing on my empty cartridge case. (A prismatic compass is invaluable for taking accurate cross-bearings.)

"Yes," I said. "Why yes, of course, they must have used it last night. I never thought of that. Good. We'll get the artillery on there to-night, and upset their ration-carts."

This pleased the fancy of Sniper 58 Morgan, and a broad grin came over his face at the thought of the Boche losing his breakfast.

"Maybe, sir, we'll see the sausages on the road to-morrow morning."

For which thought I commended him not a little: a sense of humour is one of the attributes of a good sniper, just as rash conclusions are not.

I then went down to No. 5 Post, where Jones was awaiting me, according to arrangement. There I took a second bearing, and retired to my dug-out to work out the two angles on the map. "From map to compass add: from compass to map subtract" I repeated to myself, and disposed of the magnetic variation summarily. Then with the protractor I plotted out the angles. " Exactly. The small house with the grey roof standing out by itself on the left. So that's where you live, my friend, is it ? "

Once more I was up at the new post, scrutinising the grey-roofed house with the telescope. After a long gaze, I almost jumped. I gave the telescope to Morgan. He gazed intently for a moment.

Then, " Is that a hole, sir, over the door, in the shadow, like . . . ? "

" It is," I answered

That night the machine-gun started popping as usual, when suddenly a salvo of whizz-bangs screamed over, and H.E.'s joined in the game. All round and about the little grey-roofed house flickered the flashes of bursting shells. Then the enemy retaliated, and for a quarter of an hour " a certain liveliness prevailed." Then came peace. But there was no sound all night of a machine-gun popping from Fricourt village ; on the other hand, our machine-guns had taken up the tune, with short bursts of overhead fire, searching for those Boche ration carts. And in the morning the grey-roofed cottage appeared with two tiles left on the right-hand bottom corner of the roof, and the front wall had a huge gap in it big enough to act as a mouth for fifty machine-guns. Only Morgan was disappointed : all marks of the sausages had been cleared away before dawn ! After all, are not the Germans pre-eminently a tidy people ?

III

Private Ellis had hard blue eyes that looked at you, and looked, and went on looking ; they always reminded me of the colour of the sea when a north wind is blowing and the blue is hard and bright. I have seen two other pairs of eyes like them. One belonged to Captain Jefferies, the big game shooter, who lectured on Sniping at the Third Army School. The other pair were the property of a sergeant I met this week for the first time. " Are you a marksman ? " I asked him. " Yes, sir ! Always a marksman, sir."

There is no mistaking those eyes. They are the eyes of a man who has used them all his life, and found them grow steadier and surer every year. They are essentially the eyes of a man who can watch, watch, watch all day, and not get tired of watching ; and they were the eyes of my best sniper.

For Private Ellis had all the instincts of a cunning hunter. I had no need to tell him to keep his telescope well inside the loophole, lest the sun should catch on the glass ; no need to remind him to stuff a bit of sand-bag in the loophole when he left the post unoccupied. He never forgot to let the sand-bag curtain drop behind him as he entered the box, to prevent light coming into it and showing white through a loophole set in dark earth. There was no need either to make sure that he understood the telescopic sights on his rifle ; and there was no need to tell him that the Boches were clever people. He never under-estimated his foe.

It was a warm day in early March. Private Ellis was in No. 5 Box, opposite Aeroplane Trench. This post was very cunningly concealed. Our front trench ran along a road, immediately behind which was a steep chalk bank, the road having originally been cut out of a rather steep slope. You will see the lie of the ground clearly enough on Map III. Just about five yards behind this bank was cut a deep narrow trench, and in this trench were built several snipers' posts, with loopholes looking out of the chalk bank. These loopholes were almost impossible to see, as they were very nearly indistinguishable from the shadows in the bank. Anyone who has hunted for oyster-catchers' eggs on a pebbly beach knows that black and white is the most protective colour scheme existing. And so these little black loopholes were almost invisible in the black and white of the chalk bank.

All the morning Private Ellis had been watching out of the corner of his eye a little bit of glass shining in Aeroplane Trench. Now Aeroplane Trench (as you will also see from the map) was a sap running out from the German front trench into a sunken road. From the centre sap two little branch saps ran up and down the road, and then slightly forward; the whole plan of it rather resembled an aeroplane and gave it its name. In it to-day was a Boche with a periscopic rifle ; and it was this little bit of glass at the top of the periscope, and the nose of the rifle-barrel that Private Ellis was watching. Every now and again the glass and nose-cap would give a little jump, and " plop " a bullet would bury itself in our front parapet. One of our sentries had had his periscope smashed during the morning, I was informed by a company commander with rather the air of " What's the use of you and your snipers, if you can't stop them sniping us ? " I told Ellis about the periscope, to which he replied : " It won't break us, I guess, sir—twopenn'orth of new glass for a periscope. It's heads that count." In which remark was no little wisdom.

" Crack—plop," and after a long interval another " Crack—zin—n—n—g," as a bullet ricocheted off a stone, and went away over the ridge and fell with a little sigh somewhere in the ground right away beyond Redoubt A. So it went on all the afternoon, while the sun was warming everyone up and one dreamed of the summer, and warm days, dry trenches, and short nights. Ellis had gone off rather reluctantly at midday, and the other relief was there. There was a slumbrous sensation about that brought on the feeling that there was no one really in the enemy trenches at all. Yet there was the little glass eye looking at us : it reminded one of a snake in the grass. It glittered, unblinking.

At about six o'clock I again visited the post. Ellis was back there, and watching as keenly as ever.

" No luck ? " I remarked. " I'm afraid your friend is too wily for you ; he's not going to put his head over, when he can see through a periscope as well."

Still Private Ellis said little, but his eye was as clear and keen as ever ; and still the periscope remained.

" We must shell him out to-morrow," I said, and went off.

At half-past seven we had " stood down," and I was messing with " B " Company, when I heard a voice at the top of the dug-out, and the servant who was waiting—Lewis, I think it was—said a sniper wanted to see me.

" Tell him to come down."

Private Ellis appeared at the door. Not a muscle in his body or face moved, but his eyes were glowing and glittering. " Got him, sir," was all he said.

" What ? " I cried. " Got that Boche in Aeroplane Trench ? By Jove, tell us all about it."

And so to the accompaniment of a whiskey and Perrier he told us exactly what happened. It was not till well after " stand-to," it appeared, that any change had occurred in Aeroplane Trench. Then the periscope had wobbled and disappeared below ground. Then there had been another long wait. and the outline of the sunken road had begun to get faint. Then slowly, very slowly, a pink forehead had appeared over the top, and as slowly disappeared. I wish I had been there to watch Ellis then. I can imagine him coolly, methodically sighting his rifle on the trench-edge, and waiting. "I had to wait another minute, sir; then it appeared again, the whole head this time. He thought it was too dark to be seen . . . Oh, he won't worry us any more, sir! I saw one of his arms go up, and I thought I could see him fall against the back of the trench. But it was getting so dark, I couldn't have seen him five minutes later at all."

And if Ellis couldn't, who could?

Next day, and for many days, there was no sniping from Aeroplane Trench.

CHAPTER IX

ON PATROL

"HULLO, Bill!" from Will Todd, as he passed me going up 76 Street.

"Hullo," I answered, "where are you off to?"

"Going on patrol," was the reply. "Oh, by the way, you probably know something about this rotten sap opposite the Quarry. I'm going out to find out if it's occupied at night or not."

"Opposite the Quarry?" said I. "Oh, yes, I know it. We get rather a good view of it from No. 1 Post."

"That post up on the right here? Yes, I was up there this afternoon, but you can't see much from anywhere here. The worst of it is I was going with 52 Jones; only his leave has just come through. You see, I've never been out before. I'm trying a fellow called Edwards, but I don't know him."

"If you can't get Edwards," I said suddenly, "I've a good mind to come out with you. Meet me at Trafalgar Square, and let me know."

As Will disappeared, I immediately repented of my offer, repented heartily, repented abjectly. I had never been on patrol, and a great sinking feeling came over me. I hoped with all my might that Edwards would be bubbling over with enthusiasm for patrolling. I was afraid. With all the indifference to shells and canisters that was gradually growing upon me, I had never been out into No Man's Land. And yet I had volunteered to go out, and at the time of doing so I felt quite excited at the prospect. "Fool," I said to myself.

"Edwards doesn't seem at all enthusiastic about it," said Will. "Will you really come out ?"

"Yes, rather. I'm awfully keen to go. I've never been before, either. How are you going ?"

We exchanged views on how best to dress and carry our revolvers, which instantly assumed a new interest.

"What time are you going out ?"

"Eight o'clock."

It was a quarter to already.

In the dug-out I was emptying my pockets, taking off my equipment, and putting on a cap-comforter. I had my compass with me, and put it in my pocket. I looked on the map and saw that the sap was practically due north of the Quarry. And I took a nip of brandy out of my flask. Will had gone to arrange with Captain Robertson about warning the sentries. I was alone, and still cursing myself for this unnecessary adventure. When I was ready, I stodged up 76 Street to the Quarry. It was certainly a good night, very black.

When I saw Will and Captain Robertson together on the fire-step peering over, I felt rather bucked with myself. Hitherto I had felt like an enthusiastic bather undressing, nearly everyone else having decided it was not warm enough to bathe; now it was as if I suddenly found that they were watching me as I ran down the beach, and I no longer repented of my resolution. Next moment I was climbing up on to the slimy sandbag wall, and dropping over the other side. I was surprised to find there was very little drop at all. There was an old ditch to be crossed, and then we came to our wire, which was very thin at this point. While Will was cursing, and making, it seemed to me, rather an unnecessary rattling and shaking of the wire (you know how wire reverberates if you hit a fence by the road), I looked back at our own parapet. I felt it would be a good thing to see on one's return; again, it struck me how low it was, regarded from this side; I saw a head move along the top of it. This made me jump. Already our trench seemed immeasurably far off.

I looked in front again, as the noise of Will's wire-rattling had ceased. In fact he was clean out of sight. This made me jump again, and I hurried on. It was "knife-rest" wire (see next page).

I stepped over it, and my foot came down on to more wire, which rattled with a noise that made me stand stock still awaiting something to happen.

I felt like a cat who has upset a tablecloth and all the tea things. I stood appalled at the unexpected clatter. But really it was hardly audible to *our*

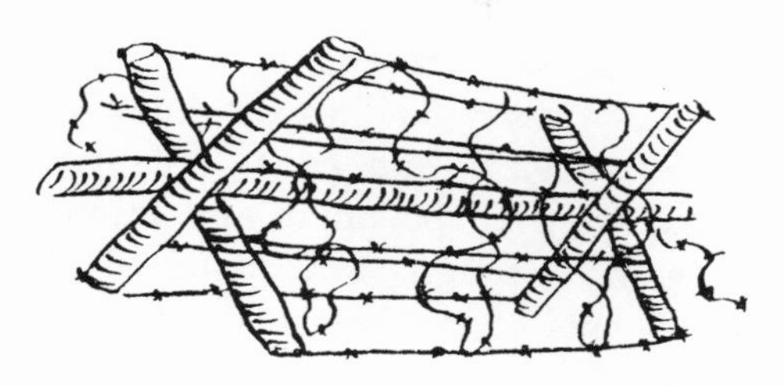

sentries, much less to the Germans at least a hundred and twenty yards away.

At last I got through and flopped down. Immediately Will's form showed up dark in front of me. When I was standing up, I had been unable to see him against the black ground. We lay about a minute absolutely quiet, according to arrangement.

I had fairly made the plunge now, and I felt like the bather shaking his hair as he comes up for the first time, and shouting out how glorious it is. I was elated. The feel of the wet grass was good under my hands; the silence was good; the immense loneliness, save for Will's black form, was good; and a slight rustle of wind in the grass was good also. I just wanted to lie, and enjoy it. I hoped Will would not go on for another minute. But soon he began to crawl.

Have you done much crawling? It is slow work.

You take knee-steps, and they are not like footsteps: they are not a hundred and twenty to the hundred yards They are more like fifty to ten yards, I should think. Anyway it seemed endless. The end of the sap was, to be precise, just one hundred and twenty-five yards from our front trench. Yet when I had gone, I suppose, forty yards, I expected to be on it any minute. Will must be going wrong. I thought of the map. Could we be going north-east instead of north? Will halted. I nearly bumped into his right foot, which raised itself twice, signalling a halt. I took out my compass, and looked at it. I shaded it with my hand, the luminous arrow seemed so bright: "rather absurd," I thought immediately, "as if the Boches could possibly see it from the trench." But we were going straight enough. Then the figure in front moved on, and I came up to where he had halted. It was the edge of a big shell-hole, full of water; I put my left hand in up to the wrist, I don't know why.

Still the figure crawled on, with a sort of hump-backed sidle that I had got to know by now. It was interminable this crawling . . .

"Swis—s—sh." A German flare shot up from ever so close. It seemed to be falling right over us. Then it burst with a "pop." I had my head down on my arms, but I could squint out sideways. It seemed impossible we should not be seen; for there, hardly twenty yards away, was the German wire, as clear as anything. Meanwhile the flare had fallen behind us. Would it never go out? I noticed the way the blades of grass were lit up by it; and there was an old tin or something. . . . I started as a rat ran across the grass past me. I wondered if it were a German rat, or one of ours.

Then at last the flare went out, and the blackness was intense. For a while longer we lay still as death; then I saw Will's foot move again. I listened intently, and on my right I heard a metallic sound. Quite close it was; it sounded like the clank of a dixie. I peered hard in the direction of the sound. Faintly I could distinguish earth above the ground-line. I had not looked to my right when the flare went up, and realised, as Will already had done, that we were out as far as the end of the sap. It was perhaps ten yards off, due right. I lay with my ear cocked sideways to catch the faintest sound. Clearly there was someone in the sap. But there was a wind swishing in the grass, and I could not hear anything more. Then my tense attitude relaxed, and I gradually sank my chin on my arm. I felt very comfortable. I did not want to move . . .

"Bang!!" and then a flame spat out; then came that gritty metallic sound I had heard before, and another "Bang!" I kept my head down and waited for the next, but it did not come. Then I heard a most human scroopy cough, which also sounded *very* near. The "bangs" were objectionably near; I literally shrank from them. To tell the truth, I had the "wind up" a bit. Those bullets seemed to me vicious personal spits that were distinctly unpleasant and near; and I wanted to get away from so close a proximity to them. I remembered a maxim of some famous General to the intent that if you are afraid of the enemy, the best thing was to remember that in all probability he was just as afraid of you. The maxim did not seem to apply somehow here. At the first "bang" I had thought we were seen; but I now realised that the sentry was merely blazing off occasional shots, and that the bullets had just plopped into our parapet.

Then Will turned round, and I did the same. Our business was certainly ended, for there was no doubt about the sap being occupied. Then I heard a thud behind us, and looking up saw the slow climbing trail of a canister blazing up into the sky; up it mounted, up, up, up, hovered a moment, then turned, and with a gathering impetus blazed down somewhere well behind our front trench.

"Trafalgar Square," I thought, as I lay doggo, for the blaze lit up the sky somewhat.

"Bomp." The earth shook as the canister exploded.

"Thud," and the process was repeated exactly as before, ending in another quaking "Bomp!"

I enjoyed this. It was rather a novel way of seeing canisters, and moreover a very safe way.

Two more streamed over.

Then our footballs answered, and burst with a bang in the air not so *very* far over into the German lines. The trench-mortar fellow was evidently trying short fuses, for usually our trench-mortar shells burst on percussion.

Then in the distance I heard four bangs, and the Boche 4·2's started, screaming over at Maple Redoubt. I determined to move on.

Then suddenly came four distant bangs from the right of our lines (as we faced them), and with "wang—wang . . . wang—wang" four whizz-bangs burst right around us, with most appalling flickers. "Bang—bang . . . bang—bang" in the distance again, and I braced every muscle tightly, as you do when you prepare to meet a shock. Behind us, and just in front, the beastly things burst. I lay with every fibre in my body strained to the uttermost. And yet I confess I enjoyed the sensation!

There was a lull, and I began crawling as fast as I could. I stopped to see if Will was following. "By God," I heard, "let's get out of this." So I was thinking! Then as I went on I saw the edge of a crater. Where on earth?

I halted and pulled out my compass. Due south I wanted. I found I was bearing off to the right far too much, so with compass in hand I corrected my course. Some crawling this time! It was not long before we could see wire in the distance. Then I got up and ran. How I got through that wire I don't know; I tore my puttees badly, and must have made a most unnecessary rattling. After which I fell into the ditch.

"Thank heaven you're all right," was the greeting from Captain Robertson. "I was just coming out after you. Those d—d artillery fellows. I sent down at once to 'phone to them to stop . . ."

And so on. I hardly heard a word. I was so elated, I could not listen. As we went back to Trafalgar Square for dinner, I heard them warning the sentries "The patrol's in." I looked up at the sandbag parapet. "In," I thought. "One does not realise what 'in' is, till one's been out."

I have been out several times later. I never had any adventures much. But always, before going out, I felt the shivers of the bather; and always, after I came in, a most splendid glow.

CHAPTER X

"WHOM THE GODS LOVE"

"NO officer wounded since we came out in October," said Edwards: "we're really awfully lucky, you know."

"For heaven's sake, touch wood," I cried.

We laughed, for the whole of our establishment was wood. We were sitting on a wooden seat, leaning our hands against wooden uprights, eating off a wooden table, and resting our feet on a wooden floor. Sometimes, too, we found splinters of wood in the soup—but it was more often straw. For this dining-room in Trafalgar Square was known sometimes as the "Summer-house" and sometimes as the "Straw Palace." It was really the maddest so-called "dug-out" in the British lines, I should think; I might further add, "in any trench in Europe." For the French, although they presumably built it in the summer days of 1915 when the Bois Français trenches were a sort of summer-rest for tired-out soldiers, would never have tolerated the "Summer-house" since the advent of the canister-age. As for the Boche, he would have merely stared if anyone had suggested him using it as a Company Headquarters. "But," he would have said, "it is not shell-proof."

Exactly. It would not have stood even a whizz-bang. A rifle-grenade would almost certainly have come right through it. As for a canister or H.E., it would have gone through like a stone piercing wet paper. But it had been Company Headquarters for so long—it was so light and, being next door to the servants' dug-out, so convenient—that we always lived in it still; though we slept in a dug-out a little way down Old Kent Road, which was certainly whizz-bang—if not canister—proof.

At any rate, here were Edwards and myself, drinking rather watery ox-tail soup out of very dinted tin-plates—the spoons were scraping noisily on the metal; overhead, a rat appeared out of the straw thatch, looked at me, blinked, turned about, and disappeared again, sending a little spill of earth on to the table.

"Hang these rats," I exclaimed, for the tenth time that day.

Outside, it was brilliant moonlight: whenever the door opened, I saw it. It was very quiet. Then I heard voices, the sound of a lot of men, moving in the shuffling sort of way that men do move at night in a communication trench.

The door flew open, and Captain Robertson looked in.

"Hullo, Robertson; you're early!"

It was not much past half-past seven.

" You've got those sand-bags up by 78 Street ? " he said, sitting down.

" Yes, 250 there, and 250 right up in the Loop. The rest I shall use on the Fort. Oh ! by the way, you know we are strafing at 12.5 ? We just had a message up from Dale. I shall knock off at 11.45 to-night ! "

" I'll see how we get on. I want to finish that traverse. Righto. I'm just drawing tools and going up now."

" See you up there in a few minutes."

And the muttering stream of " A " Company filed past the dug-out, going up to the front line. The door swung open suddenly, and each man looked in as he went by.

" Shut the door," I shouted. Our plates themselves somehow suddenly looked epicurean.

Soon after eight I was up in the front line. It was the brightest night we had had, and ideal for sand-bag work. The men were already at it. There was a certain amount of inevitable talking going on, before everyone got really started. We were working on the Fort, completing two box dug-outs that we had half put in the night before ; also, we were thickening the parapet, between the Fort and the Loop, and building a new fire-step.

" Can't see any b—— sand-bags here," came from one man.

" We'll have to pick this, sir," from another.

"Where's Mullens gone off to?" sharply from a sergeant.

But for the most part the moonlight made everything straightforward, and there was only the spitting sound of picks, the heavy, smothered noise of men lifting sand-bags, or the "slap, slap" of others patting them into a wall with the back of a shovel, that broke the stillness. On the left "A" Company were working full steam ahead, heightening the parapet and building a big traverse at the entrance

Good sand-bag work.

to the Matterhorn sap. "Robertson's traverse" we always called it afterwards. He got his men working in a long chain, passing filled sand-bags along from a big miners' sand-bag dump, the accumulation of months of patient R.E. tunnelling. These huge dumps rose up in gigantic piles whereever there was a shaft-head; and they were a windfall to us if they were anywhere near where we were working. On this occasion quite a thousand must have been passed along and built into that traverse, and the parapet there, by the Matterhorn. It was fascinating work, passing these dry, small sacks as big as medium-sized babies, only as knobby and angular under their outer cover as a baby is soft and rounded. Meanwhile the builders laid them, like bricks, alternate "headers" and "stretchers."

And so the work went on under the moon.

"Davies," I cried, in that low questioning tone that might well be called "trench voice." It is not a whisper; yet it is not a full, confident sound. If a man speaks loudly in the front trench, you tell him to remember the Boche is a hundred yards away; if he whispers in a hoarse voice that sounds a little nervy, you tell him that the Boche's ears are not a hundred yards long. The result is a restrained and serious-toned medium.

"Sirr," answered a voice close beside me, in a pitch rather louder than the usual trench-voice. Davies always spoke clear and loud. He was my orderly.

"Oh! there you are." Like a dog he had got tired of standing, and while I stood watching the fascinating progress of the erection of a box dug-out under Sergeant Hayman's direction, he was sitting on the fire-step immediately behind me. Had he been a collie, his tongue would have been out, and he would have yawned occasionally; or his nose might even have been between his paws. Now he jumped up, giving a hitch to his rifle that was slung over his left shoulder.

" I'm going round the sentries," I said.

Davies said nothing, but followed about two paces behind, stopping when I stopped, and gazing at me silently when I got up on the fire-step to look over.

The low-ground in the quarry was very wet, and the trench there two feet deep in water, so it was temporarily abandoned, and the little trench out of 76 Street by No. 1 Sniping Post was my way to No. 5 Platoon. It was a very narrow bit of trench, and on a dark night one kept knocking one's thighs and elbows against hard corners of chalk-filled sand-bags. To-night it was easy in the white moonlight. It was really not a trench at all, but a path behind a sand-bag dump. Behind was the open field. There was no parados.

All correct on the two posts in No. 5. It seemed almost unnecessary to have two posts on such a bright night. The outline of the German parapet looked clear enough. Surely the sentries must be almost visible to-night? Right opposite was the dark earth of a sap-head. Our wire looked very near and thin.

" Everything all right? "

" Yes, sir! "

I saw the bombs lying ready in the crease between two sand-bags that formed the parapet top. The pins were bent straight, ready for quick drawing. The bomber was all right; and there was not much wrong with his pal's bayonet, that glistened in the moonlight.

As usual, I went beyond our right post, until I was met by a peering, suspicious head from the left-hand sentry of "C" Company.

"Who's that?" in a hoarse low voice, as the figure bent down off the fire-step.

"All right. Officer. 'B' Company."

Then I passed back along the trench to the top of 76 Street; and so on, visiting all the sentries up to 80 A trench, and disturbing all the working-parties.

"Way, please," I would say to the hindquarters of an energetic wielder of the pick.

"Hi! make way there!" Davies would say in a higher and louder voice when necessary. Then the figure would straighten itself, and flatten itself against the trench, while I squeezed past between perspiring man and slimy sand-bag. This "passing" was an eternal business. It was unavoidable. No one ever said anything, or apologised. No one ever grumbled. It was like passing strap-hangers in the crowded carriage of a Tube. Only it went on day and night.

Craters by moonlight are really beautiful; the white chalk-dust gives them the appearance of snow-mountains. And they look much larger than they really are. On this occasion, as I looked into them from the various bombing-posts, it needed little imagination to suppose I was up in the snows of the Welsh hills. There was such a death-like stillness over it all, too. The view from the Matterhorn was across the widest and deepest of all the craters, and

I stood a long time peering across that yawning chasm at the dark, irregular rim of German sandbags. I gazed fascinated. What was it all about? The sentry beside me came from a village near Dolgelly: was a farmer's boy. He, too, was gazing across, hardly liking to shuffle his feet lest he broke the silence.

"Good God!" I felt inclined to exclaim. "Has there ever been anything more idiotic than this? What in the name of goodness are you and I doing here?"

So I thought, and so I believe he was thinking.

"Everything all right?" was all I said, as I jumped back into the trench.

"Yes, sir," was all the answer.

About ten o'clock I went back to Trafalgar Square. There I heard that Thompson of "C" Company had been wounded. From what I could gather he had been able to walk down to the dressing-station, so I concluded he was only slightly hit. But it came as rather a shock, and I wondered whether he would go to "Blighty."

At eleven I started off for the front trench again, viâ Rue Albert and 78 Street. There was a bit of a "strafe" on. It started with canisters; it had now reached the stage of whizz-bangs as well. I thought little of it, when "woo—woo—woo—woo," and the Boche turned on his howitzers. They screamed over to Maple Redoubt.

A pause. Then again, and they screamed down

just in front of us, evidently after the corner of 78 Street. I did not hesitate, but pushed on. The trench was completely blocked. Rue Albert was revetted with wood and brushwood, and it was all over the place. Davies and I climbed over with great difficulty, the whole place reeking with powder.

" Look out, sir ! " came from Davies, and we crouched down. There was a colossal din while shells seemed all round us.

" All right, Davies ? " And we pushed on. At last here was 78 Street, and we turned up to find another complete block in the trench. We again scrambled over, and met " A " Company wiring-party, returning for more wire.

" The trench is blocked," said I, " but you can get over all right."

We passed in the darkness.

Again " Look out ! " from Davies, and we cowered. Again the shells screamed down on us, and burst just behind.

" Good God ! " I exclaimed, " those wirers ! "

Davies ran back.

There was another block in the trench, but no sign of any men. They were well away by now ! But the shell had fallen between us and them before they reached the block in 78 Street !

Out of breath we arrived at the top of 78 Street, to find " A " Company just getting going again after a hot quarter of an hour. Luckily they had had no casualties. All was quiet now, and the moon looked down upon the workers as before. A quarter past eleven.

I worked my way along to the Fort and found there a sentry rather excited because, he said, he had seen exactly the spot from which they had fired rifle-grenades in the strafing just now. I got him to point out the place It was half-left, and as I looked, sure enough I saw a flash, and a rifle-grenade whined through the air, and fell with a snarl behind our trench.

" Davies," I said, " get Lance-Corporal Allan to come here with the Lewis gun."

Davies was gone like a flash.

The Lewis guns had only recently become company weapons, and were still somewhat of a novelty. The Lewis gunners were rather envied, and also rather " downed " by the sergeant-major for being specialists. But this they could not help ; and they were, as a matter of fact, the best men in my company.

Allan arrived, with one of the team carrying two spare drums of ammunition. We pointed out the spot, and he laid his gun on the parapet, with the butt against his shoulder, and his finger on the trigger, and waited.

" Flash ! "

" There he is, sir ! " from the sentry.

" Drrrrrr–r–r–r " purred the Lewis gun, then stopped. Then again, ending with another jerk There was a silence. We waited five minutes.

" I'll just empty the magazine, sir."

" Dr–r–r–r–r."

Lance-Corporal Allan took off the drum, and handed it to the other Lewis gunner. Then he handed down the gun, and we talked a few minutes. He was very proud of his gun. After a time I sent him back, and made my way along to "A" Company.

There I found Robertson. We talked. A tremendous lot of work had been done, and the big traverse was practically finished.

" I'm knocking off now," said I. It was a quarter to twelve, and I went along with the " Cease work " message.

" All right," said Robertson, " I'm just going to have another look at my wirers. I'll look in as I go down."

By the time I had reached the top of 76 Street, the trench was full of the clank of the thermos dixies, and the men were drinking hot soup. The pioneers had just brought it up. I stopped and had a taste. It was good stuff. As I turned off down the trench, I heard the Germans start shelling again on our left, but they stopped almost directly. I thought nothing of it at the time.

It was just midnight when I reached Trafalgar Square and bumped into Davidson coming round the corner.

" I was looking for you," said he. " You've heard about Tommy ? "

"Yes," I answered. "But he's not badly hit, is he?"

"Oh, you haven't heard. He died at eleven o'clock."

Died! My God! this was something new. Briefly, tersely, Davidson told me the details. He had been hit in the mouth while working on the parapet, and had died down at the dressing station. I looked hard at Davidson, as we stood together in the moonlight by the big island traverse at Trafalgar Square. Somehow I felt my body tense; my teeth were pressed together; my eyes did not want to blink. Here was something new. I had seen death often: *it* was nothing new. But it was the first time it had taken one of us. I wondered what Davidson felt; he knew Thompson much better than I. Yet I knew him well enough—only a day or so ago he had come to our billet in the butcher's shop, and we had talked of him afterwards—and now—dead——

All this flashed through my brain in a second. Meanwhile Davidson was saying,

"Well, I'm just going off for this strafe," when I heard men running down a trench.

"Quick! Stretcher-bearers. The Captain's hit," came from someone in a low voice. The stretcher-bearers' dug-out was just by where we were standing, and immediately I heard a stir inside, and a head looked out from the waterproof sheet that acted as curtain in front of it.

" Is it a stretcher-case ? " a voice asked.

" Yes," was the reply, and without more ado two stretcher-bearers turned out and ran up 76 Street after the orderly. At that moment there was a thud, and a blazing trail climbed up the sky from the left.

" D——," I muttered. " We must postpone this strafe. Davidson, we'll fix up later, see ? Only no firing now." As Davidson disappeared to his gun-position, I ran to the telephone.

" Trench-mortar officer," I said. " Quick ! "

But there is no " quick " about a signaller. He is always there, and methodically, without haste or flurry, he takes down and sends messages. There is no " quickness " ; yet there is no delay. If the world outside pulses and rocks under a storm of shells, in the signallers' dug-out is always a deep-sea calm. So impatiently I watched the operator beat his little tattoo on the buzzer ; looked at his face, as the candle-light shone on it, with its ears hidden beneath the receiver-drums, and its head swathed by the band that holds them over the ears. In the corner, the second signaller sat up and peered out of his blanket, and then lay down again.

" Zx ? Is there an officer there ? Hold on a minute, please. The officer's at the gun, sir ; will you speak to the corporal ? "

" Yes." I already had the receiver to my ear.

" Is that the trench-mortar corporal ? Well, go and tell Mr. Macfarlane, will you, to stop firing at once, and not to start again till he hears from Mr.

Adams. Right. Right. Thanks." This last to the signaller as I left the dug-out.

"Thud!" and another football blazed through the sky.

Macfarlane was the officer in charge of the trench-mortar guns of our sector. I knew him well. Davidson was in charge of the Stokes gun, which is a quick-firing trench-mortar gun. Macfarlane's shells were known as "footballs," but as they had a handle attached they looked more like hammers as they slowly curved through the air.

We had arranged to "strafe" a certain position in the German support line at five minutes after midnight. But I wanted to stop it before retaliation started. The doctor had gone up the front line, and Robertson would be brought down any minute.

Outside I met Brock. He said little, but it was good to have him there. A long while it seemed, waiting. I started up 76 Street. No sooner had I started than I heard footsteps coming down, and to make room I went back. I was preparing to say some cheery word to Robertson, but when I saw him he was lying quite still and unconscious. I stopped the little doctor.

"Is he bad, Doc?"

"Well, old man, I can hardly say. He's got a fighting chance," and he went on. Slowly I heard the stretcher-bearers' footsteps growing fainter and fainter, and there was silence. Thank God! those footballs had stopped now!

Did I guess that Robertson too was mortally wounded? I cannot say—only my teeth were set, and I felt very wideawake. In a minute both Davidson and Macfarlane came up, Davidson down 76 Street, and Macfarlane from Rue Albert. I told Macfarlane all about it, and as I did so my blood was up. I swore hard at the devils that had done this; and we agreed on a "strafe" at a quarter to one.

I stood alone at Trafalgar Square. There was a great calm sky, and the moon looked down at me. Then with a "thud" the first football went up. Then the Stokes answered.

"Bang, bang, bang, bang, bang!" Up they sailed into the air all together, and exploded with a deafening din.

"Thud—thud!"

"Bang, bang, bang, bang, bang!"

Then the Boche woke up. Two canisters rose, streamed, and fell, dropping slightly to my right.

But still our trench-mortars went on. Two more canisters tried for Davidson's gun.

I was elated. "This for Thompson and Robertson," I said, as our footballs went on methodically.

Then the whizz-bangs began on Trafalgar Square.

I went to the telephone.

"Artillery," I said briefly. "Retaliate C 1 Sector."

And then our guns began.

"Scream, scream, scream" they went over.

"Swish—swish" answered the Boche whizz-bangs.

"Phew," said Sergeant Tallis, the bombing-sergeant, as he looked out of his dug-out.

"More retaliation," I said to the signaller, and stepped out again.

A grim exaltation filled me. We were getting our own back. I did not care a straw for their canisters or whizz-bangs. It pleased me to hear Sergeant Tallis say "Phew." My blood was up, and I did not feel like saying "Phew."

"The officer wants to know if that is enough," said the telephone orderly, who had come out to find me.

"No," I answered; "I want more."

The Boche was sending "heavies" over on to Maple Redoubt. I would go on until he stopped. My will should be master. Again our shells screamed over. There was no reply.

Gradually quiet came back.

Then I heard footsteps, and there was Davidson. His face was glowing too.

"How was that?" he asked.

How was that? He had fired magnificently, though the Boche had sent stuff all round him. How was that?

"Magnificent! We've shut them up."

"I've got six shells left. Shall I blaze them off?"

"Oh, no!" said I; "I think we've avenged Tommy."

His face hardened.

" Good night, Bill ! "

But I did not feel like sleep. I still stood at the corner, waiting for I knew not what.

"Bang, bang, bang, bang, bang ! " went the Stokes gun. There was a pause, and " bang, bang, bang, bang, bang ! " came the sound of them bursting. There was a longer pause.

" Bang ! " I watched the spark floating through the sky.

" Bang ! " came the sound back from the German trench.

I waited. There was no answer. And for the first time that night I fancied the moon smiled.

[*Copy*]

DAILY SUMMARY. C 1. (LEFT COMPANY)

6 p.m. 18.3.16—3.30 p.m. 19.3.16

(a) *Operations.*

11.0 p.m. Enemy fired six rifle-grenades from F10/5. The approximate position of the battery was visible from the FORT, and Lewis gun fire was brought to bear on it, which immediately silenced it.

11.30 p.m. Enemy fired several trench-mortar shells and H.E. shells on junction of 78 Street and RUE ALBERT (F10/6), a few falling in our front line trench by the MATTERHORN. No damage was done to our trenches.

12.45 p.m. Our T.M. Battery fired 12 footballs, and our Stokes gun 32 shells at enemy's front line trench in F10/5. The enemy sent a few canisters over, but then resorted to H.E.'s. Our artillery retaliated. Our Stokes gun continued to fire until enemy was silent, no reply being sent to our last 6 shells.

7.45 a.m. Enemy fired several rifle-grenades and bombs. Our R.G.'s retaliated with 24 R.G.'s.

(b) *Progress of Work.*

F 10/6 { 30 yards of parapet thickened two feet.
25 yards of fire-step built.
20 coils of wire put out.

F 10/5 { 20 yards of parapet thickened two feet.
2 dug-outs completed.
20 yards of fire-step built.

J. B. P. ADAMS, Lt.,
O.C. "B" Coy.

CHAPTER XI

"WHOM THE GODS LOVE"—(*continued*)

AS I write I feel inclined to throw the whole book in the fire. It seems a desecration to tell of these things. Do I not seem to be exulting in the tragedy ? Should not he who feels deeply keep silent ? Sometimes I think so. And yet it is the truth, word for word the truth ; so I must write it.

In the Straw Palace next morning Davidson and I were sitting discussing last night, when the doctor looked in. He started talking about Vermorel sprayers (the portable tins shaped like large oval milk-cans, filled with a solution useful for clearing dug-outs after a gas attack). One of these was damaged, and I had sent down a note to the M.O. about it.

" How's Robertson ? " I asked at once.

" He died this morning, Bill—three o'clock this morning."

" Good God," I said.

" Pretty ghastly, isn't it ? Two officers like that in one night. The C.O. is awfully cut up about it."

" Robertson dead ? " said Davidson.

And so we talked for some minutes. The old

doctor was used to these things. He had seen so many officers fall out of line. But to us this was new, and we had not gauged it yet. You might have thought from his quiet jerky sentences that the doctor was almost callous. You would have been wrong.

"Well, I must get on," he said at last. "So long, Bill. Send that Vermorel sprayer down, will you, and I'll see to it, and you'll have it back to-night, probably."

"Righto." And the doctor and his orderly disappeared down the Old Kent Road.

Davidson and I talked alone.

"It must be pretty rotten being an M.O.," he remarked.

Then the "F.L.O." came in. He is the "Forward liaison officer," an artillery officer who lives up with the infantry and facilitates co-operation between the two. At the same moment came a cheery Scotch voice outside, and Macfarlane, the "football" officer, looked in.

"Come oot a' that!" he cried. "Sittin' indoors on a fine mornin'."

"Come in," we said.

But his will prevailed, and we all came out into the sunshine. I had not seen him since last night's little show. Now he was being relieved by another officer for six days, and I was anxious to know what sort of a man was his successor. But Macfarlane did not know much about him yet.

" Anyway," said I, " if he'll only fire like you, we don't mind."

" Och ! " grunted Macfarlane. " What's the use of havin' a gun, and no firin' it ? So long as I get ma footballs up, I'll plunk them over aw recht."

" Yes," I added. " The Boche doesn't approve of your sort."

For there were other sorts. There was the trench-mortar officer who was never to be found, but who left a sergeant with instructions not to fire without his orders ; there was the trench-mortar officer who " could not fire except by Brigade orders " ; there was the trench-mortar officer who was "afraid of giving his position away " ; there was the trench-mortar officer who " couldn't get any ammunition up, you know ; they won't give it me ; only too pleased to fire, if only . . ." ; there was the trench-mortar officer who started firing on his own, without consulting the company commander, just when you had a big working-party in the front trenches ; and lastly there were trench-mortar officers like Davidson and Macfarlane.

" Cheero, then," we said, as Macfarlane went off. " Look us up. You know our billet ? We'll be out to-morrow."

Then we finished our consultation and divided off to our different jobs.

All that day I felt that there was in me something which by all rights should have " given " : these two deaths should have made me feel different :

and yet I was just the same. As I went round the trench, with Davies at my heels, talking to platoon-sergeants, examining wire through my periscope, all in the ordinary way exactly as before, I forgot all about Tommy and Robertson. Even when I came to the place where Robertson had been hit, and saw the blood on the fire-step, and some scraps of cotton wool lying about, I looked at it as you might look at a smashed egg on the pavement, curiously, and then passed on. "Am I indifferent to these things, then ?" I asked myself. I had not realised yet that violent emotion very rarely comes close upon the heels of death, that there is a numbness, a blunting of the spirit, that is an anodyne to pain. I was ashamed of my indifference ; yet I soon saw that it was no uncommon thing. Besides, one had to "carry on" just the same. There was always a silence among the men, when a pal "goes west" ; so now Edwards and I did not talk much, except to discuss the ordinary routine.

I did not get much rest that day. In the afternoon came up a message from the adjutant that we were exploding a mine opposite the Matterhorn at 6.30 ; our trench was to be cleared from 80 A to the bombing-post on the left of the Loop inclusive. Edwards and I were the only officers in the company, so while he arranged matters with the Lewis-gun teams, I went off to see about getting the trench cleared. I had just sent off the "daily summary," my copy of which is reproduced on page 179. As I came back along 78 Street, I met Davidson again. He was looking for a new site for his gun, so as to be able to get a good fire to bear on the German lines opposite the Matterhorn. I went with him, and together we found a place behind the big mine-dump to the left of 78 Street, and close to one of our rifle-grenade batteries. As he went off to get his corporal and team to bring the gun over and fix it in position, he said something in a rather low voice.

"What?" I shouted. "Couldn't hear."

He came back and repeated it.

"Oh," I said. "Sorry. Yes, all right. I expect I'll hear from the Adjutant. Thanks."

What he said was that there would be a funeral that night at nine o'clock. Thompson and Robertson were being buried together. He thought I would like to know.

It was close on half-past six, and getting dark. The trenches were cleared, and I was waiting at the head of two platoons that strung out along 78 Street and behind the Loop. Rifles had been inspected; the men had the S.A.A. (small arms ammunition) and bomb boxes with them, ready to take back into the trench as soon as the mine had gone up. I looked at my watch.

"Another minute," I said.

Then, as I spoke, the earth shook; there was a pause, and a great black cloud burst into the air, followed by a roar of flames. I got up on the fire-step to see it better. It is a good show, a mine. There was the sound of falling earth, and then silence.

"Come on," I said, and we hurried back into the trench. Weird and eerie it looked in the half-light; its emptiness might have been years old. It was undamaged, as we had expected; only there was loose earth scattered all over the parapet and fire-step.

Then hell broke loose, a crashing, banging, flashing hell that concentrated on the German front line directly opposite. It seemed like stirring up an ant's nest, and then spraying them with boiling water as they ran about in confusion!

"Bang — bang — bang — bang — bang," barked Davidson's gun.

"Thud," muttered the football-thrower.

"Wheep! Wee-oo, wee-oo, wee-oo," went the rifle grenades. And all this splendid rain burst with a glorious splash just over the new crater. It was magnificent shooting, and half of us were up on the fire-step watching the fireworks.

Then the Boche retaliated, with canisters and whizz-bangs, and "heavies" for Maple Redoubt; and then our guns joined the concert. It was "hot shop" for half an hour, but at last it died down and there was a great calm. Some of the men were in the trenches for the first time, and had not relished the proceedings overmuch! They were relieved to get the order "Stand down!"

There were several things to be done, working-parties to be arranged, final instructions given to a patrol, Lewis gunners to be detailed to rake the German parapet opposite the Matterhorn all night. A platoon sergeant was worried about his sentries ; he had not enough men, having had one or two casualties ; and I had to lend him men from a more fortunate platoon. It was quite dark, and nearly half-past seven by the time I got back to Trafalgar Square. Edwards had started dinner, as he was on trench duty at eight o'clock. The sergeant-major was on duty until then.

Davidson looked in on his way down to Maple Redoubt.

" I say, your Stokes were bursting top-hole. We had a splendid view."

" They weren't going short, were they ? " he asked.

" No. Just right. The fellows were awfully bucked with it."

" Oh, good. You can't see a bit from where we are, and the corporal said he thought they were going short. But I'd worked out the range and was firing well over 120, so I carried on. I'm going down to have dinner with O'Brien. I think we've done enough to-night."

Then I saw that he was tired out.

" Rather a hot shop ? " I asked.

" Yes," he said in his casual way. " They were all round us. Well, cheero ! I shan't be up till about ten, I expect, unless there's anything wanted."

"Cheero!"

"It's no joke firing that gun with the Boche potting at you hard with canisters," I said to Edwards, as Davidson's footsteps died away.

"He's the bravest fellow in the regiment," said Edwards, and we talked of the time when the gun burst in his face as he was firing it, and he told his men that it had been hit by a canister, to prevent their losing confidence in it. I saw him just afterwards: his face was bleeding. It was no joke being Stokes officer; the Germans hated those vicious snapping bolts that spat upon them "One, two, three, four, five," and always concentrated their fire against his gun. But they had not got him.

"No, he's inside," I heard Edwards saying. "Bill. Telephone message."

The telephone orderly handed me a pink form. Edwards was outside, just about to go on trench duty. It was eight. I went outside. It was bright moonlight again. Grimly, I thought of last night.

"Look here," I said. "There's this funeral at nine o'clock. I've just got this message. One officer from each company may go. Will you go? I can't very well go as O.C. Company." And I handed him the pink form to see.

So we rearranged the night duties, and Edwards went off till half-past eight, while I finished my dinner. Lewis was hovering about with toasted cheese and *café au lait.* As I swallowed these glutinous concoctions, the candle flickered and went out. I pushed open the door : the moonlight flooded in, and I did not trouble to call for another candle. Then I heard the sergeant-major's voice, and went out. We stood talking at Trafalgar Square.

"Shan't be sorry to get relieved to-morrow," I said. I was tired, and I wondered how long the night would take to pass.

Suddenly, up the Old Kent Road I heard a man running. My heart stopped. I hate the sound of running in a trench, and last night they had run for stretcher-bearers when Robertson was hit. I looked at the sergeant-major, who was biting his lip, his ears cocked. Round the corner a man bolted, out of breath, excited. I stopped him ; he nearly knocked into us.

"Hang you," said I. "Stop! Where the devil . . . ?"

"Mr. Davidson, sir . . . Mr. Davidson is killed."

"Rot!" I said, impatiently. "Pull yourself together, man. He's all right. I saw him only half an hour ago."

But as I spoke, something broke inside me. It was as if I were straining, beating against something relentless. As though by words, by the cry "impossible" I could beat back the flood of conviction that the man's words brought over me. Dead! I *knew* he was dead.

" Impossible, corporal," I said. " What do you mean ? " For I saw now that it was Davidson's corporal who stood gazing at me with fright in his eyes.

He pulled himself together at last.

" Killed, sir. It came between us as we were talking. A whizz-bang, sir."

" My God ! " I cried. " Where ? "

" Just at the bottom, sir "—the man jerked his hand back down Old Kent Road. " We were just talking, sir. My leave has come through, and he was joking, and saying his would be through soon, when . . . oh, Jesus . . . I was half blinded. . . . I've not got over it yet, sir." And the man was all trembling as he spoke.

" He was killed instantly ? "

" Ach ! " said the man. He made a gesture with his hands. " It burst right on him."

" Poor fellow," I said. God knows what I meant. " Send a man with him, sergeant-major," I added, and plunged up 76 Street.

" Davidson," I cried. " Davidson dead ! "

It was close on midnight, as I stood outside the Straw Palace. Lewis brought me a cup of cocoa. I drank it in silence, and ate a piece of cake. I told the man to go to bed. Then, when he had disappeared, I climbed up out of the trench, and sat, my legs dangling down into it. Down in the trench the moon cast deep black shadows. I looked around.

All was bathed in pale, shimmery moonlight. There was a great silence, save for distant machine-gun popping down in the Fricourt valley, and the very distant sound of guns, guns, guns—the sound that never stops day and night. I pressed on my right hand and with a quick turn was up on my feet out of the trench, on the hill-side; for I was just over the brow, on the reverse slope, and out of sight of the enemy lines. I took off my steel helmet and put it on the ground, while I stretched out my arms and clenched my hands.

"So this is War," I thought. I realised that my teeth were set, and my mouth hard, and my eyes, though full of sleep, wide open: silently I took in the great experience, the death of those well-loved. For of all men in the battalion I loved Davidson best. Not that I knew him so wonderfully well—but . . . well, one always had to smile when he came in; he was so good-natured, so young, so delightfully imperturbable. He used to come in and stroke your hair if you were bad-tempered. Somehow he reminded me of a cat purring; and perhaps his hair and his smile had something to do with it? Oh, who can define what they love in those they love?

And then my mind went back over all the incidents of the last few hours. Together we had been through it all: together we had discussed death: and last of all I thought how he had told me of the funeral that was to be at 9 o'clock. And now he lay beside them. All three had been buried at nine o'clock.

"Dead. Dead," said a voice within me. And still I did not move. Still that numbness, that dulness, that tightening across the brain and senses. This, too, was something new. Then I looked around me, across the moorland. I walked along until I could see down over Maple Redoubt and across the valley, where there seemed a slight white mist; or was it only moonshine?

Suddenly, "Strength." I answered the voice. "Strong. I am strong." Every muscle in my body was tingling at my bidding. I felt an iron strength. All this tautness, this numbness, was strength. I remembered last night, the feeling of irresistible will-power, and my eyes glowed. I thought of Davidson, and my eyes glistened: the very pain was the birth of new strength.

Then, even as the strength came, I heard a thud, and away on the left a canister blazed into the air, climbed, swooped, and rushed. And the vulgar din of its bursting rent all the stillness of the night. A second followed suit. And as it, too, burst, it seemed a clumsy mocking at me, a mocking that ran in echoes all along the still valley.

"Strength," it sneered. "Strength."

And all my iron will seemed beating against a wall of steel, that must in the end wear me down in a useless battering.

"War," I cried. "How can my will batte

against war?" I thought of Davidson's smiling face; and then I thought of the blind clumsy canister. And I felt unutterably weak and powerless. What did it matter what I thought or did, whether I was weak or strong? What power had I against this irresistible impersonal machine, this war? And I remembered how an hour or so ago the trench-mortar officer had asked me whether I wanted him to fire or not, and I had answered, "Good God! Do as you d—d well like." What did it matter what he did? Yet, last night it had seemed to matter everything.

Slowly there came into my mind that picture that later has come to mean to me the true expression of war. Only slowly it came now, a half-formed image of what my spirit alone understood.

"A certain man drew a bow at a venture," I thought. What of those shells that I had called down last night at my bidding, standing like a god, intoxicated with power, and crying "Retaliate. More retaliation." Where did they fall? Were other men lying as Davidson lay to-night? Had I called down death? Had I stricken families? Probably. Nay, more than probably. Certainly. Death. Blind death. That was it. Blind death.

And all the time above me was the white moon. I looked at the shadows of my arms as I held them out. Such shadows belonged to summer nights in England . . . in Kent. . . . Oh! why was everything so silent? Could nothing stop this utter folly, this cruel madness, this clumsy death?

And then, at last, the strain gave a little, and my muscles relaxed. I went back and took up my helmet.

"Dead," the voice repeated within me. And this time my spirit found utterance:

"Damn!" I said. "Oh damn! damn! Damn!"

[*Copy*]

SPECIAL REPORT—C 1 SECTION (LEFT COMPANY)

The mine exploded by us opposite 80 A at 6.30 p.m. last night has exposed about 20 yards of German parapet. A working-party attempting to work there about 12.30 a.m. and again at 2 a.m. was dispersed at once by our rifle and Lewis-gun fire. The parapet has been built up sufficiently to prevent our seeing over it, sand-bags having been put up from inside the trench. Our snipers are closely watching this spot.

J. B. P. ADAMS, Lieut.
O.C. "B" Coy.

6.30 a.m. 20.3.16.

CHAPTER XII

OFFICERS' SERVANTS

"POOR devils on sentry," said Dixon. He shut the door quickly and came over to the fire. Outside was a thick blizzard, and it was biting cold. He sat down on the bed nearest the fire and got warm again.

"Look here, Bill, can't we possibly get any coal?"

"We sent a fellow into Bray," I answered, "but it's very doubtful if he'll get any. Anyway we'll see."

Tea was finished. The great problem was fuel. There were no trees or houses anywhere near 71 North. We had burnt two solid planks during the day; these had been procured by the simple expedient of getting a lance-corporal to march four men to the R.E. dump, select two planks, and march them back again. But by now the planks had surely been missed, and it would be extremely risky to repeat the experiment, even after dark. So a man had been despatched to Bray to try and purchase a sack of coal; also, I had told the Mess-sergeant to try and buy one for us, and bring it up with the rations. This also was a doubtful quantity.

Meanwhile, we had a great blaze going, and were making the most of it.

I was writing letters ; Dixon was reading ; Nicolson was seeing to the rum ration ; Clark was singing, " Now Neville was a devil," and showing his servant Brady how to " make " a hammock. Brady was a patient disciple, but his master had slept in a hammock for the first time in his life the night before and consequently was not a very clear exponent of the art. Apparently certain things that happened last night must be avoided to-night ; *how* they were to be avoided was left to Brady's ingenuity. Every attempt on his part to solve the problems put before him was carefully tested by Clark, and accepted or condemned according to its merit under the strain of Clark's body. At such times of testing the strains of " Neville was a devil " would cease. At last Brady hit on some lucky adjustment, and the occupant pronounced his position to be first rate. Then Brady disappeared behind the curtain that screened the servants' quarters, and the song proceeded uninterruptedly,

> " Now Neville was a devil
> A perfect little devil " ;

and Clark rocked himself contentedly into a state of restful slumber.

Meanwhile, behind the arras the retainers prepared their masters' meal. This dug-out was of the " tubular " pattern, a succession of quarter circles of black iron riveted together at the top, and so forming a long tube, one end of which was bricked up and had a brick chimney with two panes of glass on each side of it ; the other led into a small wooden dug-out curtained off. Here abode five servants and an orderly. I should here state that this dug-out was the most comfortable I have ever lived in ; as a matter of fact it was not a dug-out at all, but being placed right under the steep bank at 71 North it was practically immune from shelling. The brick chimney and the glass window-panes were certainly almost unique : one imagined it must have been built originally by the R.E.'s for their own abode ! Along the sides were four beds of wire-netting stretched over a wooden frame with a layer of empty sand-bags for mattress. In the centre was a wooden table. Over this table, in air suspended, floated Clark.

Meanwhile, as above stated, behind the arras the retainers prepared their masters' meal, with such-like comments—

" Who's going for rations to-night ? "

" It's Lewis's turn to-night, and Smith's."

" All right, sergeant."

" Gr-r-r " (unintelligible).

" Where's Dodger ? "

" Out chasing them hares. Didn't you hear the Captain say he'd be for it, if he didn't get one ? "

" Gr-r-r. He won't get any —— hares."

Here followed a pause, and a lot of noise of

plates and boxes being moved. Then there was a continued crackling of wood, as the fire was made up. Followed a lot of coughing, and muttering, and " Phew ! " as the smoke got too thick even for that smoke-hardened crew.

" Phew ! Stop it. Jesus Christ."

More coughing, the door was opened, and soon a cold draught sped into our dug-out. There was but one door for both.

" Shut that door ! " I shouted.

" Hi, Lewis, your bloke's calling. Said, 'Shut that door.' "

Then the door shut. More coughing ensued, but the smoke was better, apparently, for it soon ceased. We were each, by the way, " my bloke " to our respective retainers.

The conversation remained for some time at an inaudible level, until I heard the door open again, and a shout of " Hullo ! Dodger. Coo ! Jesus Christ ! He's all right, isn't he ? There's a job for you, sergeant, cooking that bloke. Has the Captain seen him ? Hey ! Look out of that ! You'll have the blood all over the place. Get a bit of paper."

The " sergeant " (Private Gray) made no comments on the prospect of cooking the " Dodger's " quarry, and the next minute Private Davies, orderly, appeared with glowing though rather dirty face holding up a large hare, that dripped gore from its mouth into a scrunched-up ball of *Daily Mail* held to its nose like a pocket-handkerchief.

"Look here, Dixon," I said.

"Devil's alive," exclaimed Dixon. "Then you've got one. By Jove! Splendid! I say, isn't he a beauty?" And we all went up and examined him. He was a hare of the first order. To-morrow he should be the *chef d'œuvre* in "B" Company mess at Morlancourt. For we went out of reserve into billets the next morning.

"How did you get him, Davies?"

"Oh! easy enough, sir. I'll get another if you like. There's a lot of them sitting out in the snow there. I was only about fifty yards off. He don't get much chance with a rifle, sir." (Here his voice broke into a laugh.) "It's not what you call much sport for him, sir! I got this too, sir!"

And lo! and behold! a plump partridge!

"Oh! they're as tame as anything, and you can't help getting them in this snow," he said.

At last the dripping hare was removed from the stage to behind the scenes, and Davies joined the smothered babel behind the arras.

"Wonderful fellow, old Davies," said Dixon.

"By the way, Bill," he added. "How about getting the little doctor in to-night for a hand of vingt-et-un? Can we manage it all right?"

I was Mess-president for the time, Edwards being away on a course.

"Oh! yes," I answered. "Rather. I'll send a note."

As I was writing a rather elaborate note (having

nothing better to do) requesting the pleasure of the distinguished presence of the medical officer, the man who had been to Bray for coal came and reported a fruitless errand. He seemed very depressed at his failure, but cheered up when we gave him a tot of rum to warm him up. (All rum, by the way, is kept in the company officer's dug-out; it is the only way.)

Meanwhile, the problem of fuel must be faced. A log was crackling away merrily enough, but it was the very last. Something must be done.

"Davies," I called out.

"Sir?" came back in that higher key of his.

He appeared at the door.

"Are you going down for rations?"

"Yes, sir."

"Well, look here. There's a sack of coal *ordered* from Sergeant Johnson, but I'm none too sure it'll come up to-night. I only ordered it yesterday. But I want you to make sure you get it if it is there; in fact you *must* bring it, whether it's there or not. See? If you don't, you'll be for it."

This threat Davies took for what it was worth. But he answered:

"I'll get it, sir. I'll bring something along somehow."

And Davies never failed of his word.

"Good! Do what you can."

Half an hour later he staggered in with a sack of coal, and plumped it down, all covered with snow.

The fire was burning very low, and we were looking at it anxiously. The sight of this new supply of fuel was wonderful good to the eyes. So busy were we in stoking up, that we forgot to ask Davies if he had had any trouble in getting it. After all, it did not matter much. There was the coal ; that was the point.

Behind the curtain there was a great business. Lewis and Brady had brought up the rations ; Gray was busy with a big stew, and Richards was apparently engaged in getting out plates and knives and forks from a box ; Davies was reading aloud, in the middle of the chaos, from the *Daily Mail.* Sometimes the Mess-president took it into his head to inspect the servants' dug-out ; but it was an unwise procedure, for it took away the relish of the meal, if you saw the details of its preparation. So long as it was served up tolerably clean, one should be satisfied.

At half-past seven came in Richards to lay the table. The procedure of this was first to take all articles on the table and dump them on the nearest bed. Then a knife, fork, and spoon were put to each place, and a varied collection of tin mugs and glasses arranged likewise ; then came salt and mustard in glass potted-meat jars ; bread sitting bareback on the newspaper tablecloth ; and a bottle of O.V.H. and two bottles of Perrier to crown the feast. All this was arranged with a deliberate smile, as by one who knew the exact value of things, and defied instruction in any detail of laying a table. Richards was an old soldier, and he had won from Dixon at first unbounded praise ; but he had been found to possess a lot too much talk at present, and had been sat on once or twice fairly heavily of late. So now he wore the face of one who was politely amused, yet, knowing his own worth, could forbear from malice. He gave the table a last look with his head on one side, and then departed in silence.

Suddenly the door flew open, and the doctor burst in, shuddering, and knocking the snow off his cap.

"By Jove, Dicker," he cried. "A bad night to go about paying joy visits. But, by Jove, I'm jolly glad you asked me. There's the devil to pay up at headquarters. The C.O.'s raving, simply. Some blighter has pinched our coal, and there's none to be got anywhere. Good Lord, it's too hot altogether. I couldn't stand Mess there to-night at any price. I pity old Dale. The C.O.'s been swearing like a trooper ! He's fair mad."

"Never mind," he added after a pause. "I think we've raised enough wood to cook the dinner all right. See you've got coal all right."

I hoped to goodness Dixon wouldn't put his foot in it. But he rose to the occasion and said :

"Oh, yes. We ordered some coal from Sergeant Johnson. Come on, let's start. Hi ! Richards !"

And Richards came in with the stew in a tin jug

such as is used in civilised lands to hold hot water of a morning. And so the doctor forgot the Colonel's rage.

Late that night, after the doctor had gone, I called Davies.

"Davies," I said, "where did you get that coal?"

"Off the ration cart, sir."

"Was it ours, do you think?"

"Well, sir, I don't somehow think it was. You see, the ration cart came up, and the man driving it was up by the horse—and I saw the bag o' coal there, like. So I said to Lewis, 'Lewis, you see to the rations. I'll take the coal up quick!' Then I heard the man up by the horse say, 'There's coal there for headquarters.' 'Oh, yes,' I said, 'that's all right, but this here was ordered off Sergeant Johnson yesterday,' I said. And I made off quick."

"Good Lord!" I exclaimed. "Was Sergeant Johnson there?"

"No," answered Davies. "He came later. I said to Lewis just now, 'What about that coal?' And he said Sergeant Johnson came just after and started kicking up some bit of a row, sir, about some coal; but Lewis, he said he didn't know nothing about any coal, and the man at the horse he didn't know who I was, sir; it was quite dark, you see, sir. Lewis said Sergeant Johnson got the wind up a bit, sir, about losing the coal . . ."

"Look here Davies," I remarked solemnly, "do you realise that that coal was for headquarters . . ."

"I couldn't say, sir," began Davies.

"But I can," said I. "Look here, you must just set a limit somewhere. I know I said you *must* get some coal, somewhere. But I wasn't exactly thinking of bagging the C.O.'s coal. As a matter of fact he was slightly annoyed, though doubtless if he knew it was No. 14 Davies, "B" Company orderly, he would abate his wrath. Do you realise this is a very serious offence?"

Davies' mouth wavered. He could never quite understand this method of procedure. He looked at the blazing fire, and his eyes twinkled. Then he understood.

"Yes, sir," he said.

"All right," I replied. "Don't let it occur again."

And it never did—at least, not headquarters coal.

We did not get back to Morlancourt till nearly half-past three the next day. Things were not going well in our billet at the butcher's shop. Gray, the cook, and two of the servants had been sent on early to get the valises from the quartermaster's stores, and to have a meal ready. We arrived to find no meal ready, and what was worse, the stove not lit. Coal could not be had from the stores, was the statement that greeted us.

"What the blazes do you mean?" shouted

Dixon. We were really angry as well as ravenous ; for it was freezing hard, and the tiles on the floor seemed to radiate ice-waves.

"Have you asked Madame if she can lend us a little to go on with ?" I queried.

No, they had not asked Madame.

Then followed a blaze of vituperation, and Richards was sent at the double into the kitchen. Soon Madame appeared, with sticks and coal, and lit the fire. We watched the crackles, too cold to do anything else. The adjoining room, where Dixon and I slept, was an ice-house, also tiled. It was too cold to talk even.

"C'est froid dans les tranchés," said I in execrable French.

"Mais oui, m'sieur l'officier," said Madame, deeply sympathising.

I thought of the blazing fire in 71 North, but it was too cold to say anything more. What matter if Madame imagined us standing in a foot of snow ? So we should have been for the most part had we been in the line the last two days, instead of in reserve.

Soon it began to get less icy, and the stove looked a little less of the blacklead order. It was a kitchen-range really, with a boiler and oven ; but the boiler was rather leaky. Now, as the coal blazed up, life began to ebb back again.

Confound it ! The stove was smoking like fury. Pah ! The flues were all full of soot. Dixon was rather an expert on stoves, and said that all that was needed was a brush. Where had all the servants disappeared to? Why wasn't someone there? I opened the door into our bedroom—a cold blast struck me in the face. In the middle of the room, unopened, sat our two valises, like desert islands in a sea of red tiles.

"Hang it all, this is the limit," I said, and ran out into the street, and into the next house, where the servants' quarters were. And there, in the middle of a pile of half-packed boxes, stood Gray, eating a piece of bread. Now I discovered afterwards that the boxes had just been brought in by Cody and Lewis, that Davies and Richards had gone after the coal, and were at that moment staggering under the weight of it on their way from the stores, and that Gray could not do anything more, having unpacked the boxes, until the coal came. But I did not grasp these subtle details of the interior economy of the servants' hall, and I broke out into a real hot strafe. Why should Gray be standing there eating, while the officers shivered and starved?

I returned to Dixon, and found Clark and Nicolson there; and together we all fumed. Then in came the post-corporal with an accumulation of parcels, and we stopped fuming.

"By Jove," I exclaimed, a few minutes later. "The hare. I had forgotten le—what is it, lièvre, lèvre? I forget. Never mind. Lewis, bring the hare along, and ask Madame in your best manner if she would do us the honour of cooking it for us. To-night, now."

Presently Madame came in, with Lewis standing rather sheepishly behind. She delivered a tornado of very fluent French: "eau-de-vie," "eau-de-vie," was all I could disentangle.

"Eau-de-vie ?" I asked her. "Pourquoi eau-de-vie ?"

"Brandy," explained Dixon.

"I know that," said I (who did not know that eau-de-vie was brandy ?)

"Brandy," said Dixon, "to cook the hare with. That's all she wants. Oui, oui, Madame. Eau-de-vie. Tout de suite. The doctor's got brandy. Send Lewis along to the doctor to ask him to dinner, and borrow a little brandy."

So Lewis was despatched, and returned with a little brandy, but the doctor could not come.

"Never mind," we said.

Meanwhile some tea was on the table, and bully and bread and butter ; there was no sugar, however. Richards smiled and said the rats had eaten it all in 71 North, but Davies was buying some. Whenever anything was missing, these rats had eaten it, just as they were responsible for men's equipment and packs getting torn, and their emergency rations lost. In many cases the excuse was quite a just one ; but when it came to rats running off with canteen lids, our sympathy for the rat-ridden Tommy was not always very strong.

To-day, a new reason was found for the loss of three teaspoons.

"Lost in the scuffle, sir, the night of the raid," was the answer given to the demand for an explanation.

"What scuffle?" I asked.

"Why, the box got upset, sir, the night of the raid when we all stood to in a bit of a hurry, sir."

I remembered there had been some confusion and noise behind the arras that night when the Germans raided on the left; apparently all the knives and forks had fallen to the ground and several had snapped under the martial trampling of feet when our retainers stood to arms. For many days afterwards when anything was lost, one's anger was appeased by "Lost in the scuffle, sir." At last it got too much of a good thing.

"Why this new teapot, Davies?" I said a few days later.

"The old one was lost in the scuffle, sir."

"Look here," I said. "We had the old one yesterday, and this morning I saw it broken on Madame's manure heap. Here endeth 'lost in the scuffle.' See? Go back to rats."

"Very good, sir."

That night, about ten o'clock, when Clark, Nicolson, and Brownlow (who had been our guest) had gone back to their respective billets, Dixon and I were sitting in front of the stove, our feet up on the brass bar that ran along the top-front of it, on a comfortable red-plush settee. This settee made amends for very many things, such as: a tile floor; four doors, one of which scraped most excruciatingly over the tiles, and another being glass-panelled allowed in much cold air from the butcher's shop; no entry for the servants save either through the butcher's shop or through the bedroom viâ the open window; very little room to turn round in, when we were all there; a smell of stale lard that permeated the whole establishment; and finally, the necessity of moving the settee every time Madame or Mam'selle wanted to get to either the cellar or the stairs.

But now all these disabilities were removed, everyone else having gone off to bed, and Dixon and I were talking lazily before turning in also. I had a large pan of boiling water waiting on the top of the range, and my canvas bath was all ready in the next room.

"Ah! the discomfort of it!" ejaculated Dixon. "The terrible discomfort of it all!"

"How they are pitying us at home," I replied. "'Those rabbit holes! I can't think how you keep the water out of them at all!' Can't you hear them? 'And isn't that bully beef most horribly tough and hard! Ugh! I couldn't bear it.'" I tried to imitate a lady's voice, but it was not a great success. I was out of practice.

"Yes," said Dixon, thinking of the extraordinarily good jugged hare produced by Madame. Then his thoughts turned to Davies, the hunter who was responsible for the feast.

"Wonderful fellow, old Davies," he added. "In fact they're all good fellows."

"He's a shepherd boy," I said. "Comes from Blaenau Festiniog, a little village right up in the Welsh mountains. I know the place. A few years ago he was a boy looking after sheep out on the hills all day; a wide-eyed Welsh boy, with a sheep-dog trotting behind him. He's rather like a sheep-dog himself, isn't he?"

"Gad, he's a wonderful fellow. But they all are, you know, Bill. Look at your chap, Lewis; great clumsy red-faced fellow, with his piping voice, that sometimes gets on your nerves."

"He's too lazy at times," I broke in; "but he's honest, dead honest. He was a farm hand! Good heavens, fancy choosing a fellow out of the farm-yard to act as valet and waiter! I remember the first time he waited! He was so nervous he nearly dropped everything, and his face like that fire! O'Brien said he was tight!"

"Richards talks a jolly sight too much, some-times—but after all what does it matter? They try their best; and think how we curse them! Look at the way I cursed about that stove this afternoon: as soon as anything goes wrong, we strafe like blazes, whether it's their fault or not. A fellow in England would resign on the spot. But they don't care a damn, and just carry on. This cursing's no good, Bill. Hang it all, they're doing their bit same as we are, and they have a d—d sight harder time."

"I don't think they worry much about the strafing," I said. "It's part of the ordinary routine. Still, I agree, we do strafe them for thousands of things that aren't their fault."

"They're a sort of safety-valve," he answered with a laugh. "I don't know how it is, one would never dream of cursing the men like we do these fellows. You know as well as I do, Bill, the only way to run a company is by love. It's no earthly use trying to get the men behind you, by cursing them day and night. I really must try and stop cursing these servants. After all, they're the best fellows in the world."

"The men curse all right," I said, "when they don't get their food right. I guess we're all animal, after all. It's merely a method of getting things done quickly. Besides, you know perfectly well you won't be able to stop blazing away when there's no fire or food. It creates an artificial warmth."

"D—d artificial," laughed he.

There was a silence.

"By Jove, Bill," he said at last, getting up to go to bed. "When's this war going to end?"

To which I made no reply, but moved my bath out of the icy bedroom and dragged it in front of the fire.

CHAPTER XIII

MINES

I

"THE Colonel wants to speak to O.C. 'B,' sir." It was midday.

"It's about that wire," said Edwards. "But we couldn't get any more out without stakes."

"Oh, I don't expect it's about the wire," I said, as I hurried out of the Straw Palace. "The C.O. knows we can't get the stakes."

No, it was nothing to do with the wire.

"Just a minute, sir," said the telephone orderly. "Hi! Headquarters. Is that you, George? O.C. 'B's' here now. Just a minute, sir."

A pause, followed by:

"Commanding Officer, sir," and I was handed the receiver.

"Yes, sir," I said. "This is Adams."

"Oh! that you, Adams? Well, look here—about this mine going up to-night. Got your map there? Well, the mining officer is here now, and he says . . . Look here, you'd better come down here now. Yes, come here now."

" Very good, sir," but the C.O. had rung off with a jerk, and only a singing remained in my ears.

" Got to go down and explain in person why the officer in charge of 'B' Company wirers did not get out twenty coils last night," I said to Edwards as I hurried off down Old Kent Road. "The C.O.'s in an 'I gave a distinct order' mood. Cheero ! "

On entering the Headquarters' dug-out in Maple Redoubt, I found the C.O. engaged in conversation with an artillery officer : there had been another raid last night on the left, and our artillery had sent a lot of stuff over. This was the subject under discussion.

" I think you did d—d well," said the C.O. as the officer left. " Well, Adams, I thought it would be easiest if you came down. Here's our friend from the underworld, and he'll explain exactly what he's going to do " ; and I saw the R.E. officer for the first time. He had been standing in the gloom of the further end of the dug-out.

" Look here," began the Colonel, as he laid out the trench map on the table. " *Here* is where we blow to-night at 6.0 " (and he made a pencil dot in the middle of the grass of No Man's Land mid-way between the craters opposite the Loop and the Fort. See Map III). " And here, all round here " (he drew his pencil round and round in a blacker and yet blacker circle) " is roughly where the edge of the crater will come. Isn't that right, Armstrong ? "

" Yes," was the reply, " the crater edge won't come right up to the front trench, but I don't want anyone in the front trench, as it will probably be squeezed up in one or two places."

" Exactly," said the Colonel. " Do you think this blow will completely connect up the two craters on either side ? "

" Oh, certainly," was the answer. " There's no question of it. You see, we've put in (here followed figures and explosives incomprehensible to the lay mind). " It'll be the biggest mine we've ever blown in this sector."

" A surface mine, I suppose ? " I asked.

" Almost certainly," said the R.E. officer. " You see, their gallery is only ten feet above ours, and they might blow any minute. But they're still working. We wanted to get another twenty feet out before blowing, but it isn't safe. Anyway, we are bound to smash up all their galleries there completely, though I doubt if we touch their parapet at all." He spoke almost impatiently, as one who talks of things that have been his main interest for weeks, and tries to explain the whole thing in a few words. " But," he added, " I don't want any men in that trench."

The mining officers always presumed that the infantry clung tenaciously like limpets to their trench, and had to be very carefully removed in case a mine was going up. As a matter of fact, the infantry always made a rule of clearing the trench half as far again as the mining officer enjoined, and were always inclined to want to depart from the abhorred spot long before the time decided upon!

"That's clear enough," said the Colonel. "Then from *here* to *here* (and he made pencil blobs where I have marked A and B on Map III) we will clear the trench. Get your Lewis guns placed at these two points (A and B), ready to open fire as soon as the mine has gone up. And get your bombers ready to seize the crater edge as soon as it's dark enough. You'll want to have some tools and sandbags ready, and your wirers should have plenty of gooseberries and all the stakes we can get you. Right."

As I went up 76 Street at half-past five, I realised that I had been rushing about too much, and had forgotten tea. So I sent Davies back and told him to bring up a mug of tea and something to eat. No sooner had he disappeared than I met a party of six R.E.'s, the two leading men carrying canaries in cages. They held them out in front, like you hold out a lantern on a muddy road, and they were covered from head to foot in white chalk-dust. They were doing a sort of half-run down the trench, known among the men as the "R.E. step." It is always adopted by them if there is any "strafing" going on, or on such occasions as the present, when the charge has been laid, the match lit, and the mine-shaft and galleries, canaries and all, evacuated. (The canaries are used to detect gas fumes, not as pets.)

When I reached the Fort, I found No. 7 Platoon already filing out of the trench area that had been condemned as dangerous.

" You're very early, Sergeant Hayman," I said.

I looked at my watch.

" Oh, all right," I added, " it's twenty to six; very well. Have you got all the bomb boxes and S.A.A. out ? "

" Yes, sir. Everything's clear."

" Very well, then. All those men not detailed as tool and sand-bag party can get in dug-outs, ready to come back as soon as I give orders. There will probably be a bit of ' strafing.' "

" Very good, sir."

The Lewis-gun team emerged from its dug-out twenty yards behind the Fort, in rather a snail-like fashion. I arranged where the N.C.O. and two men should stand, just at the corner of the Fort, but in the main trench (at B in map). The rest of the team I sent back to its burrow. Edwards had made all arrangements for the other team.

Ten to six. It was a warm evening early in April, and there was a deathly calm. These hushes are hateful and unnatural, especially at " stand to " in the evening. In the afternoon an after-dinner slumber is right and proper, but as dusk creeps down it is well known that everyone is alive and alert, and a certain visible expression is natural and welcome. This evening silence is like the pause between the lightning and the thunder; worst of all is the stillness after the enemy has blown a mine at "stand to," for ten to one he is going to blow another at "stand down."

The sun set in a blaze of red, and in the south the evening star glowed in a deepening blue. What will have happened by the time the day has returned with its full light and sense of security?

"Here you are, sir," I heard suddenly at my elbow, and found my mug of tea, two large pieces of bread and butter and cake, presented by Davies on a box-lid salver.

"I don't know if this is enough, sir. Lewis he wanted me to bring along a pot o' jam, sir. But I said Mr. Adams he won't have time for all that."

"I should think not. Far too much as it is. Here, put the cake on the fire-step, and take hold of this notebook, will you?" And so, with the mug in one hand, and a piece of bread and butter in the other, Scott found me as he came along at that moment, looking, as he told me afterwards, exactly like the Mad Hatter in *Alice in Wonderland*.

"What's the time?" I enquired, munching hard.

"I make it two minutes to six," said Scott.

"Go up a shixo'-clock," I said, taking a very big mouthful indeed.

"Who put the sugar in this tea?" I asked Davies a minute later.

"I did," said Davies.

"Far too much. I shall never get you fellows to understand . . ."

But the sentence was not finished. There was a faint "Bomp" from goodness knows where, and a horrid shudder. The earth shook and staggered, and I set my legs apart to keep my balance. It felt as if the whole ground were going to be tilted up. The tea splashed all over the fire-step as I hastily put it down. Then I looked up. There was nothing. What had happened? Was it a camouflet after all? Then, over the sandbags appeared a great green meadow, slowly, taking its time, not hurrying, a smooth curved dome of grass, heaving up, up, up, like a rising cake; then, like a cake, it cracked; cracked visibly with bursting brown seams; still the dome rose, towering ten, twenty feet up above the surrounding level; and then with a roar the black smoke hurtled into the air, followed by masses of pink flame creaming up into the sky, giving out a bonfire heat and lighting up the twilight with a lurid glare! Then we all ducked to avoid the shower of mud and dirt and chalk that pattered down like hail.

"Magnificent," I said to Scott.

"Wonderful," he answered.

"The mud's all in your tea, sir," said Davies.

"Dr—r-r-r-r," rattled the Lewis guns. The

Lewis gunners with me had been amazed rather than thrilled by the awful spectacle, but were now recovered from the shock, and emptying two or three drums into the twilight void. I was peering over into a vast chasm, where two minutes ago had been a smooth meadow full of buttercups and toadstools.

Suddenly I found Sergeant Hayman at my elbow. " The trench is all fallen in, sir. You can't get along at all." And so the night's work began.

At 1.0 a.m. I was lying flat down on soft spongy grass atop of a large crater-lip quite eight feet higher than the ground level. Beside me lay two bombers and a box of bombs : we were all peering out into a space that seemed enormous. Suddenly a German starlight rocketed up, and as it burst the great white bowl of the crater jumped into view. Then a few rifle-shots sang across the gulf. There followed a deeper darkness than before. Behind me was a wiring-party not quite finished ; also the sound of earth being shovelled by tired men. A strong working-party of " A " Company had been engaged for four hours clearing the trench that had been squeezed up ; all available men of " B " Company not on sentry had been digging a zigzag sap from the trench to the post on the crater-lip where I lay. Two other pairs of bombers lay out on the crater edge to right and left ; behind me the wirers had run out a thin line of stakes and barbed wire behind the new crater ; this wire passed over the sap, which would not be held by day. One wirer had had a bullet through the leg, but we had suffered no other casualties. Another hour, and I should be off duty. Altogether, a good show.

II

I was reading *Blackwood's* in a dug-out in Maple Redoubt. It was just after four, and I was lying on my bed. Suddenly the candle flickered and went out. I had to get up to ring the bell, and when I did get up, the bell did not ring, so I went out and called Lewis. The bell, by the way, was an arrangement of string from our dug-out to the servants' next door.

" Bring me a candle," I said, as Lewis appeared, evidently flushed and blear-eyed from sleep. " I don't know where you keep them. I can't find one anywhere."

Lewis fished under the bed and discovered a paper packet of candles, and lit one. " By the by," I added, " tell the pioneer servant (this was Private Davies, my orderly) to fix up that bell, will you ? And I think we'll be ready for tea as soon as you can get it. What do you say, Teddy ? Hullo, Clark ! What are you doing here ? Come in and have tea."

" Thanks, I will," said Clark, who had just come down Park Lane. " I was coming to invite myself, as a matter of fact."

" Good man," we said. Clark was no longer of " B " Company, having passed from Lewis-gun officer to the Brigade Machine-gun Corps. So we did not see very much of him.

At that moment Sergeant-Major Brown arrived and stood at the door. He saluted.

" Come in, sergeant-major."

" The tea's up, sir."

" Oh, all right," I said. " I'll go. Don't wait if tea comes in, Edwards. But I shan't be a minute."

As I went along with that tower of strength, the company sergeant-major, followed by an orderly carrying two rum jars produced from under my bed, I discussed the subject of working-parties for the night, and other such dull details of routine. Also we discussed leave. His dug-out was at the corner of Old Kent Road and Park Lane, and there I found the " Quarter " (Company Sergeant-Major Roberts) waiting with the five dixies of hot tea, just brought up on the ration trolley from the Citadel.

Sergeant Roberts saluted, and informed me that all was correct. Then the sergeant-major spilled the contents of the two jars into the five dixies, and as he did so the ten orderlies, two from each platoon, and two Lewis gunners, made off with the dixies. Then I made off, but followed by Sergeant Roberts with several papers to sign, and five pay books in which entries had to be made for men going on leave. One signed the pay-book, and also a paper to the quartermaster authorising him to pay 125 francs (the usual sum) to the under-mentioned men, out of the company balance which was deposited with him on leaving billets. I signed everything Sergeant Roberts put before me, almost without question.

"Well, Clark," I said, as we sat down to a tea of hot buttered toast, jam and cake. "How goes it ?"

"I've just been down a mine-shaft with that R.E. officer, I forget his name—the fellow with the glasses."

"I know," I replied ; "I don't know his name either, but it doesn't matter. Did you go right down, and along the galleries ? How frightfully interesting. I always mean to go, but somehow don't. Well, what about it ?"

"By Jove," said Clark. "It's wonderful. It's all as white as snow, dazzling white. I never realised that before, although you see these R.E.'s coming out all covered with white chalk-dust. First of all you go down three or four ladders ; it's awfully tricky work at the sort of halts on the way down, because there's a little platform, and very often the ladder goes down a different side of the shaft after one of these halts ; and if you don't notice, you lower your foot to go on down the same side as you were going before, and there's nothing there. The first time I did this and looked down and saw a dim light miles below, it quite gave me a turn. It's a terrible long way down, and of course you go alone ; the R.E. officer went first, and got ahead of me."

" Have some more tea, and go on."

" Well, down there it's fearfully interesting. I didn't go far up the gallery where they're working, because you can't easily pass along ; but the R.E. officer took me along a gallery that is not being worked, and there, all alone, at the end of it was a man sitting. He was simply sitting, listening. Then I listened through his stethoscope thing . . ."

" I know," I interposed. It is an instrument like a doctor's stethoscope, and by it you can hear underground sounds a hundred yards away as clearly as if they were five yards off.

" . . . and I could hear the Boche working as plainly as anything. Good heavens, it sounded about a yard off. Yet they told me it was forty yards. By Jove, it was weird. ' Pick . . . pick . . . pick.' I thought it must be our fellows really, but theirs made a different sound, and not a bit the same. But, you know, that fellow sitting there alone . . . as we went away and left him, he looked round at us with staring eyes just like a hunted animal. To sit there for hours on end, listening. Of course, while you hear them working, it's all right, they won't blow. But if you *don't* hear them ! My God, I wouldn't like to be an R.E. It's an awful game."

"By Jove," said Edwards. "How fearfully interesting! Is it cold down there?"

"Fairly. I really didn't notice."

"I must go down," I said. "We always laugh at these R.E.'s for looking like navvies, and for going about without gas-helmets or rifles. But really they are wonderful men. It's awful being liable to be buried alive any moment. Somehow death in the open is far less terrible. Ugh! Do you remember that R.E., Teddy, we saw running down the Old Kent Road? It was that night the Boche blew the mine in the Quarry. Jove, Clark, that was a sight. I was just going up from Trafalgar Square, when I heard a running, and there was a fellow, great big brawny fellow, naked to the waist, and *grey* all over; and someone had given him his equipment and rifle in a hurry, and he'd got his equipment over his bare skin! The men were fearfully amused. 'R.E.,' they said, and smiled. But, by God, there was a death look in that man's eyes. He'd been down when the Boche blew their mine, and as near as possible buried alive. No, it's a rotten game."

As I spoke, the ground shuddered, and the tea-things shook.

"There *is* a mine," we all exclaimed together.

"I wonder if it's ours, or theirs," said Edwards.

"I saw Hills, this afternoon," I answered, "and he said nothing about a mine. I'm sure he would have, if we had been going to send one up. No,

I bet that's a Boche mine. Good thing you're out of it, Clark. Oh, don't go. Well, cheero! if you must. Look us up oftener. Good luck!"

Clark departed, and I resumed *Blackwood's*.

"I say, Edwards," said I, after a while. "This stuff of Ian Hay's is awfully good. This about the signallers is *top-hole*. You can simply smell it!"

"After you with it," was the reply.

"There you are," I said at last. "It's called 'Carry On'; there have been several others in the same series. You know the 'First Hundred Thousand'?"

"No."

"Good stuff," said I. "Good readable stuff; the sort you'd give to your people at home. But it leaves out bits."

"Such as . . . ?"

"Oh, well, the utter fed-upness, and the dullness—and—well, oh, I don't know. You read it and see."

That was a bad night. The Boche mine had caught our R.E.'s this time. All the night through they were rescuing fellows from our mine gallery. Seven or eight were killed, most of them "gassed"; two of "A" Company were badly gassed too while aiding in the rescue work. This mine gas is, I suppose, very like that encountered in coal mines; and the explosion of big charges of cordite must create cracks and fissures underground that release these gases in all directions. I do not profess to write as an expert on this. At any rate they were all night working to get the fellows out. One man when rescued disobeyed the doctor's strict injunctions to lie still for half an hour before moving away from where he was put, just outside the mine shaft; and this cost him his life. He hurried down the Old Kent Road, and dropped dead with heart failure at the bottom of it. Hills told me he felt the pulses of two men who had been gassed and were waiting the prescribed half-hour; and they were going like a watch ticking. Yes, it was a bad night. I got snatches of sleep, but always there was the sound of stretchers being carried past our dug-out to the doctor's dressing-station; several times I went out to investigate how things were going. But there was nothing I could do. It was my duty to sleep: we were going up in the line to-morrow. But sleep does not always come to order.

Before dawn we "stood to," and it was quite light as I inspected the last rifle of No. 6 Platoon. They were just bringing the last of the gassed miners down to the dressing-station. I stood at the corner of Park Lane, and watched. The stretcher-bearers came and looked at two forms lying on stretchers close by me; then they asked me if I thought it would be all right to take those stretchers, and leave the dead men there another hour. I said if they wanted the stretchers, yes.

So they lifted the bodies off, and went away with the stretchers. There were several men standing about, silent, as usual, in the presence of death. I looked at those two R.E.'s as they lay quite uncovered ; grim their faces were, grim and severe. I told a man to get something and cover them up, until the stretcher-bearers came and removed them. And as I strode away in silence between my men, I felt that my face was grim too. I thought of Clark's description, a few hours back, of the man sitting alone in the white chalk gallery, listening, listening, listening. And now !

Once more I thought of "blind death." The Germans who had set light to the fuse at tea-time were doubtless sleeping the sleep of men who have worked well and earned their rest. And here . . . They knew nothing of it, would never know whom they had slain. And I remembered the night Scott and I had watched our big mine go up. "Wonderful," we had said, "magnificent." And in the morning the R.E. officer had told us that we had smashed all their galleries up, and that they would not trouble us there for a fortnight at least. "A certain man drew a bow at a venture," I said again, vaguely remembering something, but stiffening myself suddenly, and stifling my imagination.

I met Edwards by the dug-out as he returned from inspecting the Lewis guns.

"Remember," I said, "I told you the 'First

Hundred Thousand' leaves out bits? Did you see those R.E.'s who were gassed?"

Edwards nodded.

"Well," I added, "that's a thing it leaves out."

CHAPTER XIV

BILLETS

I. MORNING

"TWO hours' pack drill, and pay for a new handle," I said.

"Right—Turn!" said the sergeant-major. "Right—Wheel—Quick—March! Get your equipment on and join your platoon at once."

This last sentence was spoken in a quick undertone, as the prisoner stepped out of the door into the road. I was filling up the column headed "Punishment awarded" on a buff-coloured Army Form, to which I appended my signature. The case just dealt with was a very dull and commonplace one, a man having "lost" his entrenching tool handle. Most of these "losses" occurred in trenches, and were dealt with the first morning in billets at company orderly-room. This man had been engaged on special fatigue work the last few days; hence the reason why the loss had not been checked before, and came up on this last morning in billets.

"No more prisoners?" I asked the company sergeant-major.

"No more prisoners, sir," he answered. I then

rather hurriedly signed several returns made out by Sergeant Roberts, the company quartermaster-sergeant, and promised to come in later and sign the acquittance rolls. These are the pay-lists, made out in triplicate, which are signed by each man as he draws his pay. The original goes to the Paymaster in England, one carbon copy to the adjutant, and one is retained by the company-commander. We had paid out the first day in billets. This time "working-parties" had been tolerable. We had arrived back in billets about half-past three in the afternoon; the next morning had been spent in a march to the divisional baths at Treux (two miles away), in cleaning up, kit-inspection, and a little arm-drill and musketry practice; in the afternoon we paid out. Then followed three days of working-parties, up on the support line at Crawley Ridge; and now, we had this last day in which to do a little company work. There had been running parade at seven-thirty. Owen had taken this, and I confess that I had not yet breakfasted. So I hurried off now at 9.10 to gulp something down and be at battalion orderly-room at 9.30 sharp.

The company office was a house of two rooms; one was the "office" itself, with a blanket-clad table and a couple of chairs in the middle, and all around were strewn strange boxes, and bundles of papers and equipment. On the walls were pictures from illustrated English papers; one of Nurse

Cavell, another of howitzers firing; and several graphic bayonet-charges at Verdun, pictured by an artist who must have "glowed" as he drew them in his room in Chelsea. In the other room slept the C.S.M. and C.Q.M.S. (more familiar as the "sergeant-major" and the "quartermaster").

From this house, then, I stepped out into the glaring street. It was the end of May, and the day promised to be really quite hot. I have already explained how completely shut off from the trenches one felt in Morlancourt, sheltered as it was in a cup of the hills and immune from shelling. Now as I walked quickly along the street, past our battalion "orderly-room," and returned the immaculate salute of Sergeant-Major Shandon, the regimental sergeant-major, who was already marshalling the prisoners ready for the Colonel at half-past nine, I felt a lightness and freshness of body that almost made me think I was free of the war at last. My Sam Browne belt, my best tunic with its polished buttons, and most of all, I suppose, the effect of a good sleep and a cold bath, all contributed to this feeling, as well as the scent from the laburnum and lilac that looked over the garden wall opposite the billet that was our "Mess."

I found Edwards just going off to inspect "B" Company Lewis gunners, whom he was taking on the range the first part of the morning.

"Hullo!" he said, "you've not got much time."

"No," said I. "My own fault for getting up late. Got a case for the C.O. too. Is my watch right? I make it seventeen minutes past."

"Nineteen, I make it."

"Wish I hadn't asked you," I laughed. "No porridge, Lewis. Bring the eggs and bacon in at once. This tea'll do. There's no milk, though. What?"

Edwards had asked something. He repeated his question, which was whether I wanted Jim, the company horse, this afternoon. I thought rapidly, and the scent of the lilac decided me.

"Yes," I answered. "Sorry, but I do."

"Oh, all right; I expect I can get old Muskett to let me have one."

Muskett was the transport officer.

"Righto," said I. "Go teach thy Lewis gunners how to drill little holes in the chalk-bank."

He clattered off over the cobbles of the garden path, and in a few minutes I followed suit, running until I rounded a corner and came into view of the orderly-room, when I altered my gait to a dignified walk and arrived just as the Colonel appeared from the opposite direction.

"Parade! Tchern!!" shouted Sergeant-Major Shandon; and a moment later the four company commanders came to attention and saluted as the Colonel passed in, sprinkling "Good mornings" to right and left.

I had one very uninteresting case of drunkenness;

" A " had a couple of men who had overstayed their pass in England ; " C " had a case held over from the day before for further evidence, and was now dismissed as not proven ; while " D " had an unsatisfactory sergeant who was " severely reprimanded." All these cases were quickly and unerringly disposed of, and we company commanders saluted again and clattered down the winding staircase out into the sunshine.

I had to pass from one end of the village to the other. The orderly-room was not far from our company " Mess " and was at a cross-roads. Opposite, in one of the angles made by the junction of the four roads, was a deep and usually muddy horse-pond. But even here the mud was getting hard under this spell of warm May weather, and the innumerable ruts and hoof-marks were crystallising into a permanent pattern. As I walked along the streets I passed sundry Tommies acting as road-scavengers ; " permanent road fatigue " they were called, although they were anything but permanent, being changed every day. Formerly they had seemed to be engaged in a Herculean, though unromantic, task of scraping great rolling puddings of mud to the side of the road, in the vain hope that the mud would find an automatic exit into neighbouring gardens and ponds ; for Morlancourt did not boast such modern things as gutters. To-day there were large pats of mud lining the street, but these were now caked and hard, and even crumbling into dust, that whisked about among the sparrows. The permanent road fatigue was gathering waste-paper and tins in large quantities, but otherwise was having a holiday.

Women were working, or gossiping at the door-steps. The *estaminet* doors were flung wide open, and the floors were being scrubbed and sprinkled with sawdust. A little bare-legged girl, in a black cotton dress, was hugging a great wide loaf; an old man sat blinking in the sunshine ; cats were basking, dogs nosing about lazily. A party of about thirty bombers passed me, the sergeant giving "eyes right" and waking me from meditations on the eternal calm of cats. Then I reached the head-quarter guard, and the sentry saluted with a rattling clap upon his butt, and I did my best to emulate his smartness. So I passed along all the length of the shuttered houses of Morlancourt.

"A great day, this," I thought, as I came to the small field where "B" Company was paraded ; not two hundred and fifty men, as you will doubtless assume from the text-books, but some thirty or forty men only ; one was lucky if one mustered forty. Where were the rest, you ask ? Well, bombers bombing ; Lewis gunners under Edwards ; some on "permanent mining fatigue," that is, carrying the sand-bags from the mine-shafts to the dumps ; transport, pioneers, stretcher-bearers, men under bombing instruction, officers' servants, headquarter orderlies, men on leave, etc. etc. The company sergeant-major will make out a parade slate for you if you want it, showing exactly where every man is. But here are forty men. Let's drill them.

Half were engaged in arm-drill under my best drill-sergeant ; the other half were doing musketry in gas-helmets, an unpleasant practice which nothing would induce me to do on a sunny May morning. They lay on their fronts, legs well apart, and were working the bolts of their rifles fifteen times a minute. After a while they changed over and did arm-drill, while the other half took over the gas-helmets, the mouthpieces having first been dipped in a solution of carbolic brought by one of the stretcher-bearers in a canteen. These gas-helmets were marked D.P. (drill purposes), and each company had so many with which to practise.

When both parties were duly exercised, I gave a short lecture on the measures to be adopted against the use of *Flammenwerfer*, which is the " Liquid Fire " of the official *communiqués*. I had just been to a demonstration of this atrocity in the form of a captured German apparatus, and my chief object in lecturing the men about it was to make it quite clear that the flaming jets of burning gas cannot sink into a trench, but, as a matter of fact, only keep level so long as they are propelled by the driving power of the hose apparatus ; as water from a hose goes straight, and then curves down to the ground, so gas, even though it be incandescent, goes straight and then rises. In the trench you are unscathed, as we proved in the demonstration, when they sprayed the flaming gas over a trench full of men. Indeed, the chief effect of this *flammenwerfer* is one of frightfulness, as the Germans cannot come over until the flames have ceased. The men were rather inclined to gape at all this, but I found the words had sunk in when I asked what should be done if the enemy used this diabolical stuff against us. " Get down at the bottom of the trench, sir, and as soon as they stop it, give the ——'s 'ell ! "

The rest of the morning we spent " on the range," which meant firing into a steep chalk bank at a hundred yards. Targets and paste-pot had been procured from the pioneers' shop, and after posting a couple of "look-out" men on either side, we started range practice. The men are always keen about firing on the range, and it is really the most interesting and pleasant part of the infantryman's training. I watched these fellows, hugging their rifle-butt into their shoulder, and feeling the smooth wood against their cheeks ; they wriggled their bodies about to get a comfortable position ; sometimes they flinched as they fired and jerked the rifle ; sometimes they pressed the trigger as softly, as softly. . . . And gradually, carefully, we tried to detect and eliminate the faults. Then we ended up with fifteen rounds rapid in a minute. The " mad minute " it used to be called at home. After which we fell the men in, and Paul marched them back to the company " alarm post " outside the company office, where " B " Company always fell in ; while Owen, Nicolson, and I walked back together.

II. Afternoon

" I still maintain," said I, an hour later, as we finished lunch, " that bully-beef, some sort of sauce or pickle, and salad, followed by cheese, and ending with a cup of tea, is the proper lunch for an officer. I don't mind other officers having tinned fruit, though, if they like it," I added with a laugh.

Owen and Syme were newly joined officers for whom the sight of tinned pears or apricots had not yet lost a certain glamour that disappeared after months and months. They were just finishing the pear course. Hence my last remark.

" I bet if we allowed you to have bully every day," came from Edwards, our Mess president, " you'd soon get sick of it."

" Try," said I, knowing that he never would. I always used to eat of the hot things that would appear at lunch, to the detriment of a proper appreciation of dinner ; but I always maintained the position laid down in the first sentence of this section.

I lit a pipe and strolled out into the garden. This was undoubtedly an ideal billet, and a great improvement on the butcher's shop, where they used always to be killing pigs in the yard and letting the blood run all over the place. It was a long, one-storied house, set back about fifty yards from the road ;

this fifty yards was all garden, and, at the end, completely shutting off the road, was a high brick wall. On each side of the garden were also high walls formed by the sides of stables and outhouses; the garden was thus completely walled round, and the seclusion and peace thus entrapped were a very priceless possession to us.

The garden itself was full of life. There were box-bordered paths up both sides and down the centre, and on the inner side of the paths was an herbaceous border smelling very sweet of wallflowers and primulas of every variety. Although it was still May, there were already one or two pink cabbage-roses out; later, the house itself would be covered with them; already the buds were showing yellow streaks as they tried to burst open their tight green sheaths. In the centre of the garden ran a cross path with a summer-house of bamboo canes completely covered with honeysuckle; that, too, was budding already. The rest of the garden was filled with rows of young green things, peas, and cabbages, and I know not what, suitably protected against the ravages of sparrows and finches by the usual miniature telegraph system of sticks connected by cotton decorated with feathers and bits of rag. Every bit of digging, hoeing, weeding and sowing were performed by Madame and her two black-dressed daughters in whose house we were now living, and who were themselves putting up in the adjoining farmhouse, which belonged to them.

I said that they had done all the digging in the garden. I should make one reservation. All the potato-patch had been dug by our servants, with the assistance of Gray, the cook. Nor did they do it in gratitude to Madame, as, doubtless, ideal Tommies would have done. A quarter of it was done by Lewis, for carelessness in losing my valise; nearly half by the joint effort of the whole crew for a thoroughly dirty turn-out on commanding officer's inspection; and the rest for various other defalcations! We never told Madame the reasons for their welcome help; and I am quite sure they never did!

"The worst of this war," said I to Edwards, puffing contentedly at a pipeful of Chairman, "is this: it's too comfortable. You could carry on like this for years, and years, and years."

"Wasn't so jolly last time in," muttered the wise Edwards.

"That's exactly the point," I answered; "life in the trenches we all loathe, and no one makes any bones about it or pretends to like it—except for a few rare exciting minutes, which are very few and far between. But you come out into billets, and recover; and so you can carry on. It's not concentrated enough."

"It's more concentrated for the men than for us."

"Well, yes, very often; but they haven't the strain of responsibility. Yes, you are right though; and it's less concentrated for the C.O., still less for the Brigadier, and so on back to the Commander-in-

Chief ; and still further to men who have never seen a trench at all."

"I dare say," said Edwards ; "but, as the phrase goes, 'What are you going to do abaht it ?' Here's Jim. Old Muskett's going to send me a nag at five, so I'm going out after tea. Will you be in to tea ?"

"Don't know."

As I tightened my puttees preparatory to mounting the great Jim, Edwards started his gramophone ; so leaving them to the strains of Tannhaüser, I bestrode my charger and steered him gracefully down the garden path, under the brick archway, and out into the street.

Myself on a horse always amused me, especially when it was called an "officer's charger." Jim was not fiery, yet he was not by any means sluggish, and he went fast at a gallop. He suited me very well indeed when I wanted to go for an afternoon's ride ; for he was quite content to walk when I wanted to muse, and to gallop hard when I wanted exhilaration. I hate a horse that will always be trotting. I know it is best style to trot ; but my rides were not for style, but for pleasure, exercise, and solitude. And Jim fell in admirably with my requirements. But, as I say, the idea that I was a company-commander on his charger always amused me.

I rode, as I generally did, in a south-easterly direction, climbing at a walk one of the many roads that led out of Morlancourt towards the Bois des Tailles. When I reached the high ground I made

Jim gallop along the grass-border right up to the edge of the woods. There is nothing like the exhilaration of flying along, you cannot imagine how, with the great brown animal lengthening out under you for all he is worth ! I pulled him up and turned his head to the right, leaving the road, and skirting the edge of the wood. At last I was alone.

In the clearings of the wood the ground was a sheet of blue hyacinths, whose sweet scent came along on the breeze ; their fragrance lifted my spirit, and I drank in deep breaths of the early summer air. I took off my cap to feel the sun full on my face. On the ground outside the wood were still a few late primroses interspersed with cowslips, stubborn and jolly ; and as I rounded a bend in the wood-edge, I found myself looking across a tiny valley, the opposite face of which was a wooded slope, with all the trees banked up on it as gardeners bank geraniums in tiers to give a good massed effect. So, climbing the hillside, were all these shimmering patches of green, yellow-green, pea-green, yellow, massed together in delightful variety ; and dotted about in the middle of them were solitary patches of white cherry-blossom, like white foam breaking over a reef, in the midst of a great green sea. And across this perfect softness from time to time the bold black and white of magpies cut with that vivid contrast with which Nature loves to baffle the poor artist.

" Come on, old boy," I said, as I reached the bottom of this little valley ; and trotting up the other side, and through a ride in the wood, I came out on the edge of the Valley of the Somme. I then skirted the south side of the wood until I reached a secluded corner with a view across the valley: here I dismounted, fastened Jim to a tree, loosened his girths, and left him pulling greedily at the grass at his feet. Then I threw myself down on the grass to dream.

My thoughts ran back to my conversation with Edwards. Perhaps it was best not to think too hard, but I could no more stifle my thoughts than can a man his appetite. Responsibility. Responsibility. And those with the greatest responsibility endure and see the least; no one has more to endure than the private soldier in the infantry, and no one has less responsibility or power of choice. I thought of our last six days in the trenches. When "A" Company were in the line, the first three days, we had been bombarded heavily at "stand-to" in the evening. In Maple Redoubt it had been bad enough. There was one sentry-post a little way up Old Kent Road; by some mistake a bomber had been put on duty there, whereas it was a bayonet-man's post, the bombers having a special rôle in case of the enemy attacking. I found this mistake had been made, but did not think it was worth altering. And that man was killed outright by a shell.

In the front line "A" Company had had several killed and wounded, and I had had to lend them half my bombers; as I had placed two men on one post, a canister had burst quite a long way off, but the men cowered down into the trench. I cursed them as hard as I could, and then I saw that in the post were the two former occupants lying dead, killed half an hour ago where they lay, and where I was placing my two men. I stopped my curses, and inwardly directed them against myself. And there I had to leave these fellows, looking after me and thinking, "*He's* going back to his dug-out." Ah! no, they knew me better than to think like that. Yet I had to go back, leaving them there. I should never forget that awful weight of responsibility that suddenly seemed visualised before me. Could I not see their scared faces peering at me, even as now I seemed to smell the scent of pear-drops with which the trench was permeated, the Germans having sent over a few lachrymatory shells along with the others that night?

Ah! Why was I living all this over again, just when I had come away to get free of all this awhile, and dream? I had come out to enjoy the sunshine and the peace, just as Jim was enjoying the grass behind me. I listened. There was a slight jingle of the bit now and again, and a creaking of leather, and always that drawing sound, with an occasional purr, as the grass was torn up. I could not help looking round at last. "You pig," I said; but my tone did not altogether disapprove of complacent piggishness.

In front of me lay the blue water of the Somme Canal, and the pools between it and the river; long parallel rows of pale green poplars stretched along either bank of the canal ; and at my feet, half hidden by the slope of the ground, lay the sleepy little village of Etinehem. There was a Sunday afternoon slumber over everything. Was it Sunday ? I thought for a moment. No, it was Thursday, and to-morrow we went " in " again. I deliberately switched my thoughts away from the trenches, and they flew to the events of the morning. I could see my fellows lying, so keen—I might almost say so happy—blazing away on the range. One I remembered especially. Private Benjamin, a boy with a delicate eager face, who came out with the last draft : he came from a village close up to Snowdon ; he was shooting badly, and very concerned about it. I lay down beside him and showed him how to squeeze the trigger, gradually, ever so gradually. Oh ! these boys ! Responsibility. Responsibility.

" This is no good," I said to myself at last, and untied Jim and rode again. I went down into the valley, and along the green track between an avenue of poplars south of the canal until at last I came to Sailly-Laurette, and so back and in to Morlancourt from the south-west. It was six o'clock by the time I stooped my head under the gateway into our garden, and for the last hour or so I had almost forgotten war at last.

" Hullo," was the greeting I received from Owen. " There's no tea left."

"I don't want any tea," I answered. "Has the post come?"

There were three letters for me. As I slept at a house a little distance away, I took the letters along with me.

"I'm going over to my room to clean up," I shouted to Owen, who was reading inside the Mess-room. "What time's old Jim coming in?"

"Seven o'clock!"

"All right," I answered. "I'll be over by seven."

III. Evening

As I walked up the garden path a few minutes before seven, I had to pass the kitchen door, where the servants slept, lived, and cooked our meals. I had a vision of Private Watson, the cook, busy at the oven; he was in his shirt-sleeves, hair untidy, trousers very grimy, and altogether a very un-martial figure. There seemed to be a dispute in progress, to judge from the high pitch to which the voices had attained. On these occasions Lewis' piping voice reached an incredible falsetto, while his face flushed redder than ever.

Watson, Owen's servant, had superseded Gray as officers' mess cook; the latter had, unfortunately, drunk one or two glasses of beer last time in billets, and, to give his own version, he "somehow felt very sleepy, and went down and lay under a bank," and could remember nothing more until about ten o'clock, when he humbly reported his return to me.

Meanwhile Watson had cooked the dinner, which was, of course, very late ; and as he did it very well, and as Gray's explanation seemed somewhat vague, we decided to make Watson cook, let Gray try a little work in the company for a change, and get the sergeant-major to send Owen another man for servant. Watson had signalised the entry to his new appointment by a quarrel with Madame (the Warwicks had managed to " bag " this ideal billet of ours temporarily, and we were in a much less comfortable one the last two occasions out of trenches) ; eventually Madame had hurled the frying-pan at him, amid a torrent of unintelligible French ; neither could understand a word the other was saying, of course. Gray had been wont, I believe, to " lie low and say nuffin," like Brer Fox, when Madame, who was old and half-crazed, came up and threw water on the fire in a fit of unknown anger. But Watson's blood boiled at such insults from a Frenchwoman, and hence had followed a sharp contention ending in the projection of the frying-pan. Luckily, we were unmolested here : Watson could manage the dinner, anyway.

I entered our mess-room, which was large, light, and boasted a boarded floor ; it was a splendid summer-room, though it would have been very cold in winter. There I found a pile of literature awaiting me ; operation orders for to-morrow, giving the hour at which each company was to leave Morlancourt, and which company of the Manchesters it was to relieve, and when, and where, and the route to be taken ; there were two typed documents " for your information and retention, please," one relating to prevention of fly-trouble in billets, the other giving a new code of signals and marked "Secret" on the top, and lastly there was *Comic Cuts*. Leaving the rest, I hastily skimmed through the latter, which contained detailed information of operations carried out, and intelligence gathered on the corps front during the last few days. At first these were intensely interesting, but after seven months they began to pall, and I grew expert at skimming through them rapidly.

Then Jim Potter came in, and *Comic Cuts* faded into insignificance.

"Here, Owen," said I, and threw them over to him.

Captain and Quartermaster Jim Potter was the Father of the battalion. He had been in the battalion sixteen years, and had come out with them in 1914 ; twice the battalion had been decimated, new officers had come and disappeared, commanding officers had become brigadiers and new ones taken their place, but " Old Jim " remained, calm, unaltered, steady as a rock, good-natured, and an utter pessimist. I first introduced him in Chapter I, when I spent the night in his billet prior to my first advent into the trenches. I was a little perturbed then by his pessimism. Now I should have been very alarmed if he had suddenly burst into a fit of optimism.

"Well, Jim," we said, "how are things going? When's the war going to end?"

"Oh! not so very long now." We gaped at this unexpected reply. "Because," he added, "you know, Bill, it's the unexpected that always happens in this war. Hullo! You've got some pretty pictures, I see."

We had been decorating the walls with the few unwarlike pictures that were still to be found in the illustrated papers.

"Not a bad place, Blighty," he resumed, gazing at a picture entitled "Home, Sweet Home!" There had been a little dispute as to whether it should go up, owing to its sentimental nature. At last "The Warwicks will like it," we had said, and up it had gone. The Warwicks had our billet, when we were "in."

"Tell us about your leave," we said, and Jim began a series of delightful sarcastic jerks about the way people in England seemed to be getting now a faint glimmering conception that somewhere there was a war on.

The joint was not quite ready, Edwards explained to me, drawing me aside a minute; would old Jim mind? The idea of old Jim minding being quite absurd, we decided on having a cooked joint a quarter of an hour hence, rather than a semi-raw one now; and we told Jim our decision. It seemed to suit him exactly, as he had had tea late. There never was such an unruffled fellow as he; had we wanted to begin before the time appointed, he would have been ravenous. So he continued the description of his adventures on leave. Meanwhile I rescued *Comic Cuts* from the hands of Paul, and despatched them, duly initialled, by the trusty Davies to "C" Company. Just as I had done so the sergeant-major appeared at the door.

"You know the time we move off to-morrow?" I said.

Yes, he had known that long before I did, by means of the regimental sergeant-major and the orderly sergeant.

"Fall in at 8.15," I said. "Everything the same as usual. All the officers' servants, and Watson, are to fall in with the company; this straggling in independently, before or after the company, will stop once and for all." Lewis' face, as he laid the soup-plates, turned half a degree redder than usual.

"There's nothing more?" I said.

"No, that's all, sir."

The sergeant-major drained off his whiskey with a dash of Perrier, and prepared to go. Now was the psychological moment when one learnt any news there was to learn about the battalion.

"No news, I suppose?" I asked.

"The fellows are still talking about this 'rest,' sir. No news about that, I suppose?" said the sergeant-major.

"Only that it's slightly overdue," I answered,

with a laugh. "What do you think, Jim? Any likelihood of this three weeks' rest coming off?"

"Oh, yes; I should think so," said the quartermaster. "Any time next year."

"Good night, sir," said Sergeant-Major Brown, with a grin.

"Good night, Sergeant-Major," came in a chorus as he disappeared into the garden.

"Soup's ready, sir," said Lewis. And we sat down to dine.

The extraordinary thing about having Jim Potter in to dinner was that an extra elaborate menu was always provided, and yet old Jim himself always ate less than anyone else; still, he did his share nobly with the whiskey, so that made up for it, I suppose. To-night Edwards planned "sausages and mash" as an entrée; but, whether through superior knowledge or a mere misunderstanding, the sausages arrived seated carefully on the top of the round of beef, like *marrons-glacés* stuck on an iced cake. As the dish was placed, amid howls of execration, on the table, one of the unsteadier sausages staggered and fell with a splash into the gravy, much to everyone's delight; Edwards, wiping the gravy spots off his best tunic, seemed the only member of the party who did not greet with approbation this novel dish.

After soup, sausages and beef, and rice-pudding and tinned fruit, came Watson's special dish—cheese *au gratin* on toast. This was a glutinous concoction, and a little went a long way. Then followed *café au lait* made in the teapot, which was the signal for cigarettes to be lit up, and chairs to be moved a little to allow of a comfortable expansion of legs. Owen proposed sitting out in the summer-house, but on going outside reported that it was a little too chilly. So we remained where we were.

Edwards was talking of Amiens : he had been there for the day yesterday, and incidentally discovered that there was a cathedral there.

" I know it," said I. " I used to go there every Saturday when I was at the Army School."

" You had a good time at the Army School, didn't you ? " asked Jim.

" Tip-top time," said I. " It's a really good show. The Commandant was the most wonderful man we ever met. By the way, that concert Tuesday night was a really good show."

Jim Potter and Edwards had got it up ; it had been an *al fresco* affair, and the night had been ideally warm for it. Edwards had trained a Welsh choir with some success. Several outsiders had contributed, the star of the evening being Basil Hallam, the well-known music-hall artist, whose dainty manner, reminding one of the art of Vesta Tilley, and impeccable evening clothes had produced an unforgettably bizarre effect in the middle of such an audience and within sound of the guns. He was well known to most of the men as " the bloke that sits up in the sausage." For any fine day, coming out of trenches or going in, you could see high suspended the " sausage," whose home and " base " was between Treux and Mericourt, and whose occupant and eye was Basil Hallam. And so the " sausage bloke " was received enthusiastically at our concert.

As we talked about the concert, Owen began singing " Now Florrie was a Flapper," which had been Basil Hallam's most popular song, and as he sang he rose from his chair and walked about the room; he was evidently enjoying himself, though his imitation of Basil Hallam was very bad indeed. As he sang, we went on talking.

" A good entry in *Comic Cuts* to-night," I remarked. " ' A dog was heard barking in Fricourt at 11 p.m.' Someone must have been hard up for intelligence to put that in."

" A dog barking in Fricourt," said old Jim, warming up. " ' A dog barking in Fricourt.' What's that—Corps stuff? I never read the thing; good Lord, no! That's what it is to have a Staff— ' A dog barking in Fricourt! ' "

" The Corps officer didn't hear it," said I. " It was some battalion intelligence officer that was such a fool as to report it."

" Fool?" said old Jim. " I'd like to meet the fellow. He's the first fellow I've ever met yet who has a just appreciation of the brain capacity of the Staff. You or I might have thought of reporting a dog's mew, or roar, or bellow; but a dog's bark we should have thought of no interest whatever to the—

er—fellows up there, you know, who plan our destinies." And he gave an obsequious flick of his hand to an imaginary person too high up to see him at all.

" He's a good fellow," he repeated, " that intelligence officer. Ought to get a D.S.O."

Old Jim had two South African medals, a D.C.M. and a D.S.O.

" The Staff," he went on, with the greatest contempt he could put into his voice. " I saw three of them in a car to-day. I stood to attention : saluted. A young fellow waved his hand, you know ; graciously accepted my salute, you know, and passed on leaning back in his limousin. The ' Brains of the British Army,' I thought. Pah ! "

We waited. Jim on the Staff was the greatest entertainment the battalion could offer. We tried to draw him out further, but he would not be drawn. We tried cunningly, by indirect methods, enquiring his views on whether there would be a push this year.

" Push ! " he said. " Of course there will be a push. The Staff must have something to show for themselves. ' Shove 'em in,' they say ; ' rather a bigger front than last time.' Strategy ? Oh, no ! That's out of date, you know. Five-mile front—frontal attack. Get a few hundred thousand mown down, and then discover the Boche has got a second line. The Staff. Pah ! ! " And no more would he say.

Then Clark came in, and the Manchester Stokes

gun officer. Clark immediately joined Owen in a duet on "Florrie." Then we went through the whole gamut of popular songs, with appropriate actions and stamping of feet upon the floor. Meanwhile the table was cleared, only the whiskey and Perrier remaining. Soon there were cries of "Napoleon—Napoleon," and Owen, who bears a remarkable resemblance to that great personage, posed tragically again and again amid great applause. And then, in natural sequence, I, as "Bill, the man wot won the Battle of Waterloo," attacked him with every species of trench-mortar I could lay hands on, my head swathed in a remarkable turban of *Daily Mail.* At last I drove him into a corner behind a table, and bombarded him relentlessly with oranges until he capitulated! All the time Edwards had been in fear and trembling for the safety of his gramophone.

At length peace was signed, and we grew quiet again beneath the soothing strains of the gramophone, until at last Jim Potter said he must really go. Everyone reminding everyone else that breakfast was at seven, we broke up the party, and Owen, Paul, Jim Potter and I departed together. But anyone who knows the psychology of conviviality will understand that we had first to pay a visit to a neighbouring Mess for one last whiskey-and-soda before turning in.

As I opened the door of my billet, I heard a "strafe" getting up. There was a lively cannonade up in the line ; for several minutes I listened, until it diminished a little, and began to die away. " In " to-morrow, I thought. My valise was laid out on the floor, and my trench kit all ready for packing first thing next morning. I lost no time in getting into bed. And yet I could not sleep.

I could not help thinking of the jollity of the last few hours, the humour, the apparently spontaneous outburst of good spirits ; and most of all I thought of old Jim, the mainspring somehow of it all. And again I saw the picture of the concert a few nights ago, the bright lights of the stage, the crowds of our fellows, all their bodies and spirits for the moment relaxed, good-natured, happy, as they stood laughing in the warm night air. And lastly I thought again of Private Benjamin, that refined eager face, that rather delicate body, and that warm hand as I placed mine over his, squeezing the trigger. He was no more than a child really, a simple-minded child of Wales. Somehow it was more terrible that these young boys should see this war, than for the older men. Yet were we not all children wondering, wondering, wondering ? . . . Yes, we were like children faced by a wild beast. " Sometimes I dislike you almost," I thought ; " your dulness, your coarseness, your lack of romance, your unattractiveness. Yet that is only physical. You, I love really. Oh, the dear, dear world ! "

And in the darkness I buried my face in the pillow, and sobbed.

CHAPTER XV

"A CERTAIN MAN DREW A BOW AT A VENTURE"

IT was ten o'clock as I came in from the wiring-party in front of Rue Albert, and at that moment our guns began. We were in Maple Redoubt. The moon had just set, and it was a still summer night in early June.

"Come and have a look," I called to Owen, who had just entered the dug-out. I could see him standing with his back to the candlelight reading a letter or something.

He came out, and together we looked across the valley at the shoulder of down that was silhouetted by the continuous light of gun-flickers. Our guns had commenced a two hours' bombardment.

"No answer from the Boche yet," I said.

"They're firing on C 2, down by the cemetery."

"Yes, I hardly noticed it ; our guns make such a row. By Jove, it's magnificent."

We gazed fascinated for a long time, and then went into the dug-out where Edwards and Paul were snoring rhythmically. I read for half an hour but the dug-out was stuffy, and the smell of sand bags and the flickering of the candle annoyed me for some reason or other. Somehow "Derelicts" by W. J. Locke failed to grip my attention. Owing to our bombardment, there were no working-parties, in case the Germans should take it into their head to retaliate vigorously. But at present there was no sign of that.

I went outside again, and walked along Park Lane until I came to the Lewis-gun position just this side of the corner of Watling Street. The sentry was standing up, with his elbows on the ground level (there was no parapet) gazing alert and interested at the continuous flicker of our shells bursting along the enemy's trenches. Lance-Corporal Allan looked out of the dug-out, and, seeing me, came out and stood by us. And together we watched, all three of us, in silence. Overhead was the continual griding, screeching, whistling of the shells as they passed over, without pause or cessation; behind was a chain of gun-flickers the other side of the ridge; and in front was another chain of flashes, and a succession of bump, bump, bumps, as the shells burst relentlessly in the German trenches. And where we stood, under the noisy arch, was a steady calm.

"This is all right, sir," said Lance-Corporal Allan. He was the N.C.O. in charge of this Lewis-gun team.

"Yes," said I. "The artillery are not on short rations to-night."

For always, through the last four months, the artillery had been more or less confined to so many shells a day. The officers used to tell us they had any amount of ammunition, yet no sooner were they given a free hand to retaliate as much as we wanted, than an order came cancelling this privilege. To-night at any rate there was no curtailment.

"I believe this is the beginning of a new order of things," I said, half musing, to myself; "that is, I believe the Boche is going to get lots and lots of this now."

"About time, sir," said the sentry.

"Is there a push coming off?" said Lance-Corporal Allan.

"I don't know," I replied. "But I expect we shall be doing something soon. It's quite certain we're going to get our three weeks' rest after this turn in. The Brigade Major told me so."

Corporal Allan smiled, and as he did so the flashes lit up his face. He was quite a boy, only eighteen, I believe, but an excellent N.C.O. He had a very beautiful though sensuous face that used to remind me sometimes of the "Satyr" of Praxiteles. His only fault was an inclination to sulkiness at times, which was perhaps due to a little streak of vanity. It was no wonder the maidens of Morlancourt made eyes at him, and a little girl who lived next door to the Lewis-gunner's billet was said to have lost her heart long ago. To-night I felt a pang as I saw him smile.

" We'll see," I said. " Anyway it's going to be a good show giving the Boche these sort of pleasant dreams. Better than those one-minute stunts."

I was referring to a one-minute bombardment of Fricourt Wood, that had taken place last time we were in the line. It was a good spectacle to see the wood alive with flames, hear our Vickers' guns rattling hard behind us from the supports, and see the Germans firing excited green and red rockets into the air. But the retaliation had been unpleasant, and the whole business seemed not worth while. This continuous pounding was quite different.

I went back and visited the other gun position, and spent a few minutes there also. At last I turned in reluctantly. I went out again at half-past eleven, and still the shells were screaming over. It seemed the token of an irresistible power. And there was no reply at all now from the German lines.

The short summer nights made life easier in some respects. We " stood to " earlier, and it was quite light by three. As I turned in again, I paused for a moment to take in the scene. Davies had retired to a small dug-out, that looked exactly like a dog-kennel, and was not much larger. As Davies himself frequently reminded me of a very intelligent sheepdog, the dog-kennel seemed most suitable. I heard him turning about inside, as I stood at the door of our own dug-out.

The scene was one of the most perfect peace.

The sun was not up, but by now the light was firm and strong; night had melted away. I went back and walked a little way along Park Lane until I came to a gap in the newly erected sand-bag parados. I went through the gap and into a little graveyard that had not been used now for several months. And there I stood in the open, completely hidden from the enemy, on the reverse slope of the hill. Below me were the dug-outs of 71 North, and away to the left those of the Citadel. Already I could see smoke curling up from the cookers. There was a faint mist still hanging about over the road there, that the strong light would soon dispel. On the hill-side opposite lay the familiar tracery of Redoubt A, and the white zigzag mark of Maidstone Avenue climbing up well to the left of it, until it disappeared over the ridge. Close to my feet the meadow was full of buttercups and blue veronica, with occasional daisies starring the grass. And below, above, everywhere, it seemed, was the tremulous song of countless larks, rising, growing, swelling, till the air seemed full to breaking-point.

And there was not a sound of war. Who could desecrate such a perfect June morning? I felt a mad impulse to run up and across into No Man's Land and cry out that such a day was made for lovers; that we were all enmeshed in a mad nightmare, that needed but a bold man's laugh to free us from its clutches! Surely this most exquisite morning could not be the birth of another day of pain? Yet I felt how vain and hopeless was the longing, as I turned at last and saw the first slant rays of sunlight touch the white sand-bags into life.

"What time's this working-party?" asked Paul at four o'clock that afternoon.

"I told the sergeant-major to get the men out as soon as they'd finished tea," I replied. "About a quarter to five they ought to be ready. He will let you know all right."

"Hullo!" said Paul.

"What are you 'hulloing' about?" I asked.

Paul did not answer. Faintly I heard a "wheeoo, wheeoo, wheeoo," that grew louder and louder and ended in a swishing roar like a big wave breaking against an esplanade—and then "wump—wump—wump—wump" four 4·2's exploded beyond the parados of Park Lane.

"Well over," said Edwards.

"I expected this," I answered. "They've been too d—d quiet all day—especially after the pounding we gave them last night."

"There they are again," I added. This time I had heard the four distant thuds, and we all waited.

"Wump, wump—CRUMP." There was a colossal din, the two candles went out, and there was a shaking and jarring in the blackness. Then followed the sound of falling stuff, and I felt a few patters of earth all over me. Gradually it got lighter, and through the smoke-filled doorway the square of daylight reappeared.

"Je ne l'aime pas," said I, as we all waited, without speaking. Then Edwards struck a match and lit the candles; all the table, floor, and beds were sprinkled with dust and earth. Then Davies burst in.

"Are you all right?" we asked.

"Yessir. Are you?"

"Oh, we're all right, Davies," said I. "But there's a job for Lewis cleaning this butter up."

At length we went outside, stepping over a heap of loose yielding earth, mixed up with lumps of chalk and bits of frayed sand-bags. Outside, the trench was blocked with débris of a similar kind. Already two men had crossed it, and several men were about to do so. It was old already. There was still a smell of gunpowder in the air, and a lot of chalk dust that irritated your nose.

"I think I'll tell the sergeant-major not to get the working-party out just yet," I said to Paul. "They often start like that and then put lots more over about a quarter of an hour later." And I sped along Park Lane quickly.

As I returned I heard footsteps behind me. I looked round, but the men were hidden by a traverse. And then came tragedy, sudden, and terrible. I have seen many bad sights—every man killed is a tragedy—but one avoids and hides away the hideousness as soon as possible. But never, save once perhaps, have I seen the thing so vile as now.

"Look out!" I heard a voice from behind. And as I heard the shell screaming down, I tumbled into the nearest dug-out. The shell burst with a huge "crump," but not so close as the one that had darkened our dug-out ten minutes before. Then again another four shells burst together, but some forty or fifty yards away. I waited one, two minutes. *And then I heard men running in the trench.*

As I sprang up the dug-out steps, I saw two stretcher-bearers standing looking round the traverse. And then there was the faint whistling overhead and they pushed me back as they almost fell down the dug-out steps.

"Is there a man hurt?" I asked. "We can't leave him."

"He's dead," said one. And as he spoke there were three more explosions a little to the left.

"Are you sure?"

"Aye," said the stretcher-bearer and closed his eyes tight.

"He's past our help," said the other man.

At last, after a minute's calm, we stepped out into the sunshine. I went round the traverse, following the two stretcher-bearers. And looking between them, as they stood gazing, this is what I saw.

In the trench, half buried in rags of sand-bag and

loose chalk, lay what had been a man. His head was nearest to me, and at that I gazed fascinated; for the shell had cut it clean in half, and the face lay like a mask, its features unmarred at all, a full foot away from the rest of the head. The flesh was grey, that was all; the open eyes, the nose, the mouth were not even twisted awry. It was like the fragment of a sculpture. All the rest of the body was a mangled mass of flesh and khaki.

"Who is it?" whispered a stretcher-bearer, bending his head down to look sideways at that mask.

"Find his identity-disc," said the other.

"It is Lance-Corporal Allan," said I.

Then up came the regimental sergeant-major, and Owen followed him. They too gazed in horror for a moment. The sergeant-major was the first to recover.

"Hi! you fellows," he called to two men. "Get a waterproof sheet."

"Come away, old man," said I to Owen.

In silence we walked back to the dug-out. But my brain was whirling. "A certain man drew a bow at a venture," I thought again. That was how it was possible. No man could keep on killing, if he could see the men he killed. Who had fired that howitzer shell? A German gunner somewhere right away in Mametz Wood probably. He would never see his handiwork, never know what he had done to-day. He would never *see;* that was the point. Had he known, he would have rejoiced that there was one Englishman less in the world. It was not his fault. We were just the same. What of last night's bombardment? (The memory of Lance-Corporal Allan up by his gun-position gave me a quick sharp pang.) Had we not watched with glittering eyes the magnificent shooting of our own gunners? This afternoon's strafe was but a puny retaliation.

Slowly it came back to me, the half-formed picture that had arisen in my mind the night of Davidson's death. "A certain man drew a bow at a venture," expressed it perfectly. It was splendid twanging the bow, feeling the fingers grip the polished wood, watching the bow-string stretch and strain, and then letting the arrow fly. That was the fascinating, the deadly fascinating side of war. That was what made it possible to "carry on." I remembered my joy in calling up the artillery in revenge for Thompson's death. And then again, whenever we put a mine up, how exhilarating was the spectacle! Throwing a bomb, firing a Lewis gun, all these things were pleasant. It was like the joy of throwing stones over a barn and hearing them splash into a pond; like driving a cricket ball out of the field.

But the arrows fell somewhere. That was the other side of war. The dying king leant on his chariot, propped up until the sun went down. The man who had fired the bolt never knew he had killed a king. That was the other side of war; that was the side that counted. What I had just seen was war.

I leaned my face on my arm against the parados. Oh, this unutterable tragedy! Had there ever been such a thing before? Why was this thing so terrible? Why did I have this feeling of battering against some relentless power? Death. There were worse things than death. There were sights, such as I had just come from, as terrible in every-day life, in any factory explosion or railway accident. There was nothing new in death. Vaguely my mind felt out for something to express this thing so far more terrible than mere death. And then I saw it. Vividly I saw the secret of war.

What made war so cruel, was the force that compelled you to go on. After a factory explosion you cleared up things and then took every precaution to prevent its recurrence; but in war you did the opposite, you used all your energies to make more explosions. You killed and went on killing; you saw men die around you, and you deliberately went on with the thing that would cause more of your friends to die. You were placed in an arena, and made to fight the beasts; and if you killed one beast, there were more waiting, and more and more. And above the arena, out of it, secure, looked down the glittering eyes of the men who had placed you there; cruel, relentless eyes, that went on glittering while the mouths expressed admiration for your impossible struggles, and pity for your fate !

" Oh God ! I shall go mad ! " I thought, in the agony of my mind. I saw into that strange empty chamber which is called madness : I knew what it would be like to go mad. And even as I saw, came the thought again of those glittering eyes, and the ruthless answer to my soul's cry : " The war is utterly indifferent whether you go mad or not."

Owen was standing waiting for me. I grew calm again, and turned and put my hand on his shoulder. Together we reached the door of the dug-out.

" Oh, Bill," he said, " have you ever seen anything more awful ? "

" Only once. No, not more awful : more beastly. Nothing could be more awful."

We told the others.

" Not Allan ? " said Edwards. He was Lewis-gun officer, and Allan was his best man.

" Not Allan ? " he repeated. " Oh, how will they tell his little girl in Morlancourt ? What will she say when she learns she will never see him again ? "

" Thank God she never saw him as we saw him just now," I said, " and thank God his mother never saw him."

" If women were in this war, there would be no war," said Edwards.

" I wonder," said I.

CHAPTER XVI

WOUNDED

LANCE-CORPORAL ALLAN was killed on Tuesday the 6th of June. For the rest of that day I was all " on edge." I wondered sometimes how I could go on: even in billets I dreamed of rifle-grenades; and though I had only returned from leave a fortnight ago, I felt as tired out in body and mind as I did before I went. And this last horror did not add to my peace of mind. I very nearly quarrelled with Captain Wetherell, the battalion Lewis-gun officer, over the position of a Lewis gun. There had been a change of company front, and some readjustments had to be made. I believe I told him he had not got the remotest idea of our defence scheme, or something of the sort! My nerves were all jangled, and my brain would not rest a second. We were nearly all like that at times.

I decided therefore to go out again to-night with our wires. I had been out last night, and Owen was going to-night, but I wanted to be doing something to occupy my thoughts. I knew I should not sleep. At a quarter to ten I sent word to

Corporal Dyson, the wiring-corporal, to take his men up at eleven instead of ten, as the moon had not quite set. At eleven o'clock Owen and I were out in No Man's Land putting out concertina wire between 80A and 81A bombing posts, which had recently been connected up by a deep narrow trench. There was what might be called a concertina craze on: innumerable coils of barbed wire were converted into concertinas by the simple process of winding them round and round seven upright stakes in the ground; every new lap of wire was fastened to the one below it at every other stake by a twist of plain wire; the result, when you came to the end of a coil and lifted the whole up off the stakes was a heavy ring of barbed wire that concertina'd out into ten-yard lengths. They were easily made up in the trench, quickly put up, and when put out in two parallel rows, about a yard apart, and joined together with plenty of barbed wire tangled in loosely, were as good an obstacle as could be made. We had some thirty of these to put out to-night.

When you are out wiring you forget all about being in No Man's Land, unless the Germans are sniping across. The work is one that absorbs all your interest, and your one concern is to get the job done quickly and well. I really cannot remember whether the enemy had been sniping or not (I use the word "sniping" to denote firing occasional shots across with fixed rifles sited by day). I remember that I forgot all about Captain Wetherell and his Lewis-gun positions, as soon as I was outside the bombing post at 80A. There were about fifteen yards between this post and the crater-edge, where I had a couple of "A" Company bombers out as a covering party. But in this fifteen yards were several huge shell-holes, and we were concealing the wire in these as much as possible. It was fascinating work, and I felt we could not get on fast enough with it. After a time I went along to Owen, whose party was working on my left. Here Corporal Dyson and four men were doing well also. All this strip of land between the trench and the crater edge was an extraordinary tangle of shell-holes, old beams and planks, and scraps of old wire. Every square yard of it had been churned and pounded to bits at different times by canisters and "sausages" and such-like. Months ago there had been a trench along the crater edges; but new mines had altered these, and until we had dug the deep, narrow trench between 80A and 81A about a fortnight ago, there had been no trench there for at least five months. The result was a chaotic jumble, and this jumble we were converting into an obstacle by judiciously placed concertina wiring.

I repeat that I cannot remember if there had been much sniping across. I had just looked at my luminous watch, which reported ten past one, when I noticed that the sky in the east began to show up a little paler than the German parapet across the crater. "Dawn," I thought, "already. There is no night at all, really. We must knock off in a quarter of an hour. The light will not be behind us, but half-past one will be time to stop." I was lying out by the bombers, gazing into the black of the crater. It was a warm night, and jolly lying out like this, though a bit damp and muddy round the shell-holes. Then I got up, told Corporal Evans to come in after fixing the coil he was putting up, and was walking towards 80A post, when "Bang" I heard from across the crater, and I felt a big sting in my left elbow, and a jar that numbed my whole arm.

"Ow," I cried out involuntarily, and doubled the remaining few yards, and scrambled down into the trench.

Corporal Dyson was there.

"Are you hit, sir?"

"Yes. Nothing much—here in the arm. Get the wirers in. It'll be light soon."

Then somehow I found my equipment and tunic off; there seemed a lot of men round me; and I tried to realise that I was really hit. My arm hung numb and stiff, with the after-taste of a sting in it. I felt this could not be a proper wound, as there was no real throbbing pain such as I expected. I was surprised when I saw a lot of blood in the half light. Corporal Dyson asked me if I had a field-dressing, and I said he would find one in the bottom right-hand corner of my tunic. To my annoyance he did not seem to hear, and used one of the men's. Then Owen appeared, with a serious peering face.

" Are all the wirers in ? " I asked.

" Yes," he answered. " How are you feeling ? "

His serious tone amused me. I wanted to say, " Good heavens, man, I'm as fit as anything. I shall be back to-morrow, I expect." But I felt very tired and rather out of breath as I answered " Oh ! all right."

By this time my arm was bandaged and I started walking back to Maple Redoubt, leaning on Corporal Dyson. I wanted to joke, but felt too tired. It seemed an interminable way down, especially along Watling Street.

I had only once looked into the dressing-station, although I must have passed it several hundred times. I was surprised at its size : there were two compartments. As I stepped down inside, I wondered if it were shell-proof. In the inner chamber I could hear the doctor's quick low voice, telling a man to move the lamp : and it seemed to flash across me for the first time that there ought to be some kind of guarantee against dressing-stations being blown in like any ordinary dug-out. And yet I knew there was no possibility of any such guarantee.

" Hullo, Bill, old man," said the little doctor, coming out quickly. " Where's this thing of yours ?

In the arm, isn't it? Let's have a look. Oh yes, I see. (He examined the bandage, and the arm above it.) Well, I won't be long. You won't mind waiting a few minutes, will you? I've got a bad case in here. Hall, get him to sit down, and give him some Bovril."

And he was gone. No man could move or make men move quicker than the doctor.

I felt apologetic: I had chosen a bad time to come, just when the doctor was busy with this other man. I asked who the fellow was, and learned he was a private from "D" Company. I was very grateful for the Bovril. A good idea, this, I thought, having Bovril ready for you.

I waited about ten minutes, sitting on a chair. I listened to the movements and low voices inside. "Turn him over. Here. No, those longer ones. Good heavens, didn't I tell you to get this changed yesterday? Now. That'll do," and so on. I turned my head round in silence, observing acutely every detail in this antechamber, as one does in a dentist's waiting-room. All the time in my arm I felt this numb wasp-sting; I wondered when the real pain would start; there was no motion in this still smart.

"Now then, Bill," said the doctor. "So sorry to keep you. Let's have a look at it. Oh, that's nothing very bad."

It smarted as he undid the bandage. I don't know what he did. I never looked at it.

" What sort of a one is it ? " I asked.

" I could just do with one like this myself," said the doctor.

" Is it a Blighty one ? "

" I'd give you a fiver for it any minute," answered the doctor. " I'm not certain whether the bone's broken or not, but I rather think it is touched. I can't say, though. A bullet, did you say ? Are you sure ? "

" Very sure," I laughed.

" Well, it must be one of these explosive bullets, an ordinary bullet doesn't make a wound like yours. That's it. That'll do."

" I can't make out why there's not more pain," said I.

" Oh, that'll come later. You see the shock paralyses you at first. Here, take one of these." And he gave me a morphia tabloid.

" Cheero, Bill," he said, and I went out of the dug-out leaning on a stretcher-bearer. Round my neck hung a label, the first of a long series. " Gun-shot wound in left forearm " it contained. I found later " ? fracture. 1.15 a.m., 7.6.16."

Outside Lewis was waiting with my trench kit. He had appeared a quarter of an hour back at the door of the dressing-station, and had been told by the doctor so rapidly and forcibly that he ought to know that he would go with me to the clearing station, and that he had five minutes in which to get my kit together, that he had fairly sprinted away. Poor fellow! How should he know, seeing that he had been my servant over six months, and I had never got wounded before? But the doctor always made men double.

As I passed our dug-out, Edwards, Owen, Paul, and Nicholson were all standing outside.

"Cheero," I shouted. "Good luck. The doctor says it's nothing much. I'll be back soon."

"What about that Lewis-gun position?" asked Edwards.

"Oh," I said, "I want to keep that position on the left." Then I felt my decision waver. "Still, if Wetherell wants the other . . . I don't know."

"All right. I'll fix up with Wetherell. Good luck. Hope you get to Blighty."

I wanted to say such a lot. I wanted to say that I was sure to be back in a week or so. I wanted to think hard, and decide about that Lewis gun. I wanted to send a message to Wetherell apologising for what I had said. . . . I wanted to talk to Sergeant Andrews, who was standing there too. But the stretcher-bearer was walking on, and I must go as he pleased.

"Good-bye, Sergeant Andrews," I shouted.

Last of all I saw Davies, standing solemn and dumb.

"Good-bye, Davies. Off to Blighty."

I could not see if he answered. The relentless stretcher-bearer led me on. Was I O.C. stretcher-bearers or was I not? Why didn't I stop him?

I had not decided about that Lewis gun. At the corner of Old Kent Road, I was told I might as well sit on the ration trolley and go down on that. And in the full light of dawn, about half-past two, I was rolled serenely down the hill to the Citadel.

" Don't let go," I said to the stretcher-bearer, who was holding the trolley back. I still thought of sending up a message about that Lewis-gun position. Why could not I make up my mind ? I looked back and saw Maple Redoubt receding further and further in the distance.

" By Jove," I thought, " I may not see it again for weeks." And suddenly I realised that whether I made up my mind about the Lewis-gun position or not, would not make the slightest difference !

" Where do I go to now ? " said I.

" There's an ambulance at the Citadel," said the stretcher-bearer. " You're quite right. You'll be in Heilly in a little over an hour."

Heilly ? Why, this would be interesting, I thought. And I should just go, and have nothing to decide. I should be passive. I was going right out of the arena !

And the events of yesterday seemed a dream already.

Wednesday

I lay in bed, at the clearing station at Heilly. It was just after nine o'clock the same morning, and the orderlies were out of sight, but not out of hearing, washing up the breakfast things. Half the dark blue blinds were drawn, as the June sun was blazing outside. I could see the glare of it on the cobbles in the courtyard, as the door opened and a cool, tall nurse entered. I closed my eyes, and pretended to be asleep. I felt she might come and talk, and one thing I did not want to do, I did not want to talk.

My body was most extraordinarily comfortable. I moved my feet toes-up for the sheer joy of feeling the smooth sheets fall cool on my feet when I turned them sideways again. The pillow was comfortable; the whole bed was comfortable; even my arm, that was throbbing violently now, and felt boiling hot, was very comfortably rested on another pillow. I just wanted to lie, and lie: only my mind was working so fast and hard that it seemed to make the skin tight over my forehead. And all the time there was that buzz, buzzing. If I left off thinking, the buzzing took complete mastery of my brain. That was intolerable: so I had to keep on thinking.

At the Citadel an R.A.M.C. doctor had given me tea and a second label. He had also given me an injection against tetanus. This he did in the chest. Why didn't he do it in my right arm, I had thought: I would have rather had it there. Again, I had had to wait quite a quarter of an hour, while he attended to the "D" Company private. I had learned from an orderly that this poor fellow was bound to lose a leg, and again I had felt that I was in the way here, that I was a bother. I had then watched the poor fellow carried out on a stretcher, and the stretcher slid into the ambulance. There was a seat inside, into which I was helped. Lewis had gone in front, very red-faced and awkward. And an R.A.M.C. orderly had got in behind with me. Sitting, I had felt that he must think I was shamming! Then I remembered the first ambulance I had seen, when I first walked from Chocques to Béthune in early October! Was there really any connection between me then and me now?

Then there had been a rather pleasant journey through unknown country, it seemed. After a few miles, we halted and changed into another ambulance. As I had stood in the sunshine a moment, I had tried to make out where we were. But I could not recognise anything, and felt very tired. There was a white chalk road, a grass bank, and a house close by: that is all I could remember. And then there was another long ride, in which my one paramount idea was to rest my arm (which was in a white sling) and prevent it shaking and jarring.

Then at last we had reached a village and pulled up in a big sunlit courtyard. Again as I walked into a big room I felt that people must think I was shamming. A matron had come in, and a doctor. Did I mind sitting and waiting a minute or so? Would I like some tea? I had refused tea.

Then the doctor and an orderly came in, and the doctor asked some questions and took off my label. The orderly was taking off my boots, and the doctor had started helping! I had apologised profusely, for they were trench boots thick with mud. And then the doctor had asked me whether I could wait until about eleven before they looked at my arm: meanwhile it would be better, as I should be more rested after a few hours in bed. Bed! I had never thought of going to bed for an arm at all! What a delicious idea! I felt so tired, too. I had not been to bed all night. Then I had been helped into this delightful bed, and after scrawling a letter home to go away by the eight o'clock post (I was glad I had remembered that), I had been left in peace at about half-past four. And here I was! I had had a cup of tea for breakfast, but did not want to eat anything.

I wished I could go to sleep. Yet it was not much good now, if they were going to look at my arm at eleven. I opened my eyes whenever I was sure there was no one near me. Then I thought I might as well keep them open, otherwise they would think I had slept, and not know how tired out I felt. There was a man in the next bed with his head all bandaged; and round the bed in the corner was a screen. Opposite was an R.A.M.C. doctor, as far as I could gather; he was talking to the nurse, and looked perfectly well. I thought perhaps he might be the sort who would talk late when I wanted to sleep—he looked so well and lively; suppose he had a gramophone and wanted to play it this afternoon. I should really have to complain, if he did. Yet perhaps they would understand, and make him give it up because of us who were not so well. On my right, up at the other end of the room (was it a "ward"? yes, I suppose it was) were several voices, but I could not turn over and look at their owners, with my arm like this. How it throbbed and pulsed! Or was it aching? Supposing I got pins and needles in it. . . .

A khaki-clad padre came in. He just came over and asked me if I wanted anything, and did not worry me with talking. He had a very quiet voice and bald head. I liked both. I felt I ought to have wanted something: had I been discourteous?

The door opened, and the doctor entered, with another nurse and another doctor. Somehow this last person electrified everyone and everything. Who was he? His very walk was somehow different from the ordinary. My attention was riveted on him; somehow I felt that he knew I was there, and yet he did not look at me. They wheeled a little table up from the other end of the room, laden with glasses and bottles and glittering little silver forks and things. I could not see clearly. An orderly was reprimanded by the nurse for something, in a subdued voice. There was a hush and a tenseness in this man's presence. Yet he was calmly looking at a newspaper, and sitting on an empty bed as he did so! Apparently Kitchener was reported drowned in the North Sea: he spoke in a rich, almost drawling voice. He was immensely casual! And yet one did not mind. He walked over and washed his hands, and put on some yellowy-brown india-rubber gloves that scrooped and squelched in the basins. And then he turned round, and the other doctor (whom I had seen at four o'clock and who already seemed a sort of confidential friend of mine in the presence of this master-man) asked him, which case he wanted to see first. And as he jerked his hand casually to one of the beds, I was filled with a strange elation. This was a surgeon, I felt; and one in whom I had immense confidence. He would do the best for my arm: he would make no mistakes. I almost laughed for sheer joy!

He came at last to my bed and glanced at me. He never smiled. He asked me one or two questions. I said I was "? fracture," that my arm was throbbing but felt numb more than anything.

"I suppose we may presume there is a fracture," said he; "at any rate there is no point in looking at it here. I'll look at it under an anæsthetic," he said to me, not unkindly, but still without a smile. And a little later, as he went out, he half looked back at my bed.

"Eleven o'clock," he said to the nurse as he went out.

The tension relaxed. An orderly spoke in a bold ordinary voice. The spell was gone out with the man.

"Who is that?" I asked the nurse

"Oh! that's Mr. Bevan; he's a very good surgeon indeed."

"I know," said I, "I can feel that."

About an hour later, two orderlies whom I had not seen before came in with a stretcher, and laid it on the floor by the bed. The tall nurse asked me if I had any false teeth, and said I had better put socks on, as my feet might get cold. The orderly did this, and then they helped me on to the stretcher. My head went back, and I felt a strain on my neck. The next second my head was lifted and a pillow put under it. And they had moved me without altering the position of my arm. I was surprised and pleased at that. Then a blanket was put over me, and one of the orderlies said "Ready?"

"Yes," I said, but suddenly realised he was talking to the other orderly. I was lifted up, and carried across the room out into the courtyard. What a blazing sun! I closed my eyes.

"Dump, dump, dump." The stretcher seemed to bob along, with a regular rhythmic swaying. Then they turned a corner, and I felt a slight nausea. I opened my eyes. The stretcher was put on a table. I felt very high up.

The matron-person appeared. She was older than the nurses, and had a chain with scissors dangling on the end of it. She smiled, and asked what kind of a wound it was. Then the orderlies looked at each other, at some signal that I could not see, and lifted me up and into the next room. They held the stretcher up level with the operating table, and helped me on to it. I did some good right elbow-work and got on easily. As I did so, I saw Mr. Bevan sitting on a chair in his white overall, his gloved hands quietly folded in his lap. He said and did nothing. Again I felt immensely impressed by his competence, reserving every ounce of energy, waiting, until these less masterful beings had got everything ready.

They took off the blanket, and moved things behind. Then they put the rubber cup over my mouth and nose.

" Just breathe quite naturally," said the doctor. I shut my eyes.

" Just ordinary breaths. That is very good," said the voice, quietly and reassuringly.

I felt a sort of sweet shudder all down my body. I wanted to laugh. Then I let my body go a little. It was no good bracing myself. . . . I opened my right hand and shut it, just to show them I was not " off " yet . . .

The process of " coming to " was unpleasant and uninteresting. I do not think I distinguished myself by any originality, so will not attempt to describe it. That was a long interminable day, and my arm hurt a good deal. In the afternoon I was told that I should be pleased to hear that there was no bone broken. I was anything but pleased. I wanted the bone to be broken, as I wanted to go to "Blighty." This worried me all day. I wondered if I should get to England or not. Then in the evening the sister (I found that the nurses should be called sisters) dressed the wound. That was distinctly unpleasant. It took hours and hours and hours before it began to get even twilight. I have never known so long a day. And then I could not sleep. They injected morphia at last, but I awoke after three or four hours feeling more tired than ever.

Thursday

I can hardly disentangle these days; night and day ran into one another. I can remember little about Thursday. I could not sleep however much I wanted to; and all the time my brain was working so hard, thinking. I worried about the company: they must be in the line now. Would Edwards remember this, and that? Had I left him the map, or was it among those maps in my valise which Lewis had gone to Morlancourt to fetch?

And all the time there were rifle-grenades about; I daren't let the buzzing come, because it was all rifle-grenades really; and always I kept seeing Lance-Corporal Allan lying there. Why could I not get rid of the picture of him? Yet I was afraid

I might forget ; and it was important that I should remember. . . .

I remember the waiting to have my arm dressed. It was like waiting before the dentist takes up the drill again. I watched the man next to me out of the corner of my eye, and felt it intensely if he seemed to wince, or drew in his breath. And I remember in the morning Mr. Bevan dressed my wound. I looked the other way. For a week I thought the wound was above instead of just below the elbow. " This will hurt," he said once.

Some time in the day the man behind the screen died. I had heard him groaning all day ; and there was the rhythmic sound of pumping—oxygen, I suppose. . . . I heard a lot of moving behind the screen, and at last it was taken away and I saw the corner for the first time and in it an empty bed with clean sheets.

The man next to me, with the bandaged head, kept talking deliriously to the orderly about his being on a submarine. Once the orderly smiled at me as he answered the absurd questions.

There was one good incident I remember. After the surgeon had dressed my arm, I said, " Is there any chance of this getting me to Blighty ? " And I thought he did not hear ; he was looking the other way. But suddenly I heard that calm deliberate voice :

" Yes, that is a Blighty one. There is enough damage to those muscles to keep you in Blighty several months." And this made all the rest bearable somehow.

FRIDAY

Again the only sleep I could get was by morphia. In the morning they told me I should go by a hospital train leaving at three o'clock. I scrawled a note or two and gave them to Lewis, and instructed him about my kit. I believe they made an inventory of it. I gave him some maps for Edwards. And then he said good-bye. And I thought of him going back, and I going to England. And I felt ashamed of myself again. I wondered if the Colonel was annoyed with me.

They gave me gas in the morning. It seemed such a bother going through all that again: it was not worth trying to get better. Still I was glad, it was one dressing less! Then in the afternoon I was carried on a stretcher to the train. I hardly saw anyone to say good-bye to. I thought of writing later.

It seemed an interminable journey. By some mistake I had been put in with the Tommies. There was no difference in the structure or comfort of the officers' or Tommies' quarters; but I knew they were taking me wrong. However, I was entirely passive, and did not mind what they did. The carriage had a corridor all the way down the centre, and on each side was a succession of berths in three tiers. On the top tier you must have felt very high and close up to the roof ; on the centre one you got a good view out of the windows ; on the third and lowest tier (which was my lot) you felt that if there were an accident, you would not have far to roll ; on the other hand, you were out of view of orderlies passing along the corridor.

A great thirst consumed me as I lay waiting. I could see two orderlies in the space by the door cutting up large pieces of bread and butter. This made my mouth still drier. Then they brought in cans of hot tea, and gave it out in white enamel bowls. I longed for the sting of the tea on my dry palate, but the orderly was startled when I said, " I suppose this is all right ; I am an officer." He said he would tell them, and gave the bowl to the next man. The bowls were taken away and washed up, before a cup of tea was at last brought me. A corporal brought it ; he poured it out of a little teapot ; but I could not drink it out of a cup. My left arm lay like a log beside me, and I could not hold my right arm steady *and* raise my head. So the corporal went off for a feeding cup. I felt rather nervy and like a man with a grievance ! And when I got the tea it was nearly cold.

I say it seemed an interminable journey, and my arm was so frightfully uncomfortable. I had it across my body, and felt I could not breathe for the weight of it. At last I felt I *must* get its position altered. I called " orderly " every time an orderly went past : sometimes they paused and looked round; but they could not see me, and went on. Sometimes they did not hear anything. I felt as self-conscious and irritated as a man who calls "waiter" and the waiter does not hear. At last one heard, and a sister came and fixed me up with a small pillow under the elbow. I immediately felt apologetic, and I wondered if she thought me fussy.

The train made a long, slow grind over the rails; and it kept stopping with a griding sound and a jolt. Why did it go so slowly? At ten o'clock I begged and obtained another morphia dose, and got four hours' sleep from it again.

Saturday

I suppose it was about 7.0 a.m. when we arrived at Étretat. I was taken and laid in the middle of rows and rows of Tommies in a big sunny courtyard. I thought how well the bearers carried the stretchers: I did not at all feel that I was likely to be dropped or tilted off on to my arm. There were a lot of men in blue hospital dress on the steps of a big house. I wondered where I was: in Havre probably. It was a queer sensation lying on my back gazing up at the sun; we were tightly packed in together, like cards laid in order, face upwards. How high everyone looked standing up. Then they discovered one or two officers, and I said that I too was an officer. I felt that they rather dared me to repeat this statement. Then a man looked at my label, and said: "Yes, he is an officer." And I was taken up and carried off.

I found myself put to bed in a spacious room in which were only two beds. The house had only recently been finished, and was in use as a hospital. As soon as I was in bed, I felt a great relief again. No more motion for a time, I thought. There was a man in the other bed, threatened with consumption. We were talking, when a pretty V.A.D. nurse came in and asked what we wanted for breakfast. I felt quite hungry, and enjoyed tea and fish. I began to think that life was going to be good. I saw Cecil Todd, who had been slightly wounded a fortnight ago. I condoled with him on not getting to England. He asked me if I wanted to read. No, I did not feel like reading. I wrote a letter. Then two V.A.D. nurses came and dressed my wound. They seemed surprised to find so big a one, and sent for the doctor to see it. They dressed it very well, and gave me no unnecessary pain.

In the afternoon, I was again moved to a motor ambulance, which took me to Havre. It jolted and shook horribly. "This man does not know what it is like up here," I thought. All the time I was straining my body to keep the left arm from touching the jolting stretcher. (The stretchers slide in the ambulance.) I was a top-berth passenger; I could touch the white roof with my right hand; and there was a stuffy smell of white paint.

At last it stopped, and after a wait I was carried amid a sea of heads, along a quay. I could smell sea and the stale oily smell of a steamer. Then I was taken over the gangway with that firm, steady, nodding motion with which I was getting so familiar, along the deck, through doorways, and into a big room, all green and white. All round the edge were beds, into one of which I was helped. In the centre of the room were beds that somehow reminded me of cots. I dare say there was a low railing round the beds that gave me this impression. A Scotch nurse looked after me. These nurses were all in grey and red; the others had been in blue. I wondered what was the difference. I asked the name of the ship and they said it was the *Asturias*.

Later on a steward brought a menu, and I chose my own dinner. Apparently I could eat what I liked. The doctor looked at my wound, and said it could wait until morning before being dressed; he pleased me. I was more comfortable than I had been yet. The boat was not due out till about 1.0 a.m. At eleven o'clock I again asked for morphia, and so got sleep for another four hours or so.

SUNDAY

"I represent Messrs. Cox and Co. Is there anything I can do for any of you gentlemen this morning?"

A short, squarely built man, with a black suit, a bowler hat, and a small brown bag, stepped briskly into the room. He gave me intense pleasure: as he talked to a Scotch officer who wanted some ready cash, I felt that I was indeed back in England It was a hot sunny day; and a bowler hat on such a day made me feel sure that this was *really* Southampton, and not all a dream. Sir, whoever you are, I thank you for your most appropriate appearance.

The hospital ship had been alongside nearly an hour, I believe. It was three o'clock in the afternoon. Breakfast, the dressing of my wound again, lunch; all had followed in an uneventful succession. The throbbing of the engines as the boat steamed quietly along had been hardly noticeable at all. At last there was a bustle, and we were carried out of the room, out into the sunshine again, and along the quay to the train. Here I was given a berth in the middle tier this time, for which I was very thankful. I felt so utterly tired; and the weight of my arm across my body was intolerable.

That seemed a long, long journey too; but I got tea without delay this time, and it was hot. At Farnborough the train stopped and a few men were taken out. The rest came on to London.

"Is there any special hospital in London you want to go to?" said a brisk R.A.M.C. official, when we reached Waterloo.

"No," I answered.

He wrote on a label, and put that round my neck also.

"Lady Carnarvon's," he said.

I lay for some time on the platform of Waterloo station, gazing up at the vault in the roof. Porters and stretcher-bearers stood about, and gazed down at one in silence. Then I was moved into a motor ambulance, and a Red Cross lady took her seat in the back. My head was in the front, so that I could see nothing. Just before the car went off, a policeman put his head in.

"Any milk or anything?"

"Would you like any milk or beef tea?" the lady said.

"Milk, please."

"He says he would like a little milk," said the lady.

And then we drove off.

Monday

It was somewhere about ten o'clock Monday morning. The sister had just finished dressing my arm; the doctor had poked it about; now it lay cool and quiet along by my side. I had not slept that night again, except with morphia. I still felt extraordinarily tired, but was very comfortable. I watched the tall sister in blue with the white headdress that reminded me of a nun's cap. She was so strong and quiet, and seemed to know that my hand always wanted support at the wrist when she lifted my arm. I did not want to talk, just to lie.

Suddenly I realised that my head was no longer buzzing. I knew that I should sleep to-night—at last! My body relaxed: the tension suddenly melted away.

"Hurrah!" I thought, "I have not got to move, or think, or decide—and I can just lie for hours, for days."

At last I was out of the grip of war.

CHAPTER XVII

CONCLUSION

IT was a slumbrous afternoon in September. My wound had healed up a month ago, and I was lazily convalescent at my aunt's house in one of the most beautiful parts of Kent. The six soldiers who were also convalescent there were down in the hop-garden. For hop-picking was in full swing. I was sitting in a deck-chair with *Don Quixote* on my knees; but I was not reading. I had apparently broken the offensive power of the army of midges by making a brilliant counter-attack with a pipe of Chairman. The sun blazed mercilessly on the croquet-lawn; the balls were lying all together round one hoop: for there was a golf-croquet tournament in progress, and the mallets stood about against various hoops; one very tidy and proper mallet was standing primly in the stand at one corner. My chair was well sited under the cool shade of a large mulberry tree, in whose thick lofty branches the wind rustled with a delicious little sigh; sometimes a regular little gust would send the boughs swishing, and then a little rain of red and white mulberries would plop on to the grass, and strike the summer-house roof with a smart patter. On the grass-bank at the side of the lawn, by a blazing border of orange and red nasturtiums, a black cat was squatting with tail slowly waving to and fro, watching a fine large tabby that was sniffing at the nasturtiums in a nonchalant manner. They were the best of friends, playing that most interesting of all games, war.

I was not reading: I was listening to the incessant murmur that came from far away across the Medway, across the garden of England, and across the Channel and the flats of Flanders. That sound came from Picardy. All day the insistent throb had been in the air; sometimes faint bumps were clearly distinguishable, at other times it was nothing but one steady vibration. But always it was there, that distant growl, that insistent mutter. Even in this perfect peace, I could not escape the War.

To-day I felt completely well; the lassitude and inertness of convalescence were gone—at any rate, for the moment. My mind was very clear, and I could think surely and rapidly. The cats reminded me of the lusty family that lived in the cellar in the Cuinchy trenches, and the murmur of the guns drew my thoughts across the Channel. I tried to imagine trenches running across the lawn, with communication trenches running back to a support line through the meadow; a few feet of brick wall would be all that would be left of the house, and this would conceal my snipers; the mulberry tree would long ago have been razed to the ground, and every scrap of it used as firewood in our dug-outs ; this deck chair of mine might possibly be in use in Company Headquarters in one of the cellars. No, it was not easy to imagine war without seeing it.

I picked up the paper that had fallen at my side. There had been more terrible fighting on the Somme, and it had seemed very marvellous to a journalist as he lay on a hill some two miles back, and watched through his field-glasses : it was wonderful that the men advancing (if indeed he could really see them at all in the smoke of a heavy artillery barrage) still went on, although their comrades dropped all round them. Yet I wondered what else anyone could do but go on ? Run back, with just as much likelihood of being shot in doing so ? Or, even if he did get back, to certain death as a deserter ? Everyone knows the safest place is in a trench ; and it is a trench you are making for. Lower down on the page came a description of the wounded ; he had talked to so many of them, and they were all smiling, all so cheerful ; smoking cigarettes and laughing. They shook their fists, and shouted that the only thing they wanted to do was to get back into it ! Pah ! I threw the paper down in disgust. Surely no one wants to read such stuff, I thought. Of course the men who were not silent, in a dull stupefied agony, were smiling : what need to say that a man with a slight wound was laughing at his luck, just as I had smiled that early morning when the trolley took me down from Maple Redoubt? And who does not volunteer for an unpleasant task, when he knows he cannot possibly get it? Want to get back into it, indeed! Ask Tommy ten years hence whether he wants to be back in the middle of it again!

I wondered why people endured such cheap journalism. What right had men who have never seen war at all, who creep up on bicycles to get a glimpse of it through telescopes, who pester wounded men, and then out of their pictorial imagination work up a vivid description—what right have they to insult heroes by saying that "their wonderful spirit makes up for it all," that "the paramount impression is one of glory"? Are not our people able to bear the truth, that war is utterly hellish, that we do *not* enjoy it, that we hate it, hate it, hate it all? And then it struck me how ignorant people still were; how uncertainly they spoke, these people at home: it was as though they dared not think things out, lest what they held most dear should be an image shattered by another point of view.

Somehow people were amazed at the cheerfulness, the doggedness, the endurance under pain, the indifference to death, shown every minute during this war. I thought of the men whom I had seen in hospital. One man had had his right foot amputated; it used to give me agony to see his stump dressed every day. Another man had both legs amputated above the knees. Yet they were so wonderfully cheerful, so apparently content with life! As though alone in the blackness of night they did not long for the activity denied them for the rest of their life. As though their cheerfulness—(do not think I belittle its heroism)—*as though their cheerfulness justified the thing!*

Another thing I had noticed. An old man told me he was so struck with the heroism, the courage, the indifference to death, shown by the ordinary unromantic man. Some men had been converted, too, their whole lives changed, their vices eradicated, by this war. So much good was coming from it. People, too, at home were so changed, so sobered; they were looking into the selfishness of their lives at last. Again I thought, *as though all that justified the thing!*

Oh! you men and women who did not know before the capabilities of human nature, I thought, please take note of it now; and after the war do not underestimate the quality of mankind. Did it need a war to tell you that a man can be heroic, resolute, courageous, cheerful, and capable of sacrifice? There were those who could have told you that before this war.

There was a lull in the vibration. I turned in my chair, and listened. Then it began again.

"People are afraid to think it out," I said. "I have not seen the Somme fighting, but I know what war is. Its quality is not altered by multiplication or intensity. The colour of life-blood is a constant red. Let us look into this business; let us face all the facts. Let us not flinch from any aspect of the truth."

And my thoughts ran somewhat as follows :

First of all, War is evil—utterly evil. Let us be sure of that first. It is an evil instrument, even if it be used for motives that are good. I, who have been through war and know it, say that it is evil. I knew it before the war ; instinct, reason, religion told me that war was evil ; now experience has told me also.

It is a strange synthesis, this war : it is a synthesis of adventure, dulness, good spirits, and tragedy ; but none of these things are new to human experience ; nor is human nature altered by war. It is at war as a whole that we must look in order to appreciate its quality. And what is war seen as a whole, or rather seen in the light of my eight months' experience ? For no one man can truly appraise war.

I have seen and felt the adventure of war, its deadly fascination and excitement : it is the greatest game on earth : that is its terrible power : there is such a wild temptation to paint up its interest and glamour : it gives such scope to daring, to physical courage, to high spirits : it makes so many prove themselves heroic, that were it not for the fall of the arrow men would call the drawing of the bow good. I have seen the dulness, the endless monotony, the dogged labour, the sheer power of will conquering the body and "carrying on": there is good in that, too. In the jollity, the humour, the good-fellowship, is nothing but good also. There is good in all these things; for these are qualities of human nature triumphing in spite of war. These things are not war; they are the good in man prostituted to a vile thing.

For I have seen the real face of war: I have seen men killed, mutilated, blown to little pieces; I have seen men crippled for life; I have looked in the face of madness, and I know that many have gone mad under its grip. I have seen fine natures break and crumble under the strain. I have seen men grow brutalised, and coarsened in this war. (God will judge justly in the end; meanwhile, there are thousands among us—yes, and among our enemy too—brutalised through no fault of theirs.) I have lost friends killed (and shall lose more yet), friends with whom I have lived and suffered so long.

Who is for war now? Its adventure, its heroism? Bah! Yet this is not all.

For war spares none. It desecrates the beauty of the earth; it ruins, it destroys, it wastes; it starves children; it drives out old men, and women, homeless. And most terrible of all, it brings agony to every household: it is like a plague of the firstborn. Do not think I have forgotten you, O women, and old men. You, too, have to endure the agony of the arena; you are compelled to sit and watch us fight the beasts. Every mother is there in agony, watching her baby, and unable to stretch a finger to help. This, too, is war—the anguish of mothers whose sons perish, of wives who lose their husbands, of girls robbed for all time of marriage and motherhood.

And this vile thing is still perpetrated upon the earth among peoples who have long ago declared human sacrifice impossible and barbaric.

This then is a basal fact. We have faced it fairly. The instrument is vile. What then of the motive? What is the motive which drives us to use this evil instrument? And I see you fathers and mothers waiting to hear what I shall say. For there are people who whisper that we who are fighting are vindictive, that we lust for the blood of our enemies, that we are coarse and brutal, that we are unholy champions of what we call a just cause. Again let us face the facts. And to these whisperers I answer boldly: "Yes! we are coarse, some of us; we are vindictive; we hate; we do not deny it." For war in its vileness taints its human instruments too. When Davidson died I cried death upon his murderers. I called them devils, and worse. I am not ashamed.

That is not the point. What I or Tommy may be at a given moment is not the point. The question is, with what motives did we enter this war, agree to take up this vile instrument? We cannot help if it soils our hands. What is our motive in fighting in the arena? What provokes the dumb heroism of our soldiers? Why did men flock to the colours, volunteer in millions for the arena? You know.

I who have lived with them eight months in France, I also know. It was because a people took up this vile instrument and used it from desire of power. Because they trampled on justice, and challenged us to thwart them. Because they willed war for the sake of wrong; because they said that force was master of the world, and they set out to prove it.

Yet, it is sometimes said, war is unchristian. If men were Christian there would be no war. You cannot conquer evil by evil. I agree, if men were Christian there would be no war. I agree that you cannot conquer evil by evil; but it is war that is evil, not our motive in going to war. We are conquering an evil spirit by a good spirit, even if we are using an evil instrument. And if you say that Christ would not fight, I say that none of us would fight if the world had attained the Christian plane towards which we are slowly rising: but we are still on a lower plane, and in it there is a big war raging; and in the arena there are many who have felt Christ by their side.

That, then, is the second point. I knew that war was vile, before I went into it. I have seen it: I do not alter my opinion. I went into this war prepared to sacrifice my life to prove that right is stronger than wrong; I have stood again and again with a traverse between me and death; I have faced the possiblity of madness. I foresaw all this before I went into this war. What difference does it make that I have experienced it? It makes no difference.

Let no one fear that our sacrifice has been in vain. We have already won what we are fighting for. The will for war, that aggressive power, with all the cards on its side prepared, striking at its own moment, has already failed against a spirit, weaker, unprepared, taken unawares. And so I am clear on my second point. We are fighting from just motives, and we have already baulked injustice. Aggressive force, the power that took up the cruel weapon of war, has failed. No one can ever say that his countrymen have laid down their lives in vain.

I got up from the chair, and started walking about the garden. Everything was so clear. Before going out to the war I had thought these things ; but the thoughts were fluid, they ran about in mazy patterns, they were elusive, and always I was frightened of meeting unanswerable contradictions to my theorising from men who had actually seen war. Now my conclusions seemed crystallised by irrefutable experience into solid truth.

After a while I sat down again and resumed my train of thought :

War is evil. Justice is stronger than Force. Yet, was there need of all this bloodshed to prove this ? For this war is not as past wars ; this is every man's war, a war of civilians, a war of men who hate war, of men who fight for a cause, who are compelled to kill and hate it. That is another thing that people will not face. Men whisper that Tommy does not hate Fritz. Again I say, away with this whispering. Let us speak it out plain and bold. Private Davies, my orderly, formerly a shepherd of Blaenau Festiniog, has no quarrel with one Fritz Schneider of Hamburg who is sitting in the trench opposite the Matterhorn sap ; yet he will bayonet him certainly if he comes over the top, or if we go over into the German trenches ; ay, he will perform this action with a certain amount of brutality too, for I have watched him jabbing at rats with a bayonet through the wires of a rat trap, and I know that he has in him a savage vein of cruelty. But when peace is declared, he and Fritz will light a bonfire of trench stores in No Man's Land, and there will be the end of their quarrel. I say boldly, I know. For indeed I know Davies very well indeed.

Again I say, was there need of all this bloodshed ? Who is responsible ? Who is responsible for Lance-Corporal Allan lying in the trench in Maple Redoubt? Again I see yon glittering eyes looking down upon me in the arena. And Davies, too, in his slow simple way, is beginning to take you in, and to ask you why he is put there to fight ? Is it for your pleasure ? Is it for your expediency ? Is it a necessary part of your great game ? Necessary ? Necessary for whom ? Davies and Fritz alike are awaiting your answer.

It is hard to trace ultimate causes. It is hard to fix absolute responsibility. There were many seeds sown, scattered, and secretly fostered before they produced this harvest of blood. The seeds of cruelty, selfishness, ambition, avarice, and indifference, are always liable to swell, grow, and bud, and blossom suddenly into the red flower of war. Let every man look into his heart, and if the seeds are there let him make quick to root them out while there is time; unless he wishes to join those glittering eyes that look down upon the arena.

These are the seeds of war. And it is because they know that we, too, are not free from them, that certain men have stood out from the arena as a protest against war. These men are real heroes, who for their conscience's sake are enduring taunts, ignominy, misunderstanding, and worse. Most men and women in the arena are cursing them, and, as they struggle in agony and anguish, they beat their hands at them and cry "You do not care." I, too, have cursed them, when I was mad with pain. But I know them, and I know that they are true men. I would not have one less. They are witnesses against war. And I, too, am fighting war. Men do not understand them now, but one day they will.

I know that there are among us, too, the seeds of war: no cause has yet been perfect. But I look at the facts. We did not start, we did not want this war. We have gone into it, fighting for the better cause. Whether, had we been more Christian, we might have prevented the war, is not the point. We did not want this war: we are fighting against it.

It was the seeds of war in Germany that were responsible. And so history will judge.

But what of the future? How are we to save future generations from going down into the arena? We will rearrange the map of Europe: we will secure the independence of small states: we will give the power to the people: there shall be an end of tyrannies. So men speak easily of an international spirit, of a world conference for peace. There is so great a will-power against war, they say, that we will secure the world for the future. Millions of men know the vileness of war; they will devise ways and means to prevent its recurrence. I agree. Let us try all ways. Yet I see no guarantee in all this against the glittering eyes: I see no power in all this knowledge against a new generation fostering and harvesting the seeds of war. Men have long known that war is evil. Did that knowledge prevent this war? Will that knowledge secure India or China from the power of the glittering eyes?

I walked up and down the lawn, my eyes glowing, my brain working hard. Here around me was all the beauty of an old garden, its long borders full of phloxes, delphiniums, stocks, and all the old familiar flowers; the apples glowed red in the trees; the swallows were skimming across the lawn. In the distance I could hear the rumble of the waggon bringing up the afternoon load of hop-pokes to the oasthouse. Yet what I had seen of war was as true, had as really happened, as all this. It would be so easy to forget, after the war. And yet to forget might mean a seed of war. I must never forget Lance-Corporal Allan.

There is only one sure way, I said at last. And again a clear conviction filled me. There is only one way to put an end to the arena. Pledges and treaties have failed ; and force will fail. These things may bring peace for a time, but they cannot crush those glittering eyes. There is only one Man whose eyes have never glittered. Look at the palms of your hands, you, who have had a bullet through the middle of it ! Did they not give you morphia to ease the pain ? And did you not often cry out alone in the darkness in the terrible agony, that you did not care who won the war if only the pain would cease ? Yet one Man there was who held out His hand upon the wood, while they knocked, knocked, knocked in the nail, every knock bringing a jarring, excruciating pain, every bit as bad as yours. And any moment His will-power could have weakened, and He could have saved Himself that awful pain. And then they nailed through the other hand : and then the feet. And as they lifted the Cross, all the weight came upon the pierced hands. And when He had tasted the vinegar He would not drink. And any moment He could have come down from the Cross : yet He so cared that love should win the war against evil, that He never wavered, His eyes never glittered. Do you want to put an end to the arena? Here is a Man to follow. *In hoc signo vinces.*

I stood up again, and stretched out my hands. And as I did so a memory came back vivid and strong. I remembered the night when I stood out on the hillside by Trafalgar Square, under the moon. And I remembered how I had felt a strength out of the pain, and even as the strength came a more unutterable weakness, the weakness of a man battering against a wall of steel. The sound of the relentless guns had mocked at me. Now as I stood on the lawn, I heard the long continuous vibration of the guns upon the Somme.

"You are War," I said aloud. "This is your hour, the power of darkness. But the time will come when we shall follow the Man who has conquered your last weapon, death: and then your walls of steel will waver, cringe, and fall, melted away before the fire of LOVE."

PRINTED BY WILLIAM BRENDON AND SON, LTD.
PLYMOUTH, ENGLAND

Printed in Great Britain
by Amazon.co.uk, Ltd.,
Marston Gate.